AFRICAN MYTHOLOGY
A TO Z

Patricia Ann Lynch

African Mythology A to Z

Copyright © 2004 by Patricia Ann Lynch

Facts On File, Inc.
132 West 31st Street
New York NY 10001

Library of Congress Cataloging-in-Publication Data is available on request from Facts On File, Inc.
ISBN 0-8160-4892-4

Facts On File books are available at special discounts when purchased in bulk quantities for businesses, associations, institutions, or sales promotions. Please call our Special Sales Department in New York at (212) 967-8800 or (800) 322-8755.

You can find Facts On File on the World Wide Web at http://www.factsonfile.com

Text design by Joan M. Toro
Cover design by Cathy Rincon

Printed in the United States of America

VB PKG 10 9 8 7 6 5 4 3 2 1

This book is printed on acid-free paper.

CONTENTS

Acknowledgments

I want to thank the friends who helped me with and supported me through the enormous amount of research that has gone into this book.

Special thanks go to Brown Publishing Network for providing me the opportunity to explore the rich heritage of African mythology.

INTRODUCTION

The first impression one gets of Africa is its size. Africa is the world's second largest continent in area (after Asia). The continent spans about 5,000 miles from north to south and about 4,600 miles from east to west at its widest part in the north. The geography of Africa is as varied as one might expect in such an immense area. Strips of fertile land at northern and southern extremes of the continent gradually fade into the vast reaches of the Sahara Desert in the north and the smaller Kalahari Desert in the south. Narrow bands of brush and scrub forest and grasslands border the deserts. Tall mountains—many of which are extinct volcanoes—tower over the rolling, grassy savannas. Broad and powerful rivers cut across the continent, making their way to the sea. In the center of Africa is a great equatorial rain forest. Wherever the land was capable of supporting human life, people settled. They developed agriculture and animal husbandry, learned metalworking, founded cities, and built empires.

To refer to "Africans" or "African culture" as if the inhabitants of this enormous continent represent one people is an error. People's ways of life, religions, traditions, and mythologies vary greatly from region to region and even from one tribe to a neighboring tribe. Wherever they lived, Africans developed lifestyles, worldviews, religions, traditions, and mythologies that were as different from one another as their physical environments.

Also because of its size, outside influences on Africa varied from place to place. The great civilization of ancient Egypt dominated other cultures that developed along the Nile River. Peoples on the Red Sea coast were influenced by the peoples of southern Arabia across the sea. North Africa, which borders the Mediterranean Sea, is just 8 miles across the Strait of Gibraltar from Europe. It was settled by the ancient Phoenicians, Greeks, Romans, and Arabs, all of whom exerted their own influences on North African culture, traditions, and mythologies. Central Africa, south of the Sahara, remained uninfluenced by outside civilizations for millennia. Its peoples developed their own unique religions, worldviews, and mythologies.

Humans use mythology and ritual to establish a sense of community, identity, and an understanding of their place in the universe. These tools maintain the traditions of a culture and reflect what is most important in people's lives. We read myths not only to learn about the culture in which the myth originated, but to discover what was in the hearts and minds of the myth makers. This book explores the surviving mythological traditions of Africa outside Egypt and from the earliest known myths to the most recent. The myths of African peoples give us a glimpse into their ways of life and worldviews. Because of the vast numbers of traditions and almost limitless numbers of tales, it is impossible to represent them all in a book of this size. We have attempted to include a sampling of myths that are representative of particular cultures and that come from as wide a variety of cultures as possible.

AFRICA: A BRIEF HISTORY

Africa has a long and dynamic history that goes back millions of years. Human life began in Africa. Anthropological evidence in the form of fossil skulls, bone fragments, and other artifacts shows that the first hominids—upright primates who walked on two legs—evolved in East Africa around 5 million years ago. By 700,000 years ago, hominids who migrated out of Africa had spread throughout Asia and Europe. Fossil remains of the first modern humans—Homo sapiens—that date back 160,000 years were found in Ethiopia in 2003. This is evidence that modern humans also evolved in Africa and spread out from there.

Prehistoric African People

Some 30,000 years ago, the San people of southern Africa began painting pictures on rock outcroppings and cliffs. San rock art is a valuable aid to understanding San religion and mythology, both of which have survived to this day.

Over many thousands of years, the geography of Africa has changed more than once. Between around 5500 and 2500 B.C. the continent's climate became wetter. The northern half of Africa became a lush prairie, populated by hunters, herders, and farmers. Archaeologists have learned about these people's lives from the thousands of rock paintings discovered throughout the region. Scenes showing everyday activities, rituals, musicians, and decoratively costumed dancers give a glimpse into the customs, traditions, and ceremonial lives of these ancient people. Nothing, however, is known about their myths.

About 4,000 years ago (around 2000 B.C.) the climate changed again; it became increasingly drier. Lands that were once fertile became desert. Today, the sands of the Sahara cover the beds of ancient rivers and the ruins of cities that flourished long ago. The people of the Sahara migrated to more hospitable lands. They took with them their religions, customs, traditions, and mythology. From the Sahara, people dispersed in three directions. Some went north to the coast of the Mediterranean Sea. There, they merged with the local people and formed the Berber culture. Some settled in the fertile lands along the Nile River and later became known as Libyans. Still others migrated south into the heart of the continent.

The Rise of African Kingdoms

Some of history's oldest and most advanced civilizations developed in Africa. The civilization of Egypt arose around 5500 B.C. and flourished between 1550 and 1069 B.C. It was conquered by Alexander the Great in 332–323 B.C. The first African civilization after Egypt was Kush. The Kushites were an Egyptianized people who lived between the first and third cataracts of the Nile River. Around 3100 B.C., Egypt had conquered and colonized the region around the first cataract—known as Nubia—spreading Egyptian civilization southward. Kush grew so strong that in the eighth century B.C. it conquered Egypt and ruled it for 90 years. The Kushite religion closely resembled Egyptian religion. It contained all the major Egyptian gods, with Amon as the principal god, and the related Egyptian mythologies as well.

The Kushite dynasty ended with the Assyrian invasion of Egypt in the seventh century B.C. The Kushites retreated south. In 591, the capital moved to Meroe. By about 270, Meroe had become an empire that lasted for 500 years. In addition to Egyptian deities and mythology, Meroe had its own regional gods; among them was a lion-headed warrior god who appears in rock carvings.

While Meroe declined, the kingdom of Axum in the highlands of what is now Ethiopia grew in power. According to Greek and Roman sources, Axum was thriving by the first century A.D. Axum's language and system of writing were Semitic. After conquering Kush and acquiring territories in Arabia, Axum controlled one of the most important trade routes in the world. The Axumite religion was derived from Arabic religion and was polytheistic, or based on the belief in many gods. In Axumite mythology, gods controlled the natural forces of the universe. In the fourth century A.D., Axum's ruler was converted to Christianity. He declared Axum a Christian state—the first in the world. Axum remained a strong empire and trading power until the rise of Islam in the seventh century A.D.

Africans developed iron-making technology early, around the sixth century B.C. Beginning in the first century A.D., knowledge of iron making began to spread quickly throughout the continent. The spread of this important technology was the result of the migrations of Bantu-speaking people. Bantu is a family of closely related languages that represent the largest language family in Africa. Around the first century B.C., Bantu-speaking people migrated out of north-central Africa and spread south and east. This migration continued until about A.D. 1000. Wherever the Bantu migrated, they brought with them their language, culture, agricultural skills, knowledge of technology, traditions, and mythology. Themes common to Bantu mythology predominate in areas into which the Bantu migrated.

Islam and Trade

The most important development in the Sahel region, south of the Sahara, was the use of the camel as a means of transport. Under the influence of Islamic peoples, northern and western Africans began to use camels to transport goods across the Sahara around A.D. 750. All of the major North African kingdoms—Ghana, Mali, Songhay, and Kanem-Bornu—arose at way stations and at the southern terminal points of trade.

Ghana's power and influence were built on trade—especially trade in gold. Ghana was originally founded by Berbers but became dominated by the Soninke, a Mandé-speaking people. Fragments of the ancient Soninke traditions and mythologies survive in the DAUSI, the great EPIC of the Soninke people. Ghana was conquered by the Almoravid Berbers in a jihad, or Islamic holy war, around 1076 and ceased to be a commercial power.

According to tradition, the Sahelian kingdom of Mali was founded by the legendary hero SUNDIATA (also called Son-Jara Keita, Sundjata Keoto, or Sunjata Kayta). Many myths are told about Sundiata's exploits. After the death of Mali's most significant king, Mansa Musa (ruled 1312–37), Mali's power declined. Much of its territory was seized by Tuareg Berbers in the north and the Mossi kingdom to the south.

Mali was replaced by the Songhay kingdom, which arose from Gao, a former subject kingdom of Mali. Songhay eventually became a powerful empire. Although Songhay was a Muslim empire, the large majority of its people followed traditional African religions and retained traditional African mythologies. In the late 1500s, Songhay grew too large for imperial rulers to control its territory. Many of its subject peoples revolted, and it was defeated by the Maghreb people of Morocco in 1591. The greatest empire in African history ended in 1612.

Near Central Africa, another great empire called Kanem arose around 1200. This empire was formed by a group of tribes called the Kanuri. The historic leader of the Kanuri, Mai Dunama Dibbalemi (1221–59), was the first Kanuri to convert to Islam. At the height of their empire, the Kanuri controlled territory from Libya, to Lake Chad, to the lands of the Hausa people. By the early 1400s, Kanuri power shifted from Kanem to Bornu, a Kanuri kingdom southwest of Lake Chad. When Songhay fell, the new empire of Bornu grew rapidly. In 1846, however, Kanem-Bornu fell to the growing power of the Hausa states. Although Kanem-Bornu fell, myths of the Kanuri have survived.

Other great states arose in the forests of western Africa south of the Sahel. The greatest of these was Benin in what is now southern Nigeria. Benin was founded by Edo-speaking people around 1170. Benin is best known for its art, in particular detailed brass plaques and statuary that recount important events in Benin history, such as the arrival of the

Portuguese. Benin was still a powerful state when European powers began seizing colonial territory in Africa in the 19th century. Benin held out against the European invaders until the British dismantled the Benin state in 1897. The people of Benin and its neighbor, the Oyo empire (whose people spoke Yoruba) had elaborate PANTHEONS of deities comprising hundreds of gods and goddesses. The mythologies related to these religions are detailed and extensive.

One of the few city-states south of the Sahara that never felt the effects of Islam was Great Zimbabwe, which arose around 1085. Great Zimbabwe itself was a palace and fortress surrounded by huge stone walls made without any mortar. By the 13th century Zimbabwe dominated the Zambezi Valley both militarily and commercially as the Mwenemutapa empire. Most of the site was abandoned in the late 15th century, for unknown reasons. The people of Great Zimbabwe were the ancestors of today's Shona people and may have held the same religious and mythological beliefs.

European Influence

Historically, West Africa is associated with the slave trade, which existed before the coming of Europeans. From the mid-15th century on, Europeans played an increasingly prominent role in the trade, which grew significantly as a result. Some historians estimate that between 1450 and 1850, some 28 million Africans were forcibly removed from central and western Africa. These men and women were sent to European colonies and plantations in the Americas and the Caribbean as slaves. Displaced Africans brought their rich cultural traditions, religions, oral arts, and mythologies with them. VODUN, the religion of the Fon of Benin, is still practiced in Cuba, Haiti, and parts of the United States. African folktales about TRICKSTER animals such as the TORTOISE, HARE, and SPIDER assumed new lives in American folktales. Stories about Br'er Rabbit that originated in the American South and became popular throughout the United States in the 1800s derived from the Bantu trickster hare, KADIMBA.

The first European colony in Africa was the Portuguese colony of Angola, established in 1570. Other European colonies followed: The Dutch and British colonized South Africa, and Belgium, France, Germany, and the Netherlands established colonies throughout Africa. To end the sometimes violent conflict between nations fighting for control of African territory, European leaders met in Berlin in 1884 to establish "spheres of influence"—in other words, to divide the continent among themselves. The boundaries of present-day African countries were largely determined at the Berlin Conference. By the early 1960s, African nations achieved independence and established their own governments.

THEMES OF AFRICAN MYTHOLOGY

Africa did not develop one overall myth system, because Africa itself does not have one people, one history, or one language. African peoples speak more than 2,000 different languages. They have almost as many traditions of behavior and belief and mythologies. Still, common themes do exist. Linguists divide indigenous African languages into four distinct language families: Afro-Asiatic, Nilo-Saharan, Niger-Congo, and Khoisan. A fifth group includes Indo-European languages (Afrikaans, English, and Creole Portuguese) and Malayo-Polynesian (Malagasy, spoken on the island of Madagascar). A comparison of the mythologies of different groups within the same language family provides the following generalizations.

Afro-Asiatic (North Africa, East Africa) This language family reflects the influence of ancient Egyptian mythology, with its theme of the soul's journey after death. A related theme is the division of the world into three realms: the UNDERWORLD where the souls of the departed reside, the middle world of the living, and the upper world that is the home of the deities.

Nilo-Saharan (Central Africa) The predominant mythological theme in this language family is a recurring CREATION ACCOUNT in

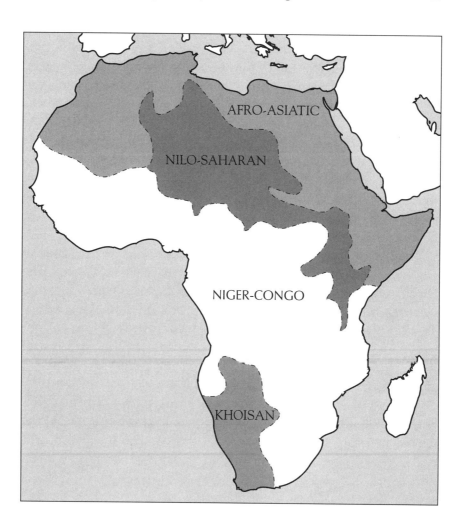

which heaven and Earth were originally close together and connected by a link (chain, leather strip, rope, spider web) that permitted humans and the divine beings to reach each other. Then something occurred that caused a separation—in various myths it was disobedience, violence, or a misunderstanding—and the LINK BETWEEN HEAVEN AND EARTH was broken. The SUPREME BEING receded from humanity, and death came into the world.

Niger-Congo (West Africa, East Africa, southern Africa) The largest of the families of languages spoken in Africa, this language family can be further divided into Bantu and non-Bantu mythologies. Bantu mythology includes a rich collection of epics—long, narrative stories recounting the deeds of a legendary or historical hero. Epic heroes traditionally undertake journeys during which they suffer terrible ordeals and confront MONSTERS, magical forces, and evil beings. The hero's travels may take him to distant lands, to the SKY world, and to the land of the dead. The hero returns home victorious and receives rewards—sometimes a kingship—for his accomplishments. Non-Bantu mythology represents sophisticated systems of COSMOLOGY. In Dogon mythology, for example, creation emerged from a series of divine words, and the human body is presented as a divine oracle. In Bambara mythology, the universe was created from the root sound *Yo*. Non-Bantu mythologies are also scharacterized by elaborate pantheons of gods and goddesses, each with a specific realm and function.

Khoisan (southern Africa) The term *Khoisan* combines the names of the Khoikhoi (formerly Hottentot) and San (formerly Bushmen) peoples. The mythology of the San is centered on the San MASTER ANIMAL, the ELAND, and the praying MANTIS, both of which are identified with the San Supreme Being, who was believed to transform himself into these creatures. San mythology is represented in rock paintings and engravings that are up to 30,000 years old, with corresponding myths that are probably just as old.

SOURCES OF AFRICAN MYTHOLOGY

Egypt and the Nile kingdoms of Nubia and Kush had long traditions of writing. It is from written records that we know about their deities, traditions, and mythologies. Similarly, the Meroic empire had a writing system acquired through its ties to the Semitic peoples of southern Arabia. The most important factor in the spread of literacy throughout Africa was the Islamic invasions, which began with the conquest of Egypt in A.D. 646. By the 1300s the kingdoms of the Sahel had been converted to Islam and became centers of Islamic learning. At first, many Africans dealt with two languages—their native languages and Arabic. Eventually, though, they began to write in their own languages using the Arabic alphabet. With literacy, Africans could record their own histories, legends, and myths. An early known example of East African literature, dated 1520 and written in Arabic, is a history of the city-state of Kilway Kisiwani. Histories of other city-states written in Swahili appeared soon after. The earliest known work of literature—a Swahili epic poem entitled *Utendi wa Tambuka* (*Story of Tambuka*)—was written in 1728.

Africa has a long and rich oral tradition that survives to this day. Cultural beliefs, traditions, histories, myths, legends, and rules for living have been passed down orally from generation to generation. The keepers of the oral tradition are BARDS—tribal poet-singers and storytellers. Bards are charged with remembering and passing along a culture's history and tradition through story and song. Almost all existing epics come from recordings of live performances by African bards (known by the French term *griot* in western Africa).

European explorers, anthropologists, and missionaries were also sources of information about African religions, customs, traditions, and mythologies. One of the most important of these persons—in terms of the quantity of records of African culture he gathered and published—was the German explorer and ethnologist Leo Frobenius (1873–1938). Between 1904 and 1935 Frobenius led 12 expeditions to Africa. His collections of African epics, legends, myths, and folktales—which include the famous Soninke and Fulbe epics—were enormous and were published in 12 volumes.

Finally, an important source of African mythology is present-day religions. The mythologies of African cultures cannot be separated from African religions. Many African religions are living religions not only in Africa but also in parts of the world where people of African descent live. It is through these contemporary religions that we have learned much about traditions, practices, and beliefs of the past.

PRONUNCIATION OF AFRICAN NAMES AND TERMS

Because so many different African languages are represented in this guide, no attempt has been made to include pronunciations of African names and terms. However, these general guidelines can be followed: Words are pronounced phonetically with all consonant and vowel sounds made; no vowels are silent, as some are in English. A final *e* is usually pronounced with a long *a* sound as in *ray*. A final *i* is usually pronounced with a long *e* sound as in *me*. A double vowel—*aa*, for example—represents a drawn-out vowel sound: *ahhh*.

Languages of the Khoisan language family are spoken with unique vocalized "clicks" made by sharply pulling the tongue away from different parts of the mouth. The following symbols indicate which part of the mouth is used:

Symbol	Technical Term	Location
|	Dental	Back of the teeth
||	Labial	Side of the teeth near the cheek
!	Alveolar	Front part of the roof of the mouth
ǂ	Alveo-palatal	Farther back on the palate, or roof of the mouth

HOW TO USE THIS BOOK

The entries in this book are in alphabetical order and may be looked up as you would look up words in a dictionary. The index at the back of the book will help you to find characters, topics, and myths. For individual entries, alternative names and spellings are provided in parentheses following the main entry, as are English translations of the African names. Cross-references to other entries are printed in SMALL CAPITAL LETTERS.

MAP OF MODERN AFRICA

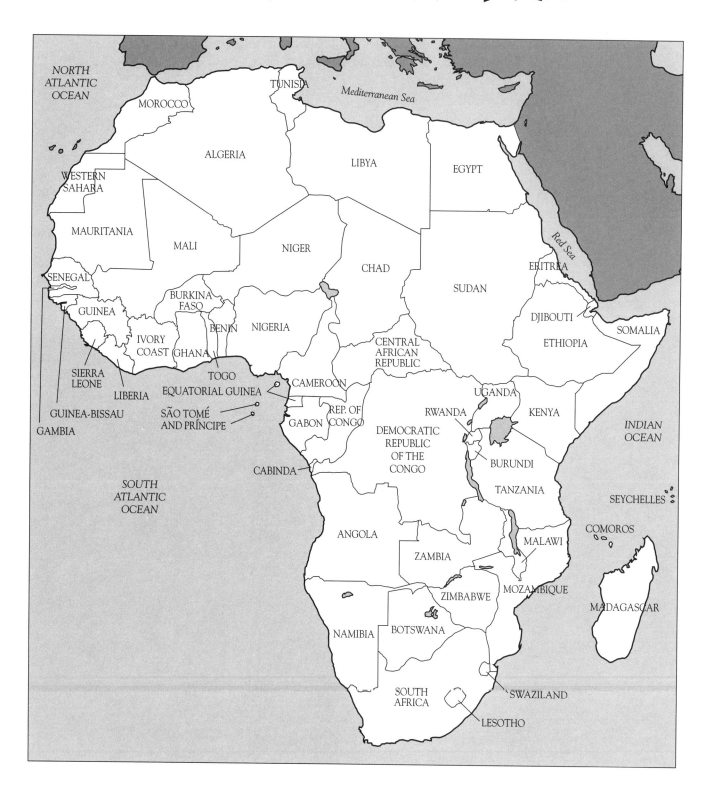

Countries and Tribal Regions

NORTH AFRICA

Algeria
Arab, Berber, Kabyle, Tuareg

Chad
Bedouin, Fulani, Maodang, Massa, Sara, Tuareg

Libya
Arab, Berber, Tuareg

Morocco
Arab, Berber, Lamtuna

Niger
Djerma, Ekoi, Fulani, Hausa, Isoko, Songhai, Tuareg

Sudan
Ama, Anuak, Azande, Bari, Beir, Bongo, Bor, Burun, Didinga, Dilling, Dinka, Fajulu, Gaalin, Jo Luo, Jumjum, Kakwa, Kuku, Lokoiya, Lotuko, Lugbara, Mahraka, Meban, Mondari, Moru, Ndogo, Nuba, Nuer, Sara, Shilluk, Topotha, Zande

Tunisia
Arab, Berber, Maktar

WEST AFRICA

Benin
Bargu, Bariba, Bini, Edo, Ewe, Fon, Igbo (Ibo), Kyama, Twi

Burkina Faso
Akan, Awuna, Bwa, Bobo-Fing, Djerema, Dogon, Gurunsi, Kasena, Korumba, Lobi, Lodagaa, Mossi, Nunuma, Talensi (Tallenzi), Tusyan

Côte d'Ivoire (Ivory Coast)
Adjuru, Agni, Akan, Anyi, Baoule, Dan, Ebrie, Guro, Kru, Kyama, Lobi, Mande, Senufo, Yakouba, Yaoure

Gambia
Mandinka, Serer

Ghana
Akan, Anlo, Ashanti (Asante), Birifor, Dagomba, Ewe, Fante (Fanti), Ga, Grunshi, Kasena, Konkomba, Kulango, Mamprusi, Moshi, Talensi (Tallenzi), Twi

Guinea

Baga, Kissi, Kono, Landumo, Lodagaa, Mdinge, Nalou, Susu, Tenda, Tomo

Guinea Bissau

Bijogo

Liberia

Bassa, Bete, Geh, Gio, Grebo, Guere, Kissi, Kono, Kpelle, Kra, Kru, Mano, Poro, Sande, Vai, Wobe

Mali

Bambara, Belle, Bozo, Dogon, Fulani, Fulbe, Habbe, Malinke, Mandé, Mandinka, Marka, Mdinge, Minyanka, Tuareg

Mauritania

Soninke

Nigeria

Abua, Afusare, Anang, Bachama, Basa, Binawa, Bini, Bura, Chamba, Chawai, Dorei, Dungi, Edo, Efik, Egede, Ekoi, Fulani, Gbari, Hausa, Ibibio, Idoma, Igbin, Igbira, Igbo (Ibo), Ijaw, Ijo, Indem, Isoko, Itsekiri, Iyala, Jen, Jompre, Jukun, Kadara, Kaibi, Kalabari, Kangoro, Katab, Kitmi, Kurama, Mama, Margi, Mumuye, Nkum, Nupe, Orri, Pabir, Piti, Pyem, Rishuwa, Rukuba, Rumaiya, Srubu, Tangale, Tiv, Urhobo, Yachi, Yako, Yoruba

Senegal

Bassari, Diola, Fulani, Mandinka, Peul (Fula), Sarakholé, Serer, Tukulor (Tukuleur), Wolof

Sierra Leone

Kono, Limba, Mendé (Mendi), Tembe

Togo

Bassari, Ewe, Fon, Konkomba, Krachi, Moba

Western Sahara

Arab, Berber

CENTRAL AFRICA

Burundi

Hutu (Bahutu), Rundi (Barundi), Tutsi (Watutsi), Twa (Batwa)

Cameroon

Bachama, Bafut, Baka, Bali, Bamenda, Bamileke, Bamoun, Bamum, Banen, Baranga, Bekom, Bulu, Duala, Ekoi, Fali, Fang, Gyelli, Keaka, Kpe, Malimba, Mambila, Mankon, Pongo, Tikar

Central African Republic
Aka, Baya, Benzele, Boloki, Fang, Pahouin, Zande

Democratic Republic of the Congo
Ake, Alur, Bachwa, Bembe, Bindji, Bushongo, Buye, Bwaka, Efe, Goma,
Hamba, Holoholo, Kongo, Kuba, Lega, Luangu, Luba, Lugbara, Lunda,
Lwalwa, Mbole, Mbuti, Mongo, Ngombe, Nyanga, Pende, Salampasu,
Soko, Solongo, Songye, Tswa, Upoto, Woyo,Yaka, Yombe, Zande

Djibouti
Affar, Issa

Equatorial Guinea
Bubi, Fang

Ethiopia
Amhara, Boran, Danakil, Galla, Ge'ez, Gelaba, Gofa, Gumuz, Hadya,
Hamar, Ingassana, Kafa, Kemant, Koma, Konso, Kuca, Kullo, Kush,
Male, Mao, Masongo, Mekan, Murle, Oromo, Sangama, Sidamo, Tigre,
Uduk (Udhuk), Walamo, Zala

Gabon
Ambete, Baka, Bakota, Benga, Bota, Douma, Fang, Kota, Lumba,
Mahongwe, Mpongwe, Punu

Kenya
Abaluyia, Boran, Digo, Duruma, Elgeyo, Embu, Gabbra, Giryama, Gush,
Kamasya, Kamba (Akamba), Karamojong, Kavirondo, Kikuyu (Gikuyu),
Kipsigis, Kony, Luhya, Luo, Maasai (Masai), Meru, Nandi, Okiet,
Oromo, Pokomo, Pokot, Rabai, Suk, Swahili, Teita, Turkana, Yugusu
(Vugusu)

Republic of the Congo
Aka, Alur, Baka, Balese, Baluba, Bambuti, Bavili, Bembe, Benzele,
Bwande, Fang, Fiote, Gbaya, Hamba, Kete, Konjo, Kuba, Kukni, Kuyu,
Kwele, Lele, Lendu, Logo, Luena, Lugbara, Lunda, Mamvu-Mangutu,
Ngombe, Nkundo, Sonata, Teke, Vili

Rwanda
Hutu (Bahutu), Nyarwanda (Banyarwanda), Rundi (Barundi), Tutsi
(Watutsi)

Somalia
Pokomo, Sanye, Somali

Tanzania
Arusha, Asu, Bena, Bondei, Chagga (Chaga), Fipa, Gogo, Haya, Hehe,
Holoholo, Kimbu, Kuulwe, Luguru, Maasai (Masai), Makonde,
Nyakyusa, Nyamwezi, Pare, Safwa, Sandawe, Shambaa, Sonjo, Sonyo,
Sukuma, Sumbwa, Swahili, Turu, Zaramo, Ziba, Zigula, Zinza

Uganda
Acholi, Alur, Amba, Ankole, Ankore, Bakene, Banyoro (Bunyoro), Basoga, Ganda, Gisu, Gwere, Jie, Karamoja, Kiga, Konjo, Kyiga, Lango, Lugbara, Luo, Madi, Nyankole, Nyankore, Nyoro, Pokot, Sebei, Teso, Teuso, Toro

SOUTHERN AFRICA

Angola
Ambo, Bacongo, Chokwe, Kimbundu, Kongo, Luba, Luena, Luimbe, Lunda, Mbangala, Mbukushu, Mbunda, Ngangela, Ovimbundu, Tshokwe

Botswana
Mbukushu, Ngawaketse, Nguni, Palapye, San, Tswana, Yeye

Lesotho
Sotho

Malawi
Chewa, Makua, Maravi, Matengo, Ngonde, Ngoni, Nyanja, Tonga, Tumbuka, Yao

Mozambique
Chopi, Konde, Lenge, Makua, Ronga, Shambala, Shangaan (Shangana), Thonga, Tonga, Tsonga, Yao

Namibia
Aikwe, Ambo, Auen, Berg Damara, Damara, Herero, Himba, Mbukushu, Nama, Naron, Ovambo, San

South Africa
Fingo, Hurutshe, Khoikhoi, Lovedu (Luvedu), Ndebele, Pedi, Pondo, San, Tembu, Thonga, Tsonga, Tswana, Venda (Bavenda), Xhosa, Zulu

Swaziland
Swazi

Zambia
Ambo, Aushi, Bauchi, Bemba, Ila, Kaonde, Lala, Lamba, Lenje, Lozi, Luapula, Luena, Lunda, Luyi, Mbundu, Nyanja, Rotse (Barotse), Totele

Zimbabwe
Karanga, Korekore, Makoni, Matabele, Ndebele, Rotse, Shangaan (Shangana), Shona, Thonga, Venda, Zezeni

Time Line of African History

Note: This time line tracks the evolution of *various* cultures, not a single monolithic and continuous one.

ca. 1000 B.C.–A.D. 350	Kingdom of Kush
ca. 630 B.C.	Greeks found province of Cyrenaica (now Libya)
814 B.C.	Phoenicians found city of Carthage—beginning of the Carthaginian empire—in what is now Tunisia
750–660 B.C.	Kushite pharaohs rule Egypt
ca. 270 B.C.–A.D. 350	Meroitic empire
149–146 B.C.	Carthage destroyed in Third Punic War
ca. 100 B.C.–A.D. 1000	Bantu migrations
96 B.C.	Ptolemy Apion bequeaths Cyrenaica to Rome
74 B.C.	Rome creates province out of Cyrenaica
ca. A.D. 1–ca. 800	Kingdom of Axum
ca. 300–1076	Kingdom of Ghana
646	Muslims conquer Egypt and begin their spread across North Africa
ca. 1000–1300s	Hausa states
ca. 1000–1505	Swahili city-states
ca. 1100–1450	Great Zimbabwe
ca. 1170–1900	Kingdom of Benin
ca. 1200–1800	Kingdom of Oyo
ca. 1230–1500	Kingdom of Mali
ca. 1250–1836	Kanem-Bornu
ca. 1250–1967	Lake kingdoms
ca. 1400–1700	Kingdom of Congo
1479	Spain enters African slave trade
1485	Diogo Cão of Portugal sails along western coast of Africa
1487	Bartolomeu Dias of Portugal reaches Cape of Good Hope
1497	Vasco da Gama of Portugal sails around Africa to India

1562	Britain begins slave trade in Africa
1570	Portuguese establish colony in Angola
1600–1894	Kingdom of Dahomey
1600–1850	Height of African slave trade
1652	Dutch establish colony at Cape of Good Hope, South Africa; colonists (called Boers or Afrikaners) begin settling large farms
1695–1901	Kingdom of Akan
1700s–mid-1800s	Era of European exploration of Africa
1795	British seize Cape Colony from Dutch
1818–28	Zulu wars against British in South Africa under Shaka
1822	Colony of Liberia formed by free African Americans; Liberia becomes independent nation in 1847
1884	Berlin Conference establishes European "spheres of influence" in Africa
1960s	End of European colonial era in Africa

A-to-Z Entries

ABASSI (ABASI) *Anang, Efik (Nigeria)* The Supreme God and Creator, who lived in the SKY. Like many other African gods, Abassi had a dual nature and was effectively two gods: Abassi Onyong, "the god above," and Abassi Isong, "the god below." According to the Efik, humans could communicate with the Supreme God through Abassi Isong. The Anang said that Ikpa Ison, a fertility goddess and earth spirit, kept Abassi in touch with earthly activities by means of a vulture. (See also BIRDS.) SPIRITS played important roles in Anang and Efik religion and mythology. These spirits included spirits of ANCESTORS, guardian spirits, and evil beings. Fifty-four spirits called *nnem* had significant religious, social, political, and economic functions. They brought sacrifices to Abassi so that he could decide how to reward the humans who had made the sacrifices.

Abassi created the world and the first man and woman. Because Abassi did not want anyone to compete with him, he decided that the people he had created could not be allowed to live on Earth. His wife, Atai, disagreed with him. She insisted that Abassi allow the couple to settle on Earth. Abassi finally permitted them to do so but with two conditions: They could neither grow their own food nor have children. To make it unnecessary for the couple to grow crops or hunt, Abassi rang a bell to summon them to the sky, where they ate all their meals with him. The woman, however, began to till the soil and produce food. Her husband agreed that the food she grew was better than the food Abassi gave them, so he joined her in the fields. The couple stopped having meals with Abassi. In time, they also began to have children. Abassi told Atai that he had been right about not letting humans live on Earth; they had forgotten him. Atai reassured him that humans would never be his equal. To keep people in their place, she sent Death into the world. (See also DEATH, ORIGIN OF.) Death slew the human couple and caused disagreements among their children.

ABEREWA *Ashanti (Ghana)* The name given to both the primordial, or first, woman and a powerful earth goddess, who was also called ASAASE YAA. Aberewa figures in a myth that explains why the SKY god, NYAME, withdrew from Earth and returned to the heavens. As Aberewa prepared food for her children, she pounded palm nuts in a mortar with her pestle. Each time she pounded the mortar, she bumped Nyame with her pestle. Annoyed, Nyame went away from Earth. In a slightly different version of this myth, each time the pestle bumped Nyame, he was bounced a little higher. When he reached the sky, he decided to stay there.

ABOSOM *Ashanti (Ghana)* The name for the PANTHEON of gods and goddesses of the Ashanti and other members of the Akan language group. The head of the pantheon is the Supreme God, NYAME. Nyame was the father of the *abosom*, the gods and goddesses of the pantheon. He sent his four sons to Earth, where they became identified with bodies of water. Beneath the *abosom* are minor deities called *asuman*; and beneath the *asuman* are SPIRITS that animate trees, animals, and charms (see AMULETS AND TALISMANS). Lower still are the *nsamanfo*, the spirits of the ANCESTORS. The *abosom* derived their power from Nyame and were said to come from him and be part of him. They served as intermediaries and messengers between Nyame and other beings. The Ashanti religion is a living religion in western Africa. The following list briefly describes some of the Ashanti deities.

Apo   One of Nyame's sons; associated with a body of water.

Asaase Afua   One of Nyame's daughters; the goddess of fertility and procreation.

Asaase Yaa   One of Nyame's daughters; a powerful earth goddess. ASAASE YAA ruled over Earth's barren places and was also regarded as the mother of the dead. In some accounts she is given as the mother of ANANSI the SPIDER.

Bia (or Bea)   The eldest of Nyame's sons and Nyame's favorite.

Bosomtwe   One of Nyame's sons; associated with a body of water.

Nyame   The SUPREME BEING and creator of the universe. Nyame was one of a trinity, or triad, of gods. He represented the natural universe; NYANKOPON represented its *kra*, or life-giving power; and ODOMANKOMA represented the creative force that made the visible world. (Not all Akan people make these distinctions among the three names of the deity.)

Tano   The second of Nyame's sons; god of the Tano River. He was also invoked as a war god. TANO cheated his brother Bia out of his inheritance.

ABRADI   *Ama, Nyimang (Sudan)*   The Supreme God and Creator, who lived in the SKY. Abradi was all-powerful and above all SPIRITS, whose power came from him. Although no one had ever seen Abradi, people called on him for help when drought, famine, or epidemics struck. One tale explains why Abradi and the spirits were distant from Earth and human activities. In the beginning, the sky was so close to Earth that it pressed down on people and interfered with their everyday activities. Women had to bend low over their cooking pots in order to stir the food. One woman became so annoyed that she reached up and stabbed the sky with her stirring rod. This angered the sky (personified by Abradi, the sky god) so greatly that the sky and all the spirits moved far away from the Earth.

In a myth about the ORIGIN OF DEATH, when someone died, Abradi told the people that the person would come to life again the next day if they just set the body aside. So it was—anyone who died came back to life the next morning. Once, however, when

a man died, a RABBIT reached the people before Abradi did. Rabbits did not get along with people, and this rabbit wanted to cause mischief. It told the people to bury the dead man or else Abradi would destroy them. Frightened, the people buried the man. When Abradi found out what they had done, he decreed that from then on death would be permanent.

ABUA   *Abua (Nigeria)*   The first man to settle on Earth. The Supreme God, Ake, sent Abua and his wife, Egupe, down from the heavens to populate Earth. The couple climbed down to Earth on a rope. (See also LINK BETWEEN HEAVEN AND EARTH.) The children they produced established the first human settlements and towns. See also HUMANS, ORIGIN OF.

ABUK   *Dinka (Sudan)*   The primordial, or first, woman, who was elevated to divine status; patron goddess of women and gardens. Abuk presided over women's activities, especially the cultivation of millet. Her emblem was a small SNAKE. In the beginning, a rope linked Earth and the heavens, home of the Supreme God, NHIALIC. (See also LINK BETWEEN HEAVEN AND EARTH.) Nhialic permitted Abuk and her husband, Garang (the first man), to plant and grind just one grain of millet a day for food. One day Abuk felt especially hungry, so she planted several millet grains. She used a long-handled hoe to do the planting. At that time the SKY was very close to Earth, and Abuk accidentally struck Nhialic with her hoe. This angered the god so much that he severed the rope between Earth and the heavens and withdrew from involvement with human affairs. Because of this, people had to work hard for their food, and illness and death came into the world. (See also DEATH, ORIGIN OF.)

In some traditions, Abuk was the mother of DENG, a RAIN and fertility god and the intermediary between humans and the Supreme God.

ABU NUWAS (ABU NOWAS, ABU NU'AS) (747?–ca. 813) *Arab (Madagascar, Mauritius, Tanzania, Zanzibar)*   An eighth-century Persian poet who became a TRICKSTER-hero in areas of East Africa where Arabic cultural influences were felt. The historical Abu Nuwas (whose full name was Abu Nuwas

Abu Nuwas, an eighth-century Persian poet, appears in many tales as a trickster. *(drawing by Kahlil Gibran)*

al-Hasan ibn Hani al-Hakami) was born in al-Ahwaz, Persia (now Ahvaz, Iran). He gained the favor of the caliphs Harun al-Rashid and his son, al-Amin, and enjoyed great success at court in Baghdad until his death. Abu Nuwas is considered one of the great poets of the golden age of Arabic literature. His verse was creative and marked with humor and irony. This sense of humor and the poet's lifelong pursuit of pleasure may account for his appearance in hundreds of tales as a jester and trickster. Abu Nuwas appears as a character in *The Thousand and One Nights* (also known as *The Arabian Nights' Entertainment*), a collection of ancient tales from Persia, India, and Arabia.

The following tale demonstrates how Abu Nuwas's cleverness amused his sponsors. One day, Abu Nuwas went to the sultan, sobbing, and told him that his wife had died. The sultan told Abu Nuwas that he would get him another wife. The sultana, the sultan's wife, had the perfect maiden in mind. Abu Nuwas and the maiden agreed to marry. The sultan gave them many presents and 1,000 gold pieces as well. Abu Nuwas and his new wife gave no thought to the future and spent the money freely until nothing was left. Abu Nuwas thought of a clever plan. He went to the sultan and told him that his new wife had died, but he had no money with which to bury her. The sultan gave him 200 gold pieces. Then Abu Nuwas's wife went to the sultana and told her that Abu Nuwas had died, but she had no money with which to bury him. The sultana gave her 200 gold pieces. When the sultan saw the sultana that evening, she told him that Abu Nuwas was dead. He responded that it was not Abu Nuwas who was dead but his wife. To settle the matter, they sent a servant to Abu Nuwas's house to determine who actually had died. Abu Nuwas had his wife lie down. Then he covered her with a sheet like a corpse and showed the servant his "dead" wife. The sultana refused to believe the servant's report, so she sent a second servant to Abu Nuwas's house. This time, Abu Nuwas pretended to be dead. The sultan and sultana decided to find out the truth for themselves. When they reached the house of Abu Nuwas, they found the couple lying still as corpses under a sheet. The sultan declared that he would give 1,000 gold pieces to anyone who could tell him the truth about the matter. At that point, Abu Nuwas sat up and told the sultan to give the money to him. Both the sultan and sultana burst into laughter at the way they had been fooled, and the sultan sent the money to Abu Nuwas.

ABU YAZID (ABUYAZIDU) (d. 947) *Berber (Algeria, Morocco, Tunisia)*   The historical figure on whom the mythical hero BAYAJIDA may have been based. Abu Yazid was a leader of the Zanata tribe, one of the most important Berber tribes in North Africa. He adopted the Kharajide faith, converted his tribe to it, and spread the religion across North Africa. This brought him in conflict with the Fatimid caliphs who ruled North Africa. During the time of the second Fatimid caliph, Imam al-Qaim (ruled 933–945), Abu Yazid conquered many important towns. Imam al-Qaim sought refuge in the city of Mehdiya in Morocco, to which Abu Yazid laid siege in 945. Abu Yazid's siege was unsuccessful, but al-Qaim died during it. The imam was succeeded by his son, al-Mansur, who continued trying to quell Abu Yazid's revolt. Abu Yazid withdrew to Susa, which al-Mansur then attacked. Abu Yazid was driven off to Morocco. He continued his revolt until he was finally defeated at Fort Kutama. Seriously wounded during the battle, he died soon afterward. Despite their enmity, al-Mansur respected Abu Yazid for his bravery. After Abu Yazid's death, al-Mansur took care of all of his family.

ADROA *Lugbara (Democratic Republic of the Congo, Sudan, Uganda)* The Supreme God and Creator, who—like many other African gods—had two aspects. He was, therefore, in effect two gods: Adroa and Adro. Adroa (or Adronga) was the SKY god. Adroa was transcendent—lying beyond the limits of experience and knowledge—and remote from humanity. Adroa was thought of as *onyiru,* "good." Adro was the earth god, immanent—existing within the realm of reality—and close to humanity. He was thought of as *onzi,* "bad"; his children were the ADROANZI. Adro onzi (literally, "bad god") was associated with death. To gain Adro's favor, people sacrificed children to him. Later, rams were substituted for children as sacrificial victims.

Adroa created the first man and woman—a pair of TWINS, Gborogboro and Meme. Meme gave birth to all the animals and then to another pair of male-female twins. These first sets of twins were not really human; they had supernatural powers and could perform magical deeds. After several generations of male-female miraculous twins, the hero-ANCESTORS Jaki and Dribidu were born. Their sons were said to be the founders of the present-day Lugbara clans.

ADROANZI *Lugbara (Democratic Republic of the Congo, Sudan, Uganda)* The children of Adro, the earthly aspect of ADROA. The *adroanzi* were guardian SPIRITS of the dead. They frequented streams, large trees, and rocks and followed people at night. If the people they followed looked back, the *adroanzi* killed them.

AFTERWORLD The place where souls went after death. In many African traditions—as in cultures throughout the world—the home of the dead was the UNDERWORLD, a subterranean world ruled over by a deity. Commonly, the underworld was a reflection of the world of the living. In their subterranean village, dead souls carried out their customary daily activities—cultivating the fields, clearing brush, preparing food.

In some traditions, dead souls went to the heavens to live with the SUPREME BEING. (See DJAKOMBA; IIGAMAB; ǂGAO!NA; XU.) According to Bambara tradition, when the first humans died, they did not actually die. They moved closer to the Creator and became ANCESTORS. Usually the Supreme Being brought the souls of the dead to the heavens. ǂGao!na, the !Kung Creator, took the SPIRITS of the dead to live with him in the SKY. The spirits of the dead lived on the lower floor of ǂGao!na's house; ǂGao!na lived on the upper floor with his wife and children. Xu, the Heikum Creator, lived in the sky on the first floor of a two-storied house. The second story was occupied by the souls of the dead. The dead sometimes made their own way to the afterworld. The Edo people of Nigeria bury the dead with their feet pointing west, toward the ocean. The dead are believed to set off in canoes across the sea to reach the spirit world in the dome of the sky.

In still other cultures, when the dead were buried, their bodies were believed to become earth; the dead symbolically became united with the earth god or goddess. (See ALA; AMA.)

For the Oromo of Ethiopia, life after death was lived as a shadowlike existence in Ekera, the afterworld.

AGBÈ *Fon (Benin)* In the Fon PANTHEON of deities (known as the VODUN), chief of the Sea Pantheon, one of the four pantheons into which the Vodun is divided. Agbè was the third-born son of the Creator, MAWU-LISA. He had a female twin named Naètè, who was also his wife. When Mawu-Lisa divided up the realms of the universe among her children, she told Agbè and Naètè to inhabit the sea and command the waters.

AGÈ *Fon (Benin)* In the Fon PANTHEON of deities (known as the VODUN), the god of the hunt; the fourth-born son of the Creator, MAWU-LISA. When Mawu-Lisa divided up the realms of the universe among her children, she gave Agè command of the game animals and birds and put him in charge of uninhabited land.

AGEMO *Yoruba (Nigeria)* A CHAMELEON that was the servant of OLORUN, the head of the Yoruba PAN-

THEON of deities (known as the ORISA). Agemo carried messages between Olorun and the other *orisas*.

Agemo was instrumental in helping Olorun win a contest against OLOKUN, goddess of the sea. Olokun was skilled at weaving and dyeing cloth, and she believed that this skill made her superior to all the *orisas*, including Olorun. Olokun challenged Olorun to a contest to determine which of them was more knowledgeable about making cloth. Olorun sent Agemo to Olokun with the message that if her cloth were as magnificent as she claimed, he would enter the contest. He asked Olokun to show the best examples of her weaving to Agemo, who could report back to Olorun on their quality. One by one, Olokun brought out pieces of cloth dyed in brilliant colors. As she showed each cloth to Agemo, his skin turned the exact color of the cloth. Finally, Olokun brought out a cloth that had a pattern in several different colors. When Agemo's skin reproduced the colors and pattern perfectly, Olokun felt defeated. She thought that if a mere messenger could duplicate what she had created, Olorun's abilities must be even greater. Olokun instructed Agemo to return to Olorun with the message that she acknowledged his greatness.

AGIPIE *Turkana (Kenya)* A god with a dual nature, or two different aspects, each of which warred with the other. One aspect of Agipie was a benevolent SKY god. His other aspect was a dangerous earth god who was associated with lightning and drowning. A thunderstorm occurred whenever the two gods hurled lightning bolts at one another as they fought. See also THUNDER AND LIGHTNING.

AHA NJOKU See IGBO PANTHEON.

AI See SAGBATA.

AIDO-HWEDO *Fon (Benin)* The cosmic serpent (see SNAKE), a servant of the Creator, MAWU-LISA. Aido-Hwedo existed before Mawu-Lisa and participated in the creation of the universe (see FON CREATION ACCOUNT). Aido-Hwedo carried the Creator in his mouth as she created the world. Wherever they rested there are mountains, which were built up from Aido-Hwedo's excrement. When the Creator was finished, Aido-Hwedo curled himself around and under the Earth, where he continues to hold everything in the universe in its place. Aido-Hwedo was seen as the RAINBOW or as light reflected in water.

AIGAMUXA See MONSTERS.

AIWEL LONGAR *Bor, Dinka (Sudan)* A mythical hero who was regarded as the ANCESTOR of the Bor. Tales about Aiwel are examples of ENFANT-TERRIBLE tales—a classification of stories about children whose births are unusual and who have supernatural powers. Different myths tell somewhat different versions of Aiwel's life.

According to one myth, an elderly woman with one daughter was weeping because her husband had died and she had no son. A river god took pity on her and impregnated her with his waters. She bore a son she named Aiwel. He was born with a full set of teeth, which was a sign of spiritual power. The infant Aiwel was also able to walk and talk. When his mother discovered his abilities, he warned her that she would die if she told anyone about this. She did tell someone, and she died. Aiwel went to live with his father, the river god, until he was grown. Then he returned to the village with an ox whose hide had every color on it. Aiwel became known by the name of the ox—Aiwel Longar. He took over the herd of cattle that had belonged to his mother's husband.

During a period of drought and famine, all the villagers' cattle became thin and started to die except those belonging to Aiwel Longar. His cattle remained fat and healthy. Some young men spied on him to find out his secret. They saw that when Aiwel touched the ground, grass and water sprang up. When the young men reported what they had seen, they died. Aiwel told the villagers they should all leave to escape the famine. He offered to take them to a land of plenty, but they refused and set off on their own.

When the people tried to cross a river, Aiwel threw spears at them. One man was able to seize Aiwel and hold him until he became too tired to fight. Then Aiwel said that the people could cross, and he gave them his spears. He told them that he would leave and not return unless they needed his help.

In the second version of the myth, an elderly woman with one daughter lived by catching fish in the river. One day she was splashed by a river being and became pregnant. Eight years later, she bore a son she named Aiwel. Her daughter would not accept Aiwel as her brother because her mother was long past her childbearing years. Aiwel lived as an outcast, herding the headman's cattle to stay alive. He was given a cow by Fadol, the headman. The cow gave birth to a yellow calf that grew into a spotted bull. Because of this miracle, Aiwel became known as Aiwel Longar.

During a period of drought and famine, all the cattle were thin and dying except for Fadol's cattle that Aiwel herded. Fadol followed Aiwel one day and saw that when Aiwel struck the ground, grass and water sprang up. When Aiwel saw him, Fadol fell dead. However, Aiwel touched Fadol and restored him to life. After the two men returned to the village, Fadol gave Aiwel cattle and two beautiful women as wives. Aiwel became headman in Fadol's place.

Aiwel's spear was the symbol of his power and divinity. Priests of the present-day clan of the Spear-Masters trace their origins to him. These priests are the link between the people and the gods and are responsible for spearing to death the sacrificial oxen.

AJA See ORISA.

ÀJÀPÁ See IJAPA.

AJOK (ADYOK, NAIJOK) *Lotuko (Sudan)* The Supreme God and Creator. Although Ajok was benevolent, humans had to make constant prayers and sacrifices to maintain his good nature. In a tale about the ORIGIN OF DEATH, a quarrel between a husband and wife led Ajok to make death permanent. The couple's child had died, and the mother begged Ajok to bring the child back to life. When he did, the woman's husband became angry. He scolded his wife and killed the child. Ajok declared that he would never again bring anyone back to life; from that time on, death would be permanent.

AKOMA MBA *Fang (Cameroon, Equatorial Guinea, Gabon)* The hero of an EPIC of the Fang that is an example of an ENFANT-TERRIBLE tale—a classification of stories about fabulous children with extraordinary powers. After Akoma Mba was miraculously born, he became a danger to his family because of his unpredictable behavior. He became a well-known warrior who went to war against and conquered various peoples. Eventually he became the ruler of the Ekang people.

AKONGO *Ngombe (Democratic Republic of the Congo)* The Supreme God, who in the beginning had close relations with humans and served as their guardian and protector. However, people became increasingly quarrelsome. When the argument among humans became especially intense, Akongo left them and went to live in the forest. No one ever saw him again.

ALA (ALE, ALI) *Igbo (Nigeria)* The earth goddess and goddess of fertility; daughter of the Supreme God, CHUKU. Although Chuku created human souls, he was a distant god. In contrast, Ala—considered the mother of the Igbo people—was close to humans. Everything came from her; she bore the Earth from her womb and took Earth's people under her protection. As the goddess of fertility, Ala made the seed in women's wombs grow. She gave children life and watched over them throughout their lives. As ruler of the UNDERWORLD, she accepted the dead into her body (the earth) and ruled over the ANCESTORS buried there. When the dead were buried, the Igbo believed that they turned into earth and became united with Ala. See also IGBO PANTHEON.

ALATANGANA See KONO CREATION ACCOUNT.

AL-KAHINA (d. 701) *Lamtuna (Mauritania, Morocco)* A half-legendary, half-historic Berber heroine and queen. Originally named Zaynab al-Nafzawiya, she became known as Dahia al-Kahina, "the prophetess." According to legend, al-Kahina directed the most determined resistance to the seventh-century Arab invasion of North Africa. Around 690, she assumed personal command of the North African armies. Under her leadership, the North Africans were victorious, and the Arabs were briefly forced to retreat. However, the Arabs were relentless, and in 701 the North Africans were defeated. Al-Kahina took her own life. Before she did so, she instructed her sons to go to the Arab camp, accept Islam, and join with the Arabs.

According to one legend, the emir Abu Bakr ibn Umar married al-Kahina when she promised to give him great wealth. (The historical Abu Bakr lived in the 11th century.) Al-Kahina blindfolded Abu Bakr and by magical means took him into an underground chamber, where he saw rooms filled with gold, silver, and gems. Other legends say that al-Kahina had JINN (evil supernatural beings) for her servants and that she was a witch.

AL-KHIDR (AL-KHADIR, The Green One) *Arab (Algeria, Libya, Morocco, Western Sahara)* A legendary Islamic hero. According to legend, he was given the name "the Green One" when he sat on some barren land and it turned green with vegetation. Al-Khidr was associated with the sea and became the patron saint of wayfarers. In some legends, he was a companion of Alexander the Great. He accompanied Alexander in his search for the Fountain of Life. Alexander did not find the Fountain of Life, but al-Khidr did. He became immortal after he drank from (or fell into) the fountain.

In the *Qur'an (Koran)*, al-Khidr appears as a servant of Allah (God) who was sent to test the prophet Musa (Moses). Moses and al-Khidr met on the shores of Algeria. Al-Khidr had the ability to see the future. Moses wanted to follow him, but al-Khidr warned him that this would be difficult for Moses. He said that if Moses followed him, he must be patient and refrain from asking any questions, no matter what happened. Moses was tested when al-Khidr scuttled a boat, killed a young boy, and repaired the wall of a city whose inhabitants had refused them food. On each occasion, Moses lost patience with al-Khidr and demanded an explanation for his strange actions. Finally, al-Khidr told Moses that they had to separate, because Moses was unable to see the wisdom of al-Khidr's actions. Al-Khidr then explained that everything he had done was on Allah's orders. He had scuttled the boat to hide it from a tyrant who would steal it; the tyrant was going to die the next day, and the boat's owners could then retrieve it. He had killed the boy because he would have caused his parents to turn away from the true religion. He repaired the wall because it hid a treasure that would have been lost if

people saw it. Through these tests, Moses learned humility.

AMA (MA) *Jukun (Nigeria)* The Creator, possibly a fusion of two or more deities. Ama was sometimes regarded as male and at other times as female. In her female aspect, Ama was an earth goddess and world mother—the female counterpart of CHIDO, the SKY god. Chido was the god above, and Ama was the goddess below. Ama created Earth, the heavens, and everything that lives and grows. As the personification of the Earth, Ama ruled Kindo, the UNDERWORLD, from which all living things came and to which they returned after death.

Ama was compared to a potter. Much as a potter builds up a pot with strips of clay, Ama created the human body by building it up bone by bone. When Ama finished creating a human, Chido descended to Earth and breathed life into the person's body. (See also HUMANS, ORIGIN OF.) When Ama created crops to nourish humans, Chido sent the RAIN and made the crops ripen.

AMADLOZI *Zulu (South Africa)* The SPIRITS of the ANCESTORS of the Zulu people. Humans could invoke the help of the spirit world by calling on the *amadlozi*.

AMMA *Dogon (Burkina Faso, Mali)* The Creator, a deity who in some versions of the DOGON CREATION ACCOUNT was male and in others was female. Amma created the universe and everything in it. He created the Earth by throwing a lump of clay into the heavens. He created the SUN and MOON by shaping two earthenware bowls, one wrapped in red copper (the Sun) and the other wrapped in white copper, or brass (the Moon). He created the STARS by breaking off a piece of the Sun, shattering it, and casting the pieces into space. (In a different version of the myth, he created the stars by throwing bits of clay into the heavens.) For the Dogon, the universe was centered on a world axis pillar called Amma's House Post. The post supported the SKY, which the Dogon thought of as the roof of Amma's house.

AMOKYE *Ashanti (Ghana)* The woman who welcomed the souls of dead women to ASAMANDO, the

Land of the Dead. (See also UNDERWORLD.) Traditionally, Ashanti women were dressed for burial in *amoasie* (loincloths) and beads, which they gave to Amokye as payment for admitting them to Asamando.

AMULETS AND TALISMANS Threatened by hunger, natural elements, beasts of prey, and unknown forces, Africans—like many other people around the world—enlisted the aid of magic or supernatural powers to overcome forces that could cause harm. Amulets and talismans are objects believed to have special powers to protect or bring good luck. Amulets are magical charms used for protection and to ward off evil. Some amulets were believed to have broad powers, providing general protection. Others were used for specific purposes, such as helping hunters achieve success. Talismans are general good luck charms.

Amulets can be either natural or crafted by hand. Natural amulets are of many kinds: the feathers of birds; animal hooves, horns, teeth, and claws; bones; stones; plants and grasses. For example, the teeth of LIONS and CROCODILES were regarded as powerful MEDICINE against wild beasts, especially if a hunter wore them and returned from the hunt successfully. Crafted amulets include carved figures of animals, beaded ornaments, and jewelry such as bracelets, anklets, and rings. Charms are sometimes carried in a pouch called a mojo bag in some cultures, a *wanga* (*oanga*) bag in others. The bag is kept hidden. The belief is that if another person touches someone's charm, the luck will go away.

Charms that seemed to work were widely copied and eventually became standardized into symbolic magical devices. The following list gives some of the most common charms and their uses:

Charm	Use
animal carving	ensure a good hunt
animal teeth	protect against wild animals
anklet	protect a child
bamboo whistle	defend against witchcraft
bundle of sticks	guard the home
copper ring	prevent snakebites
goatskin pouch	ward off illness
iron bracelet	promote fertility

Amulets such as this one from the Yaka people of Democratic Republic of the Congo were worn or carried for protection during the hunt or while on a journey. *(National Museum of African Art/Smithsonian Institution)*

In North Africa, where Arabic influences are strong and the primary religion is Islam, the most important good luck charm is the *khamsa*—a representation of a hand. The hand symbolizes the hand of Fatima, the daughter of the prophet Muhammad, who is seen as a protective figure. The hand symbolizes strength, power, and generosity. Its five fingers represent the five principles of Islam; according to tradition, the number 5 has magical powers of protection against the "evil eye"—a malicious stare that supposedly could bring bad luck, illness, or even death. Many Moroccans, among other people, wear silver hand pendants around their necks, hang embroidered hands in their homes, and paint hand symbols on the outside of buildings. Frequently the palm of the hand is engraved with patterns; often it contains a symbol for an eye. The use of silver for *khamsa* charms is related to the belief that silver has magical qualities and represents purity.

Many Berber women paint designs on their hands with henna (a temporary dye) or even permanently tattoo them. These designs are believed to ward off evil spirits and provide protection from bad luck and illness. At birth, a Berber girl is given a necklace—an amulet with compartments containing herbs and seeds that are believed to have magical powers to protect the newborn baby.

ANANSASEM (ANANSESEM) *Akan (Ghana)* SPIDER stories, named after the Ashanti TRICKSTER hero ANANSI; a class of folktales told by the Akan-speaking people of Ghana. These are stories told for entertainment and are distinguished from myths. The example that follows is a tale in which Anansi proved to the other animals that he was older than any other creature.

The animals had gotten into an argument about which of them was the oldest. They went to Anansi and asked him to be the judge. In turn, each animal told why it was the oldest. The guinea fowl said that when he was born, there was a great grass fire. Since there was no one in the world but him, he had put out the fire. The fire had burned his legs, and they were still red. The parrot claimed that when he was born, there were no tools or weapons. He had made the first iron tool with his beak, which is why parrots' beaks are bent. The ELEPHANT claimed that when he was created, the Supreme God gave him such a large nose that there was very little material left. This is why other animals have short noses. The RABBIT said that day and night had not existed when he was born. The porcupine said that when he came into the world, it was still soft. When all the animals had finished, Anansi announced that he, in fact, was the oldest creature. When he was born, Earth itself did not exist. When Anansi's father died, there was no ground in which to bury him, so Anansi had buried his father in his head. The animals had to agree that Anansi was indeed the oldest of them all.

ANANSI (ANANSE) *Ashanti (Ghana)* The SPIDER, a TRICKSTER and CULTURE HERO. Anansi is one of the most popular characters in West African mythology. He is often referred to as Kwaku (Father) Anansi. As a trickster figure, Anansi was renowned for his cleverness and ingenuity. In some stories, Anansi served as the intermediary of the SKY god NYAME, his father. (In other tales, Nyame was Anansi's friend rather than his father.) As a culture hero, Anansi was regarded as the CREATOR of the SUN, MOON, and STARS and therefore responsible for day and night. He also brought RAIN and taught humans how to sow grain.

One story tells how Anansi came to own all the tales that are told. In the beginning, all tales belonged to Nyame. Anansi wanted to own the stories himself, so he offered to buy them. Nyame told Anansi that he was willing to sell the stories, but the price was high. He wanted three things: Mmoboro, the hornets; Onini, the great PYTHON; and Osebo, the LEOPARD. Anansi was confident that he was clever enough to perform these tasks. He first cut a gourd and made a small hole in it. He then poured water on himself and on the tree where the hornets lived. Anansi then told the hornets that they were foolish to stay in the rain, and he offered the gourd as shelter. When the hornets flew into the gourd, Anansi plugged up the hole and took the hornets to Nyame. Next, Anansi cut a bamboo pole and went to visit Onini, the python. He told Onini that he and his wife had been arguing over whether Onini was shorter or longer than the pole. Onini suggested that Anansi measure him against the pole, and he stretched out along it. Anansi convinced Onini to let him tie the python to the pole to keep him straight. He then carried the bound python to Nyame. To capture Osebo, the leopard, Anansi first dug a pit and covered it with branches and leaves. When Osebo fell into the pit, Anansi offered to rescue him. He bent a tall tree toward the ground and tied it in place. Next, he tied a rope to the top of the tree and dropped the other end of the rope into the hole. He told Osebo to tie his tail to the rope. When Anansi released the rope that held down the tree, the tree sprang upward, leaving Osebo dangling in the air. Anansi had no trouble capturing the helpless leopard. When Anansi presented Osebo to Nyame, the sky god agreed that the price had been paid. From that day onward, all stories belonged to Anansi.

Another Anansi story explains why some people are wiser than others. In the beginning, Anansi was renowned for his wisdom, because he owned all the wisdom in the world. No one did anything without first seeking Anansi's advice. However, not everyone seemed grateful for Anansi's wise counsel. To punish people for their lack of gratitude, Anansi decided to stop giving advice and to repossess all the wisdom he had given out. He went from house to house, collecting all the bits of wisdom. He stored the wisdom in a large pot (or a gourd), which he planned to hide at the top of a tall tree. Anansi tied a rope around the pot and hung it on his chest. When he tried to climb the tree, however, the dangling pot prevented him from getting a good grip. After Anansi had made several unsuccessful attempts to climb the tree, his son, Ntikuma, shouted that he might have an easier time of it if he hung the pot on his back. Anansi angrily responded that he must have failed to gather up all of the world's wisdom, since Ntikuma still seemed to possess some. With the pot on his back, Anansi quickly reached the top of the tree, but his anger made him clumsy. As he tried to tie the pot to the tree, it slipped from his hands. The pot fell to the ground and smashed on a rock, setting free all the bits of wisdom. People came from all over to snatch up as much wisdom as they could. The first to arrive were able to collect a great deal of wisdom, but the latecomers found very little left to collect. (In a slightly different version of the tale, Anansi ignored his son's advice and fell to the ground, scattering his collection of wisdom.)

See ANANSASEM for a story about why Anansi is the oldest animal.

ANCESTORS   In many traditions throughout Africa, ancestors are not truly dead in the final sense of the word. Although unseen, they are forces in the lives of the living and can be called on for guidance and protection. Ancestor cults have a prominent place in the mythologies of the people of East Africa and southern Africa, with the exception of the nomadic Maasai. SPIRITS of ancestors were members of every African PANTHEON of deities; in the hierarchy of the pantheon, most were considered superhuman beings, not deities.

In the tradition of the Bambara of Mali, when the first humans died, they did not disappear. They moved closer to the Creator and became ancestors. For the Bambara, death is viewed as a positive transition in the direction of the Creator. Living humans appeal to the ancestors to intercede with the Creator for them or to exercise power on their behalf. A major component of Bambara religion involves ritual communication with the ancestors.

Ancestral spirits were usually seen as spiritual guardians who protected the community against enemies. People expected ancestral spirits to continually guard the living. The Zulu of South Africa invoked

Ancestral figures of the Dogon of Mali (© *The Hamill Gallery of African Art, Boston, MA*)

the help of the spirit world by calling on the *amadlozi*, the ancestors of the Zulu people. Ancestral spirits known as *ombwiri* (or *ombuiri*) functioned as guardians for a number of ethnic groups in Central Africa, particularly in Gabon. The *ombwiri* took a personal interest in the affairs of their descendants. Depending on their feelings toward the chosen descendant, these spirits could bring well-being and wealth or inflict illness and misfortune. They could appear in dreams, in visions available to members of the *ombwiri* cult, and during ceremonies in which narcotic herbal preparations were consumed.

According to the tradition of the Fon of Benin, the *tohwiyo* (founders) were the divine founding ancestors of the Fon clans. The *tohwiyo* started the clans, instituted their laws, and organized their cults.

The *mizhimo*—the ancestral spirits of the Ila and Kaonde of Zambia—mediated between humans and the Supreme God, LEZA. The RAIN chief of the Bari and Fajulo of Sudan received his rainmaking tools and powers from the ancestors and interceded with the Supreme God through the ancestors. According to the Ashanti of Ghana and other members of the Akan language group, living persons could communicate with the *nsamanfo*—the spirits of the ancestors—in dreams or meditative states.

The Dogon of Burkina Faso and Mali have two categories of ancestors: those who lived before death entered the world and those who lived after death came to humanity. Ancestors in the first category were considered immortal; those in the second category were mortal.

ANIMALS Animal tales in the African tradition amuse and entertain, provide explanations, and comment on human weaknesses and values. Animal TRICKSTER heroes are common. Chief among these are the TORTOISE (see IJAPA), SPIDER (see ANANSI; GIZO; WAC), HARE (see KADIMBA), FOX, and JACKAL.

Animals have symbolic relationships to the gods. Rams, for example, were sacred to SHANGO, the Yoruba god of THUNDER AND LIGHTNING. Shango is frequently depicted with ram's horns. A CHAMELEON named AGEMO was the servant of the Yoruba SUPREME BEING, OLORUN. KHONVOUM, the Supreme God of the Pygmies, communicated with humans through either a chameleon or an ELEPHANT named Gor, "The Thunderer."

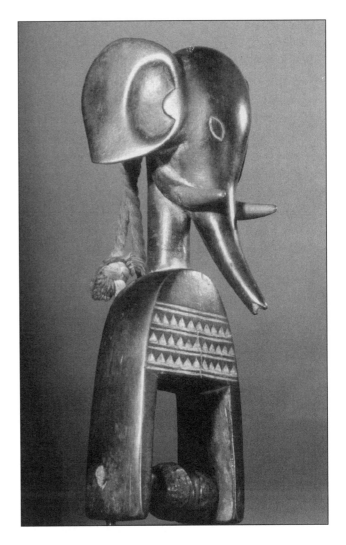

This elephant figure from the Baule/Guro culture of Côte d'Ivoire is actually a pulley. (© Werner Forman/ Art Resource, NY)

In tales throughout the continent about the ORIGIN OF DEATH, animals served as messengers to humanity from the Supreme Being. Typically, one animal bore the message that humans would die but be reborn, and the other carried the message that death would be permanent. The most frequently paired messenger animals were the chameleon and the LIZARD. Other animals used as messengers were the DOG, duck, FROG, hare, MOLE, and TOAD. In some tales the goat, HYENA, and RABBIT were associated with the origin of death in various ways.

Animals are also ritual guardians of sacred places. They are often seen as signs of communication from the spirit world, and their appearance in a place may mark it as sacred.

SNAKES, particularly the PYTHON, play prominent roles in African mythology. A serpent named AIDO-HWEDO carried the Fon Creator, MAWU-LISA, in his mouth as she created the world. CHINAWEZI, the cosmic serpent of the Lunda people, governed the Earth and its waters. Snakes were commonly associated with RAIN and the RAINBOW. (See BUNZI; MBUMBA.)

Where hunting was the way of life, the MASTER ANIMAL—the primary source of food for a people—was revered. In traditional hunting societies, people believed that if their deaths were honored, animals would appear and offer themselves willingly. By killing the animal, the hunter enabled it to enter the spirit world, from which it would return to nourish humanity. When the master animal was not treated properly, the consequences could be terrible for the people who depended on it. See BUFFALO for a tale in which the mistreatment and death of the Baronga master animal had a devastating effect. See ELAND for tales about the master animal of the San.

The origin of animals is part of the creation accounts of most African cultures. In many traditions, animals, plants, and humans were made by the Creator after the Earth was first formed. The gift of specific animals is described in various myths. The Maasai of Kenya, for example, were given cattle by the CULTURE HERO NAITERU-KOP (or in some versions, the Supreme God EN-KAI), who lowered them down from the SKY. In another Maasai myth, livestock emerged from a termite hole in the ground.

For other myths involving animals, see BAT, CROCODILE, LEOPARD, and LION.

ANTAR (ANTARA, ANTARAH) (ca. 525–615)
Bedouin (Algeria, Libya, Morocco, Western Sahara) A warrior and poet celebrated as a hero who rose from slave birth to the status of a tribal chief. Antar's full name was Antarah ibn Shaddad al-Absi. His greatness gave rise to many legends about his deeds, which are retold in the Arabic EPIC *Sirat Antar (Romance of Antar)*. Antar represented the ideal of a Bedouin chief: rich, generous, brave, and kind. Rather than being born to rule, he achieved leadership through his strength of character and his powerful spirit. He was the champion of the weak and oppressed and famed for his courage and gallantry.

According to legend, Antar was the son of an Ethiopian slave woman and Shaddad, chief of the Abs tribe. His father did not acknowledge him as his son, so Antar was treated as a slave. At the age of 15, he proved himself in a battle with a neighboring tribe. Shaddad, proud of his son's ability as a warrior, freed him. In time, Antar became the tribe's chief. As a poet, Antar was praised by his contemporaries, as he is by present-day critics. Although Antar was not a Muslim, one of his poems received the highest honor possible for an Islamic writer—it was displayed at the entrance to the great temple at Mecca.

As the story is told in the *Sirat Antar*, Antar was unaware that the chief was his father. He fell in love with his cousin Ibla (or Abla) and sent her love poetry. This angered her father, who was Antar's uncle Malik. Malik and Shaddad plotted to kill Antar. However, when they saw Antar kill a lion with his bare hands, they did not go through with their plan. Antar later discovered that Shaddad was his father. He demanded that Shaddad acknowledge this, but Shaddad only beat him and drove him off.

Antar then set off on the quest typically undertaken by epic heroes. According to the legend, he conquered Algeria and Morocco and fought with the king of Ethiopia. He also struggled against SPIRITS and other supernatural forces. His travels took him far beyond North Africa—to Spain, Iraq, Iran, Syria, and Rome. Antar returned home victorious and wealthy. He continued to press his suit to marry Ibla against her family's opposition and was forced to kill a jealous rival. At last Ibla's family gave in, and Antar carried his bride off in a silver litter with supports of gold.

AREBATI (AREBATE, BAATSI, TORE) *Efe, Mbuti (Democratic Republic of the Congo)* In Efe and Mbuti mythology, the Supreme God and Creator, god of the SKY and associated with the MOON. The Efe and Mbuti are two of the 10 populations of Pygmies. Among some other Pygmy groups, KHONVOUM is the Supreme God and Creator, rather than Arebati. Some groups make no distinction between Arebati and Tore. For others, Arebati is a lunar deity, and Tore is a god of the forests and hunting.

Arebati created the world and the first man, whom he made from clay with the Moon's help. After fashioning the man's body, Arebati covered the clay with a skin and poured blood into the skin to bring the human to life. (See also HUMANS, ORIGIN OF.)

In the beginning, there was no death. When people grew old, Arebati made them young again. One day, however, a woman did die, so Arebati went to bring her back to life. He asked a FROG to move the woman's body, but a TOAD demanded that he be the one to do this. Arebati allowed the toad to sit with the woman's body on the edge of a pit, which symbolized a grave. He warned the toad that if they fell into the pit, great misfortune would come. The clumsy toad knocked the woman's body into the pit and fell in after her. As Arebati had warned, misfortune came. The woman did not come back to life, and from then on all people were fated to die. (See also DEATH, ORIGIN OF.)

In a different myth about the origin of death, the Supreme God (called Baatsi in the Efe story and Tore in the Mbuti myth) had told humans that they could eat the fruit of any tree but the *tahu*. As long as humans obeyed this rule, Baatsi took them to live in the sky with him when they grew old. One day a pregnant woman craved *tahu* fruit and had her husband pick some for her. The Moon saw this and told the Creator. Baatsi was so angry with humans because of their disobedience that he sent death as a punishment.

ARUAN *Kyama (Benin, Côte d'Ivoire)* A mythical king of the Kyama people. Aruan was one of two sons born to King Ozolua on the same day by different wives. According to legend, the child that cried first would be the heir to the kingdom. Although Aruan was born first, he made no sound. His half-brother Esigie cried out when he was born, so he became the heir. However, King Ozolua favored Aruan over Esigie. When Aruan was grown, Ozolua gave him the royal necklace and a magical sword. He instructed Aruan to choose a place and plant the sword in the ground. That place would become the new capital of the kingdom, and Ozolua was to be buried there. Esigie tricked Aruan into planting the sword in an undesirable location. One of Aruan's slaves dug a great pit there and filled it with his tears, creating a magical lake that he said would be Aruan's home.

When Ozolua died, Esigie had him buried in Benin before Aruan could claim the body. Esigie then demanded that Aruan give him the royal necklace. When Aruan refused, the two went to war. Aruan wore a large bell on his chest. He told his servants that if he lost, he would ring the bell. He instructed them to throw his wives, slaves, and all of his possessions into the lake at the sound of the bell. Unfortunately, as Aruan entered Esigie's city, the bell fell off and rang loudly against the ground. Before Aruan could return to stop them, his servants carried out his orders. Aruan cursed the lake and threw himself into it. The myth says that every five days he emerged from the lake and wandered around moaning in anguish over the loss of all he had.

ARUM *Uduk (Ethiopia)* The Supreme God and Creator, who made everything in the universe, including humans. According to the myth, a *birapinya* tree linked the heavens and Earth. (See also LINK BETWEEN HEAVEN AND EARTH.) This great tree reached up to the SKY, which was much closer to Earth than it is now. Humans traveled back and forth between the sky and Earth by means of this tree, and the sky people used it to visit villages on Earth. One day, however, an elderly woman became angry because she thought she had been wronged, so she cut down the tree. There was no longer any way to get to the heavens, and the sky moved far away from Earth. Before this, death had not been permanent. After the destruction of the tree, death became final. (See also DEATH, ORIGIN OF.)

ARWE See SOLOMONIC DYNASTY, FOUNDING OF.

ASAASE YAA (ABEREWA, ASASE YA) *Ashanti (Ghana)* In the Ashanti PANTHEON of deities (known as the ABOSOM), the daughter of the Supreme God, NYAME. Asaase Yaa was the goddess of the barren places of the Earth. In some tales, she appears as the mother of the TRICKSTER and CULTURE HERO ANANSI the SPIDER.

Another name by which Asaase Yaa was known was ABEREWA. According to myth, Aberewa had a long, sharp sword that could fight by itself. When she ordered the sword to fight, it slaughtered everyone it encountered. When she commanded the sword to stop fighting, it did. The Ashanti tell a story about Anansi and Aberewa's sword. Once, there was famine in the land, and the only food available was in the storehouse of Nyame. In order to become Nyame's agent and sell his food supplies to the people, Anansi agreed to let his head be shaved daily. However, the shaving was painful, and people made fun of the way he looked. When Anansi could no longer stand this situation, he stole some food and fled to Aberewa's house. When he asked the goddess for her protection, she granted it.

One day, when Aberewa left the house, Anansi stole her sword. He returned with it to Nyame and offered to use the sword to protect Nyame whenever he needed help. Nyame accepted Anansi's offer. When an enemy army approached, Anansi ordered the sword to fight. It slew all of the enemy forces. However, Anansi could not remember the command to make the sword stop. With no enemies left to kill, the sword turned on Nyame's army. When only Anansi was left alive, it killed him too. Then it stuck itself into the ground and turned into a plant with leaves so sharp they cut anyone who touched them. The plant still cuts people, because no one has ever given the sword the command to stop.

ASAMANDO   *Ashanti (Ghana)*   The land of the dead (see also UNDERWORLD). A woman named Amokye welcomed the souls of dead women at the river that souls crossed to reach Asamando. In payment, she received from them their *amoasie* (loincloths) and beads. Ashanti women prepared for burial were dressed in *amoasie* and beads so that they could give these to Amokye at the river crossing. In a well-known Ashanti tale, a young man made a journey to Asamando in search of the SPIRITS of his dead wives (see KWASI BENEFO).

ASHANTI PANTHEON   See ABOSOM.

ASIS (ASISTA)   *Kipsigis, Nandi (Kenya)*   The Supreme God, personified by the SUN. Working through the Sun, Asis created all of Earth's creatures from air, earth, and water. Asis first created the Sun, MOON, SKY, and Earth. Next he created the first four living beings: a human, the ELEPHANT, the SNAKE, and the cow. Although distant, Asis was the force behind everything; he gave humans everything that was good. The *oiik*, the SPIRITS of the dead, mediated between Asis and humans. If humans upset the balance of nature, the *oiik* punished them.

ATAA NAA NYONGMO   *Ga (Ghana)*   The Supreme God, who created the universe and everything in it and was associated with the SKY. Ataa Naa Nyongmo was considered a nurturing god, an important quality for the deity of an agricultural society. He controlled the RAIN, the SUN's light, and the growth of plants. If humans failed to perform rites properly or violated his commandments, he punished them by withholding the things necessary for life or by causing catastrophic natural events such as earthquakes.

ATAI   *Efik (Nigeria)*   The wife of ABASSI, the Supreme God and Creator. After Abassi created the first man and woman, Atai convinced him to allow the couple to live on the Earth. Abassi set two conditions on the humans: They could neither grow their own food nor have children. When the couple violated these prohibitions, Atai sent Death to Earth. (See also DEATH, ORIGIN OF.) Death killed the couple and caused discord among their children.

ATUNDA (That Which Destroys and Creates Again)   *Yoruba (Nigeria)*   A being who was the slave of the Creator, ORISA-NLA. In the beginning, there was just formless space in which Orisa-nla and Atunda lived. One day, while Orisa-nla was working in a hillside garden, Atunda rebelled against the Creator. He rolled a huge boulder down the slope. When the boulder struck Orisa-nla, he shattered into hundreds of fragments. Each fragment became an ORISA, part of the Yoruba PANTHEON of gods and goddesses.

AZŌ   See SAGBATA.

BAATSI *Mbuti (Democratic Republic of the Congo)*
The first man, who was created by the Supreme God, Tore, with the help of the MOON. (See also HUMANS, ORIGIN OF.) Tore made Baatsi by kneading clay into the shape of a man, which he covered with a skin. When Tore poured blood into the skin, the man came to life. The Creator told Baatsi that he would live in the forest and produce many children. Baatsi's children could eat the fruit of every tree but one, the *tahu* tree. Baatsi warned his many children of this prohibition and then went to live with Tore in the SKY. One day, however, a pregnant woman had such a craving for *tahu* fruit that she could not resist. Her husband got the fruit for her and hid the peel, but the Moon saw him. When the Moon told Tore what the humans had done, Tore became so angry that he sent death as a punishment. (See also DEATH, ORIGIN OF.)

In Efe tradition, Baatsi was another name for the Supreme God AREBATI.

BACHWEZI See CHWEZI.

BAGANDA PANTHEON See LUBAALE.

BAMBARA CREATION ACCOUNT *Bambara (Mali)* There are several different versions of the Bambara creation account, each of which offers conflicting descriptions of the relationships among the principal figures. According to legend, in the beginning there was nothing but the emptiness of the void. The universe began from a single point of sound—the sound *Yo*. Everything—including human consciousness—came from this root sound. Yo—the primeval creative spirit—created the structure of the heavens, the Earth, and all living and nonliving things. Yo brought into being the creator figures FARO, PEMBA, and Teliko. Faro (who was male in this account) was

a water spirit. He created seven heavens corresponding to the seven parts of the Earth and fertilized them with RAIN. Teliko was the spirit of the air. He created a set of TWINS who were the ancestors of the first humans. Pemba created the Earth. He then mixed together his saliva and dust and created a woman, MUSOKORONI, who became his wife. Together they created all the animals and plants. Jealous of Pemba's growing power, Musokoroni planted him in the ground. She then left and wandered the world, creating disorder and unhappiness and bringing illness and death to humanity. (See also DEATH, ORIGIN OF.) Before Musokoroni died herself, though, she taught humans the skill of agriculture. Faro uprooted Pemba and took over responsibility for the harmony of life on Earth.

In another account, in the beginning the Supreme God, Bemba, created a set of twins. They were a male creator figure, Pemba, and his sister, Musokoroni, the goddess of disorder. Musokoroni rebelled against Bemba, and she and Pemba left the heavens. They went down to Earth on an umbilical cord. (See also LINK BETWEEN HEAVEN AND EARTH.) Then they severed the cord, which broke their connection to the heavens. On Earth the twins behaved recklessly, which drew Bemba's wrath. Despite the god's anger, the twins continued their wild ways. Musokoroni had sexual relations with her twin, Earth itself, trees, the wind, and the SUN's rays. Bemba was determined to end this activity. He created a second set of twins—a female creator figure named Faro and her brother, Koni—and sent them to Earth in a golden canoe.

Bemba intended the two sets of twins to join together to create humans and animals to populate Earth. However, Musokoroni was jealous of Faro, and she tried to turn humans against her. She lured

A bard in a marketplace embellishes the story he tells with music played on a bamboo flute. (© Craig Aurness/ CORBIS)

human men to herself, had sexual relations with them, and then destroyed them. As punishment, Bemba sent a FLOOD to cleanse Earth. Musokoroni died in the flood. Faro paddled around in her golden canoe rescuing humans and animals so that they could repopulate Earth.

In a different account in which Musokoroni is not mentioned, the two creator figures Faro and Pemba emerged from the forces of creation. Faro created the SKY, and Pemba created the Earth. Faro had a male twin, Koni, who was also her husband. The Supreme God sent a flood to cleanse the Earth. Faro gathered humans into an ark that drifted for seven days. After Faro and the humans emerged from the ark, they built the first village and planted seeds. After the first rain fell, those seeds grew into all of the plants and trees on Earth. Then Faro created animals and ordered night and day, the seasons, and life itself.

For another creation account involving Pemba and Faro, see MANDE CREATION ACCOUNT.

BARD A poet-singer skilled in composing and reciting verses about heroes and their deeds. EPICS—long, narrative stories that recount the deeds of a legendary or historical hero—are performed by bards. In African traditions, epics may be told in prose or as dramatic poetry; they are usually interspersed with songs. Almost all existing epics come from recordings of live performances by the African bards and storytellers who were charged with remembering and passing along a culture's history and tradition through story and song. In western Africa, bards were known by the French term *griot*. (See also ORAL TRADITION.)

Among the Fulbe, or Fulani, people of Sudan, a nobleman customarily set out in quest of adventures accompanied by a bard (*mabo*) who also served as his shield bearer. In this way, the bard served as the witness of the lord's heroic deeds, which he then celebrated in an epic poem called BAUDI.

BAT The bat is the only mammal that can truly fly rather than just glide. Bats are nocturnal. They are able to fly and hunt in complete darkness by means of echolocation, which uses echoes of the bat's own supersonic squeaks to locate obstacles and prey. Many bats live largely on insects; some are carnivorous;

some live on flower nectar and pollen; and one group—the flying foxes—are fruit-eaters. Because of their nocturnal nature and ability to negotiate their way in darkness, bats have been viewed as creatures of mystery and are frequently feared.

A legend told by the Kono of Sierra Leone explains why bats sleep during the daytime. Long ago, the SUN shone during the day, the MOON shone during the night, and there was never any true darkness in the world. Then the Supreme God, Yataa, put darkness into a basket and told a bat to take it to the Moon. When the bat grew tired and hungry, it set the basket down and flew off to look for food. Other animals found the basket, opened it, and let the darkness escape. To this day the bat sleeps during the daytime and flies around at night, trying to recapture the darkness.

BAUDI *Fulbe, or Fulani (Mali, Niger)* Ancient EPICS containing the myths and legends of the Fulbe people. The hero of several Fulbe legends was Goroba-Dike (also written as Goroo-Bâ-Dicko), a member of the Ardo royal family. Being a younger son, Goroba-Dike had no inheritance. He was so angry because of his lack of status that he left the land of the Ardo and wandered around the lands of

This royal stool from Cameroon is decorated with a motif of bat heads. *(© Réunion des Musées Nationaux/ Art Resource, NY)*

the Bammana people in a destructive mood. Out of fear, the Bammana gave Goroba-Dike's BARD gold and begged him to help them. The bard convinced Goroba-Dike to return to his own people, who owed him a kingdom.

In order to determine the situation in Ardo, Goroba-Dike disguised himself as a peasant and went to work for a blacksmith. The smith told him that Kode Ardo, the daughter of the king, Hamadi Ardo, wore a tiny ring on her little finger. She had declared that she would marry only the man whose finger the ring would fit—someone with the delicate bones of a true Fulbe. Men came from all over to try to fit the ring on their fingers, but it fit none of them. Goroba-Dike, still dressed in rags, was the last to try—and the ring fit. Kode Ardo protested that she could not marry a ragged, filthy peasant. Her father insisted that she had set the test, and Goroba-Dike had passed it. The two were married.

Burdama, or Tuaregs, had been stealing the Fulbe cattle, so Hamadi Ardo sent his army against them. Mounted on a donkey, Goroba-Dike left to join the battle, with his wife jeering at him. During the battle, he transformed himself into a richly dressed warrior on a splendid horse. He agreed to help the king's sons-in-law win the battle if each of them gave him one of their ears in payment. After each battle, Goroba-Dike changed back into a peasant riding a donkey. At one point, the Burdama kidnapped Kode Ardo. Goroba-Dike—in his heroic form—rescued his wife but was badly wounded. Not recognizing him as her husband, Kode Ardo bound up his wound with a part of her dress. That night, Kode Ardo saw that her husband had been wounded, and she recognized the cloth that covered his wound. When she asked her husband for an explanation, he revealed that he was the son of a king. He displayed the ears he had taken to prove that he was the hero of the battles. In gratitude, King Hamadi Ardo handed over his kingdom to Goroba-Dike.

BAYAJIDA (ABU YAZID, ABUYAZIDU) *Hausa (Niger, Nigeria)* The legendary hero of the Hausa, who was said in some accounts to be the son of the king of Baghdad; his Arabic name was Abuyazidu. (See also ABU YAZID.) The Hausa claim to be originally of Arab descent through Bayajida.

According to tradition, Abuyazidu commanded a large army. After fighting a war against enemies that had attacked Baghdad, Abuyazidu wandered about with his army until they reached Bornu in the northern part of Nigeria. He allied himself with the Sultan of Bornu and helped the ruler defend his territory in several wars. During this time people began to call him Bayajida. Bayajida married the sultan's daughter, Magira. As Bayajida's wealth, power, and fame grew, however, the sultan became envious and decided to kill him. Magira learned of her father's plan and warned Bayajida. The couple fled Bornu and settled in Garum Gabas. Bayajida left the pregnant Magira there and continued on his travels.

Bayajida reached the town of Daura, which was ruled by a woman named Daurama. An elderly woman agreed to let him stay in her house. When Bayajida requested a drink of water, the woman told him that there was none. The town had just one well, in which a great SNAKE lived. Villagers could draw water from the well only when the entire community came together and formed a group strong enough to hold the snake off. Undaunted, Bayajida took a bucket, went to the well, and began to draw up water. As the bucket rose, the giant snake clung to the rope attached to the bucket. Bayajida bravely grasped the snake's head with one hand and cut it off. He left the snake's body by the well but put its head into his sack, which he carried back to the woman's house.

When people passed by the well the next morning, they saw the snake's dead body and brought the news to Queen Daurama. Astonished, the queen declared that she would give the rule of half her land to whoever brought her the head of the snake. Many people claimed that they had killed the snake, but no one was able to produce its head. Finally, the woman who had housed Bayajida came forward and told about her unusual guest. Queen Daurama summoned Bayajida, and he produced the snake's head. When Daurama offered Bayajida half her land, he refused. Instead, he requested the queen's hand in marriage. She accepted, and they lived a long, happy life together. Their son, Bawo, ruled Daura after their death. Bawo's six sons became the founders and rulers of six of the seven Hausa states. The son of Bayajida by his first wife, Magira, founded and ruled the seventh Hausa state.

Ashanti sculpture featuring a bird (© Werner Forman/ CORBIS)

BIA   See ABOSOM; TANO.

BIGO BYA MUGENYI   A late Iron Age settlement in Uganda, said to have been built by the CHWEZI, or Bachwezi, a semimythical people who migrated into the area of what is now Uganda and founded the ancient kingdom of Bunyoro. Bigo Bya Mugenyi was an enormous enclosed area—covering nearly four square miles—that contained villages and forts. The settlement was surrounded by a 12-foot ditch dug into the bedrock. It was occupied from about A.D. 1000 to 1500.

BIRDS   Because of their ability to fly, birds were often seen as intermediaries or messengers between the SKY deities and humans. In the tradition of the Anang of Nigeria, a vulture kept the Supreme God,

ABASSI, in touch with earthly activities. For the Kamba of Kenya, birds were the messengers the Creator sent to humans to tell them that death would be permanent. (See DEATH, ORIGIN OF; MULUNGU; NGAI.) WAKA, the Supreme God of the Galla of Ethiopia, sent a bird to tell humans that they would be immortal. The bird, however, gave the opposite message, bringing death to the world. A Fon tale relates how a bird called Wututu (or Otutu) intervened in a quarrel between the gods SAGBATA and Hevioso. The gods' dispute had caused a great drought on Earth. Wututu was able to reconcile the gods, and the drought ended.

Birds were sometimes associated with evil or seen as evil themselves. According to the Kaonde of Zambia, the Supreme God, LEZA, gave a honey bird three sealed calabashes (a kind of gourd) to take to the first humans. The bird was to tell the humans that they could open the first two gourds, which contained seeds, but not the third one. They could open that only after Leza went down to Earth and taught them about its contents. On the way, however, the curious honey bird opened all three calabashes. The first two held seeds, but in the third were all the evils of the world—death, disease, poisonous reptiles, and beasts of prey. Leza was unable to recapture these evils, and so they remained in the world. In a Krachi myth, a ground toucan developed a liking for human flesh. It killed and ate every person it met. (See WULBARI.)

For the Xhosa of South Africa, birds were associated with heaven and the SUPREME BEING. In a Xhosa tale about the hero GXAM, CROWS—which were considered miraculous birds of God—had the power to restore the hero's vision after he had been blinded. For the Xhosa, lightning was a bird—Impundulu or Intakezulu—whose wingbeats produced thunder. (See also THUNDER AND LIGHTNING.) Impundulu was greatly feared as a messenger of death. In a myth told by the Sara of Chad and Sudan, a crow was responsible for the scattering of humans, fish, and plants throughout the world. (See WANTU SU.)

In some cultures, birds were revered for various powers they were supposed to have. In West Africa, ibis were revered for their supposed oracular powers—their ability to predict future events.

In the KONO CREATION ACCOUNT, there was no light in the world until a man named Sa gave birds the ability to sing. Their voices called light into the world. In the SHANGAAN CREATION ACCOUNT, a bird was responsible for the ORIGIN OF HUMANS. N'wari, the bird god, laid an egg in a reed. The first human hatched from this egg.

In one section of the great EPIC of the Soninke people, the DAUSI, a buzzard was responsible for the recovery of Tabele, the great war drum that had been stolen by JINN (evil spirits).

BOOK OF THE GLORY OF KINGS (*Kebra Negast*)   See SOLOMONIC DYNASTY, FOUNDING OF.

BUFFALO   The African buffalo is a formidable animal. There are two types: the large savannah, or plains, buffalo and the much smaller forest buffalo. The savannah buffalo weighs more than 1,500 pounds on average and stands 6 feet tall at the shoulders. Cows, or female buffalo, are lighter and smaller than bulls, or male buffalo. Buffalo bulls are dark brown or black, but buffalo cows are reddish in color. The buffalo's heavy, curved horns have a span of 3 feet and are a powerful weapon. Buffalo are swift runners, able to sustain speeds of 37 miles per hour on open ground. They are fearless fighters against their enemies—human or animal.

The buffalo cow is closely associated with female deities in various African traditions. The shape of the

The buffalo—a primary food source for some African people—is the subject of many myths. (© *Susan Van Etten*)

buffalo's horns resembles a crescent MOON—a symbol of the goddess as an archetype. Buffalo cows are a symbol of female reproduction and of the goddess's regenerative powers—her ability to renew and restore life. This power is seen in the continuing renewal of the supply of game. The goddess associated with game animals offers them as food for humans and then brings forth more animals. The need of hunters to join with the goddess's power is reflected in a Yoruba myth in which the goddess OYA—in her aspect of Red Buffalo Woman—was pursued by the god OGUN, Chief of Hunters, until he made her his wife.

The buffalo was the MASTER ANIMAL—the primary source of food—of the Baronga of South Africa, who called it "the Miracle Worker of the Plains." According to Baronga belief, there was a covenant, or pact, between the master animal and humans. The people took care of the master animal, which in turn assured the supply of buffalo for the hunt. A Baronga myth illustrates the dire consequences of breaking this covenant.

A young Baronga woman married a man from a faraway village and asked her parents for a buffalo to accompany her to her new home and be her servant. Her parents refused—the master animal was not the servant of humans. When the woman left the village with her new husband, though, the buffalo accompanied them, visible only to her. In the woman's new home, the buffalo performed all of the woman's work—fetching water, carrying firewood, and clearing fields. In the woman's home village, a plate was always filled with food for the buffalo. However, the young woman never thought to feed her servant, and the buffalo grew weak with hunger. When he complained, his mistress told him to take food from the villagers' gardens. Angered at the theft of their crops, the villagers set up a guard at night. The buffalo could not remain invisible while eating, and so he was seen. The young woman's husband killed him. Horrified, the young woman tried several times to restore the buffalo to life. Her husband interrupted her each time, and she had to give up. She returned home to tell her people about the death of the Miracle Worker of the Plains. Devastated, the villagers killed themselves and their children rather than face starvation.

In a myth about the origin of game animals that was told by the Kabyl of Algeria, the primordial buffalo, Itherther, emerged from a dark place under the ground with a female calf named Thamuatz. They produced a young bull that drove off his father and mated with his mother and his newborn sister. Itherther wandered into the mountains. Every time he thought of Thamuatz, his semen ran into a natural bowl of rock. The SUN used this semen to create all the game animals.

BUMBA *Bushongo (Democratic Republic of the Congo)* The Supreme God, first ANCESTOR, and creator of the universe. See BUSHONGO CREATION ACCOUNT.

BUNYORO PANTHEON See CHWEZI.

BUNZI *Woyo (Democratic Republic of the Congo)* A cosmic serpent (see SNAKE) that brought the RAIN. Bunzi was the daughter of Mboze, the Great Mother, who brought life to and watched over human beings. When Mboze gave birth to a serpent, her husband knew he was not the serpent's father, so he killed Mboze. Bunzi assumed her mother's rainmaking powers. When a RAINBOW appeared in the sky, people knew that it was Bunzi.

BUSHONGO CREATION ACCOUNT *Bushongo (Democratic Republic of the Congo)* In the beginning, only darkness and water existed. Bumba, the Supreme God, was alone. Stricken with stomach pain, Bumba began to vomit. First, he vomited up the SUN, and for the first time there was light. Then Bumba vomited up the MOON and the STARS. He vomited again, and various animals, birds, and fish appeared. Last, Bumba vomited up human beings. (See also HUMANS, ORIGIN OF.) The creatures that came out of Bumba created other animals. A heron created all the birds, a CROCODILE made reptiles and lizards, a beetle created all the other insects, and so on. Bumba's three sons finished the task of creating the world. When all their work was done, Bumba gave the completed world to humans.

CAGN See IKAGGEN.

CHAMELEON A tree-dwelling lizard with a prehensile tail, independently movable eyes, and the unusual ability to change the color and markings of its skin to blend in with its surroundings. This mysterious skill led people to attribute magical powers to the chameleon. The Mensa of Ethiopia believed that the chameleon had medicinal, or healing, properties. A chameleon would be placed on the head of a person who had a headache. When the chameleon changed color, this meant that it had taken the ailment into itself. The chameleon was then thrown away, taking the headache with it.

Chameleons play a variety of roles in the mythology of different tribal groups. In a Yao myth about the ORIGIN OF HUMANS, only animals lived on Earth until a chameleon found the first man and woman in its fish trap (see MULUNGU). According to the Fon, the smooth skin of the chameleon reflected what was happening behind people's backs. When enemies came from behind, their approach would be reflected in the chameleon's skin. Therefore, the Great God MAWU-LISA sent a chameleon to Earth with the first humans to protect them.

Chameleons often appear in myths as messengers—intermediaries between the SUPREME BEING and other deities or humans on Earth. In the Yoruba tradition, a chameleon named AGEMO carried messages between OLORUN, the Supreme God, and the other deities of the Yoruba PANTHEON. In myths about the ORIGIN OF DEATH, a chameleon was frequently one of two messengers sent by the Creator to tell humans whether death would be temporary or permanent. In these myths, the chameleon carried the message that people would die but would be reborn. Typically, a faster-moving animal—a LIZARD, BIRD, or HARE—arrived first and gave people the message that death would be permanent. When the chameleon finally arrived, people did not accept its message of rebirth and renewal. The Supreme Gods CHIUTA, LESA, MULUNGU, NGAI, NYAMBE, QAMATHA, UMVELINQANGI, UNKULUNKULU, and ZIMU sent chameleons with messages of eternal life. In some myths, it was humans who used chameleons as messengers (see MODIMO; TILO).

This wooden dance mask from Nigeria has a chameleon—the servant of the Yoruba Supreme God Olorun—on its crest. (*© Werner Forman/Art Resource, NY*)

In some cultures, chameleons were held to be unlucky. For a chameleon to enter a Zulu hut was the worst possible omen.

CHARMS   See AMULETS AND TALISMANS.

CHIDO *Jukun (Nigeria)*   The SUPREME BEING and SKY god; the male counterpart of the earth goddess AMA. When Ama created humans, Chido descended to Earth and breathed life into them. When Ama created nourishing crops, Chido sent the RAIN and caused the crops to ripen. Chido was identified with the SUN and with heavenly phenomena in general.

CHINAWEZI *Lunda (Angola, Democratic Republic of the Congo)*   The cosmic serpent (see SNAKE) that governed the Earth. Chinawezi was the mother of all things. In the beginning, she divided up the world with her husband, Nkuba, the lightning. (See also THUNDER AND LIGHTNING.) Nkuba went into the SKY, where he created the RAIN with his urine. Chinawezi controlled the waters and made the rivers swell when she heard thunder.

CHINEKE   See CHUKU.

CHIUTA *Tumbuka (Malawi)*   The Supreme God—powerful, self-created, and all-knowing. Although humans could not approach Chiuta, he kept in contact with their activities. When there was an earthquake, it was the voice of Chiuta asking whether his people were still there. Chiuta was associated with natural phenomena such as RAIN and THUNDER AND LIGHTNING.

In a myth about the ORIGIN OF DEATH, Chiuta sent a CHAMELEON and a LIZARD to take two messages to humans. The chameleon's message was that when humans died, they would be reborn; the lizard's message was that death would be permanent. Because the chameleon was so slow, the lizard arrived first with its message. When the chameleon finally arrived, it was too late—the people had accepted the lizard's message, and the permanence of death was established.

CHUKU (CHI, Great Spirit) *Igbo (Nigeria)*   The Supreme God, the Creator from whom all good came,

and the head of the IGBO PANTHEON of deities. Chuku was a triad, or trinity, of gods. His three aspects were Chukwu, the Great God; Chineke, the creative spirit; and Osebuluwa, who governed and directed all things. Chuku's symbol was the SUN, and he brought RAIN to make plants grow.

As with many other African gods, Chuku became separated from his creations. In the beginning, the SKY in which Chuku lived was close to Earth and could be touched by humans. However, the sky was so close that whenever a woman pounding her mortar with a pestle lifted the pestle high, she hit the sky. Chuku told the woman to stop, but she paid no attention. In anger, he moved far above Earth, where the sky has been ever since. ALA, Chuku's daughter, remained close to humans and was considered the mother of the Igbo people.

The Igbo myth about the ORIGIN OF DEATH reverses the usual tale in which the SUPREME BEING sent two messengers to people, one to tell them that they would be reborn after death and the other to tell them that death would be permanent. In the Igbo tradition, when death entered the world, the people sent a DOG to ask the Creator to restore the dead to life. However, a TOAD overheard the message. Wanting to punish humans, the toad raced ahead of the dog and told Chuku that humans did not want to be returned to life after they died. Chuku accepted this request and could not reverse his decision when the dog arrived with the correct message.

CHUKWU   See CHUKU.

CHWEZI (BACHWEZI, CWEZI) *Nyoro (Uganda)*   The PANTHEON of SPIRITS that constitutes the traditional religion of Bunyoro-Kitara, one of the four main kingdoms that compose the Republic of Uganda. Traditionally, there were 19 Chwezi spirits, who were variously associated with harvest, healing, plenty, smallpox, royalty, weather, cattle, and so on. Each spirit was identified with one of the long-dead—and perhaps mythical—Chwezi who had once ruled the kingdom of Bunyoro.

Historically, the Chwezi, or Bachwezi, were an unknown people that migrated into the area of what is now Uganda and founded the ancient kingdom of Bunyoro. Historians do not agree about who these people were, where they came from, where they went, or even whether they existed at all. At its peak, the kingdom was said to have covered the whole of central, western, and southern Uganda; western Kenya; northern Tanzania; and the eastern part of the Democratic Republic of the Congo. According to the ORAL TRADITION, the Chwezi were demigods who had one leg in this world and the other in the UNDERWORLD, but who had assumed the characteristics of human beings. They were said to have been tall and light skinned, great magicians, and skilled hunters. Legends record just three Chwezi kings: Ndahura, his half-brother Mulindwa, and his son Wamara. The first ruler, Ndahura, was also revered as the god of smallpox.

During Wamara's rule, disease and famine led to the decline of the Chwezi. They consulted the diviners, who killed an ox and cut it open to study its entrails, or intestines—but the ox had none! A strange diviner from the north appeared and said that he would solve the riddle. He cut open the ox's head and hooves, releasing its missing entrails together with a dark cloud of soot. The diviner's interpretation was that the absence of the entrails meant that the rule of the Chwezi in Bunyoro was at an end. The cloud of soot signified that dark-skinned strangers from the north would take over the kingdom. The entrails' presence in the hooves meant that the Chwezi would go far away. Their presence in the head signified that the Chwezi would continue to rule somewhere. The Chwezi left Bunyoro, and to this day no one knows where they went. One legend says that because of their semidivine status the Chwezi disappeared into the underworld. According to another legend, they drowned themselves in Lake Albert, which is on the border of Uganda and the Democratic Republic of the Congo.

See also BIGO BYA MUGENYI.

COSMIC EGG One of the themes of African creation accounts is the "cosmic egg myth," in which an egg was the beginning of life. In the FANG CREATION ACCOUNT, MEBEGE, the Supreme God, was lonely with only a SPIDER, Dibobia, for company. Because they were alone, Dibobia told Mebege to create the Earth. Using hair from his underarm, material from his brain, and a smooth stone, Mebege produced an egg, which he gave to Dibobia. The spider lowered the egg into the sea. When the egg cracked, three people came out of it. Mebege and Dibobia withdrew and left the creation and ordering of the world in their hands.

In the MANDE CREATION ACCOUNT, the Supreme God MANGALA existed alone as a round, energetic presence (an egg). Within him were two sets of TWINS. Mangala used the matter within himself to create a seed that was the world. However, the seed did not hold together well and blew up. Mangala tried again, placing two sets of twin seeds in an egg. This time, Mangala's creation was successful.

Similarly, in the DOGON CREATION ACCOUNT, AMMA, the Creator, existed alone in the shape of an egg. Within this cosmic egg were the material and structure of the universe. As in the Mande story, Amma's first creation failed. Amma then planted a seed within herself that became two placentas, each containing a set of twins. One of the twins broke out and tried to create his own universe, but he failed. Amma used a bit of this twin's placenta to create the Earth.

COSMOLOGY The belief system of a people with respect to the creation, structure, and natural order of the world or universe. In African traditions, some groups of people had a relatively simple cosmology (or cosmogony) in which the Creator—usually a SKY god—was said to have made the heavenly bodies and Earth and continues to govern, or order, their movements. Other traditions, such as that of the Dogon of Burkina Faso and Mali, have more complex cosmologies. See also DOGON COSMOLOGY; KONGO COSMOLOGY.

CREATION ACCOUNT Every culture has its creation account—a story that explains how the universe, SUN, MOON, STARS, Earth, humans, animals, and all that forms the world came into being. Almost universally throughout Africa, one SUPREME BEING was held to be responsible for the creation of everything in existence. Creation accounts are as diverse as the cultures of different tribal groups.

One of the themes of African creation accounts is the "COSMIC EGG myth," in which an egg was the beginning of life. (See DOGON CREATION ACCOUNT;

FANG CREATION ACCOUNT; MANDE CREATION ACCOUNT.) A second theme is that of the sacred word through which creation proceeds or that is given to humanity by the Creator. (See BAMBARA CREATION ACCOUNT.)

In some African traditions, the first humans emerged from a hole in the ground. (See SAN CREATION ACCOUNT; XHOSA CREATION ACCOUNT.) In other traditions, life began in a reedy swamp or on land created on the primordial waters. (See BUSHONGO CREATION ACCOUNT; SHANGAAN CREATION ACCOUNT; YORUBA CREATION ACCOUNT; ZULU CREATION ACCOUNT.) SNAKES are central to the creation accounts in some traditions. In the FON CREATION ACCOUNT, AIDO-HWEDO, the cosmic serpent, carried the Creator, MAWU-LISA in his mouth as she created the world. In the IGWIKWE CREATION ACCOUNT, the Creator, Pishiboro, died from the bite of a puff adder, but his death created the world.

See also KONO CREATION ACCOUNT; MAKONI CREATION ACCOUNT; SHONA CREATION ACCOUNT.

CREATOR See SUPREME BEING.

CROCODILE A carnivorous, lizardlike reptile found throughout most of Africa south of the Sahara. Crocodiles average 16 feet in length and prey upon a wide variety of animals—antelope, buffalo, young hippos, fish—as well as on humans. Crocodiles are found in sub-Saharan Africa wherever there is water—lakes, rivers, freshwater swamps, and brackish pools.

In the tradition of the Yoruba of Nigeria, crocodiles were associated with kingship. The crocodile's ability to both walk on land and swim in water acted as a metaphor for the belief that kings also lived in two realms—the world of ordinary life and the world of the gods and spirits.

In a myth of the Habbe of Mali, crocodiles helped the Habbe escape from enemies by carrying them across the Niger River on their backs. (See NANGA-BAN.) In the BUSHONGO CREATION ACCOUNT, a crocodile created all of the other reptiles and lizards.

Crocodiles, which prey on humans as well as other animals, sometimes appear in myths as MONSTERS that threaten heroes. In a myth cycle of the

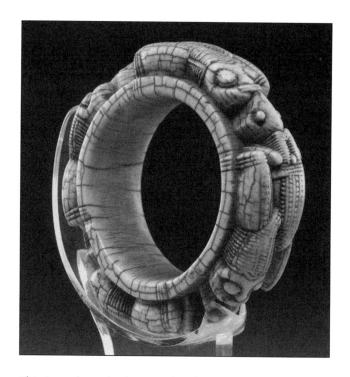

This ivory bracelet is carved with representations of crocodiles, a symbol of royal power for the Yoruba of Nigeria. Traditionally, only the king could wear ivory ornaments. *(Detroit Institute of Art)*

Ambundu people of Angola, the child-hero SUDIKA-MBAMBI wanted to marry the daughter of KALUNGA, the lord of the UNDERWORLD. Among the tests to which Kalunga subjected him was the slaying of the crocodile Kimbiji kia Malenda, master of the underworld abyss. Sudika-mbambi was swallowed by the great reptile. He was later restored to life by his brother Kabundungulu, who managed to slay the crocodile.

CROW A large, glossy-feathered, gregarious black bird with a distinctive *caw*. For the Xhosa of South Africa, crows were birds of God. In a Xhosa tale about a hero named GXAM, crows magically restored the vision of the blinded hero.

In a myth of the Sara of Chad and Sudan, the Supreme God, WANTU SU, gave his nephew, Wantu, a drum that contained bits of everything that existed in the SKY world. Wantu was supposed to give the things the drum contained to humans. However, as Wantu climbed down the rope that was the LINK

BETWEEN HEAVEN AND EARTH, a crow struck the drum. The drum fell to Earth and broke, scattering animals, fish, and plants throughout the world. (See also DRUMS AND DRUMMING.)

CULTURE HERO   A mythic archetype that appears universally across cultures—a transformer who in a mythic age at the beginning of the world helped shape human culture into its familiar form. A culture hero is a historical or mythological hero who changed the world through invention or an important discovery, such as FIRE or agriculture. The stories of culture heroes give insights into the culture that created them. Through their lives or the mythological tales about them, we learn the values, hopes, and histories of past cultures.

African culture heroes include NAITERU-KOP, who gave the gift of cattle to the Maasai of Kenya; ≠GAO!NA, who gave the !Kung of Angola and Namibia bows and arrows, digging sticks, fire, and the knowledge of how to make things; and TSOEDE, who founded the kingdom of Nupe (Nigeria) and saved his people from slavery. Not all culture heroes are human. According to the Ashanti of Ghana, ANANSI the SPIDER was a TRICKSTER-hero who taught humans how to sow grain. A FOX gave fire to the Uduk of Ethiopia and taught humans to speak.

DANCE Dance plays an important role in African ceremonial and religious life. It is a powerful means of prayer to both the SUPREME BEING and lesser SPIRITS. Dances serve a variety of purposes, among them to invite the presence of particular spirits or to honor the dead. Dance can also be a form of storytelling, as when music and dance are included in the performance of an EPIC. In a ceremony called the Sigi, the Dogon of Mali perform a ritual dance that retells the DOGON CREATION ACCOUNT. The dance also ensures the continued support of the ANCESTORS.

Among the !Kung of Namibia, dance is an important part of healing rituals. The dance energizes a spiritual power within the dancer that enables him or her to enter a different level of consciousness and heal other people. For the San of Botswana, Namibia, and South Africa, a dance that serves to heal the community is an important ritual. The dance transforms spiritual power and energy into MEDICINE that can heal both physical and psychological problems.

DAUSI *Soninke (Mauritania)* An EPIC set in the heroic period of Soninke history. The Soninke people lived in the African Sahel, the semidesert southern fringe of the Sahara that stretches from present-day Senegal in the west to the Nile River in the east. The Soninke culture peaked around 500 B.C. Fragments of Soninke history and traditions survive in the *Dausi*, which was composed by an unknown BARD around the fourth century A.D. Troubadours—wandering musicians and storytellers—performed the *Dausi* into the 12th century. Much of the *Dausi* has been lost, mainly because Islamic influences supplanted a great deal of traditional African culture.

Gassire's Lute One of the better preserved sections of the *Dausi* is "Gassire's Lute," in which the hero Gassire is responsible for the first disappearance of WAGADU, the Soninke goddess. *Wagadu* is the name of both the goddess and the legendary city of the Fasa people. Other names for Wagadu were Dierra, Agada, Ganna, and Silla—the names of cities in the Sahel. The epic begins:

> Four times Wagadu stood there in all her splendor. Four times Wagadu disappeared and was lost to human sight: once through vanity, once through falsehood, once through greed, and once through dissension. Four times Wagadu changed her name. First she was called Dierra, then Agada, then Ganna, then Silla. Four times she turned her face. Once to the north, once to the west, once to the east, and once to the south. For Wagadu, whenever men have seen her, has always had four gates: one to the north, one to the west, one to the east, and one to the south. Those are the directions whence the strength of Wagadu comes, the strength in which she endures no matter whether she be built of stone, wood, or earth, or lives but as a shadow in the mind and longing of her children.
>
> From *African Genesis*.
> Leo Frobenius and Douglas C. Fox
> (New York: Benjamin Blom, 1966).

"Gassire's Lute" tells the story of the first loss of Wagadu—through vanity. At that time, Wagadu was called Dierra. Her last king was Nganamba Fasa. The Fasa fought against the Burdama and the Boroma every day. However, Nganamba was very old. His son, Gassire, was a grown man with eight sons of his own, and Gassire wanted to be king. One night, Gassire went to a wise man for advice. The wise man told Gassire that his father would die, but Gassire would not inherit his father's sword and shield. Instead, Gassire would carry a lute—and Gassire's lute would

Dogon men wearing traditional masks perform a dance in Sanga, Mali. (© Wolfgang Kaehler/CORBIS)

cause the loss of Wagadu. Angered, Gassire called the man a liar.

Still angry the next day, Gassire insisted on fighting the Burdama alone. He fought so fiercely that the Burdama threw away their spears and fled. The Fasa heroes gathered up the spears and sang Gassire's praises. Never before had so many spears been won for Wagadu. Afterward, Gassire went into the fields alone, where he heard a partridge sing that all must die, but the *Dausi*—the song of its battles—would not die. The *Dausi* would outlive all kings and heroes. Wagadu would be lost, but the *Dausi* would endure. Gassire returned to the wise man and asked him if he knew the *Dausi* and whether it could outlive life and death. The wise man answered only that Gassire was hurrying to his end and that since he could not become king, he would become a bard. Gassire told a smith to make him a lute. The smith responded that he would, but the lute would not sing. When the lute was finished, Gassire discovered that the smith had been right—it would not sing. He complained to the smith. The smith responded that the lute was just a

piece of wood. It could not sing until Gassire gave it a heart. He told Gassire to carry the lute into battle on his back where it could absorb blood, breath, and pain and become a part of Gassire's people.

Gassire went into battle with his oldest son, carrying the lute on his back. When his son was killed, Gassire carried the body home on his back. His son's blood seeped into the lute. On each of the next six days, Gassire went into battle with one of his sons. Each son in turn was killed, and Gassire carried each one home on his back with his son's blood seeping into the lute. The people became angry at this senseless killing and told Gassire that it had to stop; he must leave Dierra. Gassire went into the desert with his remaining son, his wives, and his warriors. In the night, while the others slept, Gassire heard the lute singing the *Dausi*. At the same time, King Nganamba died, Gassire's anger left him, and Wagadu disappeared for the first time.

The Rediscovery of Wagadu Lagarre is the hero of a section of the *Dausi* that relates the rediscovery of Wagadu. Lagarre was the youngest of seven sons of

King Mama Dinga. The king had said that Wagadu would be found again when Tabele, the great war drum, was beaten. However, the drum had been stolen by the JINN, evil SPIRITS that had tied it to the sky.

One day, Mama Dinga told his servant that he felt he would die soon. He ordered the servant to send his eldest son—his heir—to him after midnight so that he could tell him things he needed to know. The servant, however, had been mistreated by the six older sons of the king. Only Lagarre, the youngest, had treated him kindly. The servant told Lagarre to dress himself in his brother's robe and arm ring and to go to the king in his brother's place. The king, who was blind, was fooled by the disguise. He gave Lagarre instructions to follow that would enable him to understand the language of animals, birds, and the jinn. He could then ask the jinn where the drum Tabele was.

Lagarre followed his father's instructions and then went to the jinn. The jinn, in turn, sent him to the animals and birds. Each creature sent Lagarre on to another, until at last he came to Koliko, the buzzard. Koliko told Lagarre that he knew where Tabele was, but he was too old and weak to fly to it. To help Koliko grow strong again, Lagarre had to bring him the heart and liver of a young horse and a young donkey every day for seven days. At the end of the seven days, Koliko was able to fly to where Tabele was tied to the sky, but he was not strong enough to break its ties. Lagarre fed Koliko for three more days, and the buzzard was able to release Tabele and bring it back to Earth. Koliko told Lagarre to wait three days before he beat the drum. On the third day, Lagarre beat Tabele, and Wagadu appeared before him.

DA ZODJI *Fon (Benin)* In the Fon PANTHEON of deities (known as VODUN), the firstborn son of the Creator, MAWU-LISA. Da Zodji was chief of the Earth Pantheon, one of the four pantheons into which the great gods of the Fon are divided. He was the great serpent power (see SNAKE), and he assisted in the ordering of the universe. Da Zodji had a female twin named Nyohwè Ananu, who was also his wife. The two produced several children who were the SAGBATA gods—the gods of the Earth Pantheon. Mawu-Lisa divided the realms of the universe among the children of Da Zodji and Nyohwè Ananu.

DEATH, ORIGIN OF   Almost universally in myths throughout Africa, in the beginning there was no death. In some myths, the SUPREME BEING made people young again after they grew old. In other tales, people died but were reborn. In still others, people went to the heavens and lived with the Creator, sometimes in a different form. Then death entered the world. The reasons for the coming of death are many and varied.

In some stories, humans lost the possibility of eternal life through greed, curiosity, stubbornness, arrogance, desperation, or some other weakness. In a Boloki tale, a man offered humans a choice of two bundles. One was large and contained beads, cloth, knives, mirrors, and other objects. The smaller bundle, the man said, contained everlasting life. The women dressed themselves in the beads and cloth and greedily carried away the large bundle. The man disappeared with the smaller bundle, and people lost their chance at immortality.

Death was often inflicted on humans as a punishment for disobedience. ABASSI, the Supreme God of the Efik of Nigeria, punished humans with death when they disobeyed his command that they could neither grow their own food nor have children. ABRADI, the Supreme God of the Ama and Nyimang of Sudan, punished people with death when they followed a RABBIT's instructions rather than his. AREBATI, the Supreme God of the Efe and Mbuti of the Democratic Republic of the Congo, condemned humans to die when a woman ate the forbidden fruit of the *tahu* tree. JOK, the Supreme God of the Acholi, Alur, and Lango of Uganda, planned to give humans the fruit of the Tree of Life and make them immortal. However, when humans delayed coming to the heavens for the gift, Jok gave all the fruit to the heavenly bodies. None was left for humans.

A common theme in many stories about the origin of death is the "failed message." In the basic story, two creatures are sent to humans, the first with a message of life and the second with a message of death. Either the first message does not get delivered, or the second message is delivered first, and people accept it. No reason is usually given for the sending of the second messenger. It may only have been to introduce the factor of chance. Possibly the Creator had not made up his mind and decided to let the issue depend on which messenger arrived first. In one myth in which a reason is given, NGAI—the Supreme God of the Kikuyu of Kenya—changed his mind. The idea behind the message of life was not that humans would be exempt from death but that they would return to life after death.

Most often the creature that carried the message of life was a CHAMELEON. (See CHIUTA; LESA; MDALI; MULUNGU; NGAI; NYAMBE; QAMATHA; TILO; UMVELINQANGI; UNKULUNKULU; ZIMU.) The second creature was frequently a LIZARD. Other creatures include a TOAD, HARE, salamander, and BIRDS of different kinds. Osawa, the Supreme God of the Ekoi of Cameroon, sent a duck with the message of life and a FROG with the message of death. When a DOG was the messenger of life, it was usually distracted by food and overtaken by another animal that carried the message of death. (See NGEWO.) In some myths, the message of death was delivered deliberately and maliciously, not simply because a faster animal overtook a slower-moving one. (See IKAGGEN.) Frequently a lizard, out of spiteful mischief, changed the message. (See QAMATHA.)

Another theme relates to the severing of the LINK BETWEEN HEAVEN AND EARTH. In many stories, heaven and Earth were once connected—by a chain, rope, spider web, string, strip of leather, tree, or umbilical cord. When the link was severed, heaven became inaccessible, and death and illness entered the world. (See ARUM; KWOTH.)

Sometimes death entered the world by accident. In a tale told by the Luba of Democratic Republic of the Congo, a dog and a goat were supposed to guard a path along which Death and Life would try to pass. Following an argument, the goat went home, leaving the dog to guard the path alone. The dog fell asleep, and Death was able to slip by unnoticed. The goat returned and caught Life, preventing it from reaching humanity. According to the Limba of Sierra Leone, the Supreme God, KANU, created a MEDICINE that would make humans immortal. Kanu told a SNAKE to carry the medicine to humans, but a toad took it instead. When the toad began to hop, all the medicine spilled out. Kanu refused to make more.

According to the Banyoro of Uganda, the permanence of death came about because of human indifference. At one time, only animals died permanent deaths. Ruhanga, the Supreme God, brought people back to life after they died. All that he required was that the living express joy when someone was resurrected. One woman refused to dress up and go to greet the newly risen because she was unhappy over her dog's death. When Ruhanga heard this, he decided that if people did not care what happened to the dead, they might as well stay dead, and he never resurrected humans again.

DENG (DENKA, Rain) *Dinka (Sudan)* A RAIN and fertility god who was the intermediary between humans and the SUPREME BEING. Deng was sometimes regarded as the son of God; sometimes as the son of the goddess ABUK. He was closely linked with the Supreme God, NHIALIC. In some areas, Deng and Nhialic were regarded as one and the same.

One tale of Deng's origins has elements of the ENFANT-TERRIBLE category of myths—tales about children with unusual births and supernatural powers. A pregnant young woman appeared from the SKY. The people celebrated her arrival and built a house for her. When her son was born, he had a full set of adult teeth—a sign of spiritual power—and he wept tears of blood. The woman told the people that her son would be their leader. As she spoke, the rain fell in torrents, giving the boy his name, Deng (Rain). According to legend, Deng ruled over the people for many years. When he was old, he disappeared in a storm.

DIBOBIA See FANG CREATION ACCOUNT; SPIDER.

DITAOLANE (LITUOLONE, Diviner) *Sotho (Lesotho)* A mythic hero with supernatural powers. The myth about Ditaolane is an example of an ENFANT-TERRIBLE tale—a story of a child with an unusual birth and extraordinary powers. At the time of Ditaolane's birth, a fearful beast named Kammapa had devoured almost all of humanity. The only human left alive was Ditaolane's mother, who had hidden herself. When her child was born, he had a necklace of divining charms around his neck. Because of this, she named the boy Ditaolane (Diviner). In the time it took for her to gather straw for a bed, the boy grew to adult size and was able to speak wisely.

Ditaolane noticed the emptiness of the world and questioned his mother about it. When she told him about Kammapa, Ditaolane took a knife and went in search of the monster. Kammapa swallowed Ditaolane, but the hero was not harmed. He used his knife to slash the monster's intestines, and Kammapa fell dead. When Ditaolane cut his way out of the beast's body, everyone who had been devoured by Kammapa emerged with him.

Rather than being grateful to Ditaolane, however, the people he had freed feared him and plotted to kill him. Ditaolane's skill at divination gave him advance warning, so people's attempts to slay him failed. One day, when he was being pursued by his enemies, Ditaolane turned himself into a stone. Frustrated by his inability to find Ditaolane, one of the warriors picked up the stone and threw it across a river. The stone turned back into Ditaolane, and he went on his way.

In a different version of the myth, Ditaolane grew tired of stopping attempts on his life. He gave himself up to his pursuers and allowed himself to be killed. When he died, his heart flew out of his body as a bird.

DJAKOMBA (DJABI, DJAKOBA) *Bachwa (Democratic Republic of the Congo)* The Supreme God and Creator, a SKY god whose voice was thunder and who struck people down with lightning. (See also THUNDER AND LIGHTNING.) Djakomba created everything, including the first humans, who were the Bachwa. The Bachwa call themselves "children of Djakomba." While on the one hand, Djakomba gave humans life and food to sustain them, he also sent illness and death. After death, though, people went to live with Djakomba in the heavens, where they no longer suffered any hardships.

DJO *Fon (Benin)* In the Fon PANTHEON of deities (known as the VODUN), the sixth-born son of the Creator, MAWU-LISA. When Mawu-Lisa divided up the realms of the universe among her children, she told Djo to live between Earth and the SKY as god of the air. Mawu-Lisa also entrusted Djo with responsibility for the life span of humans, and she gave him knowledge of human language.

DOG Dogs have lived as the companions and helpers of humans since prehistoric times. The loyalty of dogs toward humans is well recognized. This loyalty plays a role in myths told by the Anuak of Sudan in which a dog helped humans gain a place on Earth and have a long life (see JUOK).

In another Anuak myth, a dog was responsible for the gift of FIRE to humans. A dog was caught in the rain and became soaked. He asked people for shelter, but they turned him away. Finally, a kind woman took him in. He asked her where her fire was, but she told him she had none. He then told her to make a pile of dried grass. The dog urinated on the grass, and it burst into flame. He taught the woman how to keep the fire alive by placing sticks in it and blowing on it. Then he told her that when other people asked her for fire, she should charge them for it because they had treated him unkindly.

However, dogs are also very fond of food, and this weakness plays a role in African myths about the ORIGIN OF DEATH. In a myth told by the Isoko and Urhobo of Nigeria, in the beginning people lived forever, and the world became overpopulated. Humans and animals argued over what should be done. A TOAD said that the solution was for people to die. A dog—because of its close association with humans—disagreed and argued that the Supreme God, OGHENE, should just make the world larger. The humans sent the dog and the toad to tell Oghene what they felt. The argument presented by the one that arrived first would be accepted. Convinced that his speed would make him the winner, the dog stopped for a meal on the way and fell asleep. The toad arrived first, and Oghene accepted its opinion. This is how death came into the world. In myths of the Mende of Ethiopia (see NGEWO) and the Dagomba of Ghana, a dog that carried the message of life was distracted by food and overtaken by another animal that carried the message of death. WULBARI, the Krachi Creator, gave a dog a MEDICINE that would restore dead people to life. The dog saw a bone in the road and put the medicine down. While the dog was gnawing on the bone, a goat took the medicine and scattered it all over the grass. This is why death is permanent for people, but grass dies and comes back to life each year.

In an Igbo myth, humans sent a dog to the Supreme God, CHUKU, to ask him to restore the dead to life. The dog meandered along slowly and was

In the tradition of the Kongo of Democratic Republic of the Congo, Kozo, the double-headed dog, is a powerful figure that mediates between the worlds of the living and the dead. Wooden carvings such as this were used in rituals to solve problems or bring wealth. *(© The British Museum/Topham-HIP/The Image Works)*

overtaken by a toad that had overheard the message. The toad wanted to punish humans, so it gave Chuku the message that humans did not wish to be restored to life. Chuku agreed to that request and could not reverse himself when the dog arrived with the correct message. Death became permanent.

In a Nandi legend, a dog was directly responsible for the origin of death. The dog told humans that all people would die as the MOON did. Unlike the Moon, he said, they would not be reborn unless they gave him milk from a gourd and beer to drink through a straw. The people laughed and gave him milk and beer on a stool. The dog became angry because they had not served him in the same way as a human. He decreed that all people would die and only the Moon would return to life.

Dogs were sacred to OGUN, the Yoruba divinity of iron, knives, the forge, and war.

DOGON COSMOLOGY *Dogon (Burkina Faso, Mali)* The Dogon people have an elaborate cosmology based on Sirius, the brightest STAR in the SKY. The Dogon call Sirius *sigi tolo* and say that it has a tiny, invisible companion star they call *po tolo*, "deep beginning." (Sirius actually does have a white dwarf companion whose presence was theorized in 1844; it was first seen through a telescope in 1862.) According to the Dogon, all things emerged from this invisible star. The Dogon also say that *po tolo* used to be where the SUN is now, but it and all of the other stars moved away. Only the Sun remained close to Earth.

The Dogon say that *po tolo* is at the center of the sky, meaning that it exerts an important influence on other heavenly bodies. It is a center in motion that governs the rest of the stars and keeps them in their proper places. *Po tolo* also regulates Sirius, which it is said to circle once every 50 years. The spinning of *po tolo* constantly seeds the world with new life. The Dogon have preserved ceremonial MASKS used in a ceremony related to the stars of the Sirius system that has been performed at least since the 13th century.

The Dogon associate *po tolo* with the *fonio* grain (*po*), a cereal native to Africa. *Po*, an extremely tiny grain, was the first of eight seed grains that the Creator, AMMA, made. The Dogon liken the star *po tolo* to the *po* grain in size and color—*po* is tiny and white, just as *po tolo* is tiny and white. Sirius (with its companion) sets in the evening sky in mid-June, shortly before the rainy season begins. Its disappearance signals the planting season. *Po* is scattered rather

This 17th-century brass plaque from Benin shows a drummer playing two drums typical of the region. Such drums were made from hollow logs. (*© Werner Forman/Art Resource, NY*)

than planted—its scattering seeds the fields with new life, just as *po tolo* is believed to seed the Earth with new life. Sirius reappears as a morning star during the rainy season, when the new crops are growing. For the Dogon, the harvesting of the *po* crop is seen as a sacrifice the grain makes: Its death gives humans life and ensures its own rebirth the next growing season.

DOGON CREATION ACCOUNT *Dogon* (Burkina Faso, Mali)

In the beginning, the Creator, AMMA, was in the shape of an egg. (See also COSMIC EGG.) The egg was divided into four sections representing earth, air, FIRE, and water; this also established the four cardinal directions. The first time Amma tried to create Earth, she failed. The second time, she planted a seed in herself that formed two placentas, each containing a pair of TWINS. One twin, Ogo, broke out of the placenta and tried to create his own universe. He was unsuccessful, and Amma used a fragment of Ogo's placenta to create the Earth. Amma killed Ogo's twin, Nommo, and scattered his body parts around the world to bring a sense of order to it. She then brought the parts back together and restored Nommo to life. Nommo created four SPIRITS that became the ANCESTORS of the Dogon people. Amma sent Nommo and these spirits to Earth in an ark to populate the world.

DRUMS AND DRUMMING

Historically, drumming has accompanied various modes of communication, including singing, dancing, and storytelling. In western Africa, people used drums to send and receive spiritual messages, to communicate over long distances, to aid healing, and to celebrate ritual events and the change of seasons. Specific drum rhythms and their associated dances continue to have significant meaning in Africa. Drums accompany most ceremonies and social rituals—including birth, puberty, marriage, death, and burial.

In many world cultures, both within and outside Africa, drums have accompanied poetry. For the Akan-speaking people of Ghana, however, drums themselves have traditionally been used as a means of transmitting poetry. On state occasions, poems were drummed to the chief and to the community as a whole. The explanation for how drums could "talk" is that many African languages are tonal. The relative tone of a word—high or low—determines its meaning. Since drums have only tone and volume as variables, they cannot produce word-for-word imitations of speech. But drum texts contain set phrases that drummers use; listeners who know the same language can recognize these phrases.

Many rules governed Ashanti drummers. A drummer could never carry his own drums or teach his own son the art of drumming. Women were prohibited from touching drums.

In legend, drums were instruments of great power. In one episode of the *DAUSI*, the EPIC of the Soninke people, the great war drum of the Soninke was stolen by JINN (evil spirits). When the drum was recovered and struck by the hero Lagarre, Wagadu—the lost Soninke goddess—reappeared.

The sacred drum of the Venda of South Africa and Zimbabwe—called Ngoma-lungundu, the Drum of the Dead—was regarded as the voice of God. The drum was brought to southern Africa by the Senzi people, who migrated from the north and became the Venda. It had belonged to the departed ANCESTORS of the Senzi. No one except the high priest and the king was permitted to beat or even see the drum. With it, the king could perform miracles. During the Senzi migration, the drum was enclosed so that its six carriers could not see it. The king, Mwali—who had become an ancestor-god—spoke through the drum and told the carriers never to let the drum touch the ground. It fell to the ground during one stop when its carriers failed to secure it tightly enough to a tree. As punishment, Mwali sent a storm and LIONS that killed many people. On a second occasion, wind blew the drum over and caused it to fall to the ground. This time, enemies massacred the Senzi and captured the drum. With the help of Mwali, it was later recovered.

Drums were also associated with plenty. WANTU SU, the Supreme God of the Sara of Chad and Sudan, gave his nephew a drum with a little of everything that existed in the heavens to bring to humans on Earth. Unfortunately, on his way down, the nephew dropped the drum. It broke and scattered everything it held all over the Earth.

DZIVAGURU *Shona (Zimbabwe)* The god of water, who controlled the seasons and called on RAIN to fall whenever he felt it was needed. For people whose survival depends on a reliable source of rain, the benevolence of the rain deity is crucial. Dzivaguru was a generous and benevolent god. He roamed throughout the land performing acts of kindness and magic.

EBELE *Igbo (Nigeria)* A mythical hunter who was regarded as the ANCESTOR of the Igbo people. No one knew where Ebele came from. He appeared one day and took up residence in the town of Ohanko. At that time, Ohanko was at war with two towns to the south. Many people had been killed in the conflict, which was fought with spears and poisoned arrows. What distinguished Ebele from other warriors was his possession of a flintlock rifle. He went to the aid of the people of Ohanko and slew several enemies with his gun. The others, who had never seen a gun before, fled in terror at the seemingly magical way it had killed their comrades. The people of Ohanko hailed Ebele as their savior, and he became a prominent resident of the town. Years later, Ebele negotiated an agreement in a dispute between two opposing groups of people in the town. The solution was for one group to leave Ohanko and the other to stay. Ebele then became the town's chief.

ECLIPSE The total or partial obscuring of one celestial body by another. A solar eclipse occurs when the MOON passes directly between Earth and the SUN. Where the cone of the Moon's shadow falls on Earth, the Sun is eclipsed. A lunar eclipse occurs when Earth is directly between the Sun and the Moon. The Moon is eclipsed as it passes through Earth's shadow. Because eclipses are unusual and dramatic, people of many African cultures tried to explain them.

In the tradition of the Fon of Benin, the Creator MAWU-LISA had two aspects, female and male. The female aspect, MAWU, was given command of the night and was associated with the Moon. The male aspect, LISA, was given command of the day and was associated with the Sun. When there was an eclipse of the Moon or the Sun, it was said that Mawu and Lisa were engaged in intercourse.

According to the Arabs and Berbers of Morocco, a solar eclipse occurred when a jinni—an evil spirit—swallowed the Sun (see JINN). When the jinni vomited up the Sun, it would begin to shine again. The Jukun of Nigeria believed that a lunar eclipse occurred when the Sun caught the Moon. The Jukun beat drums to make the Sun release the Moon.

EGG, COSMIC   See COSMIC EGG.

EKAGA   See TORTOISE.

EKERA   See AFTERWORLD.

ELAND The largest antelope of Africa, standing more than 6 feet high at the shoulder. A fully grown male may weigh more than 1,500 pounds. Both male and female elands have heavy, spirally twisted horns of up to 3 feet or more in length. The eland was the MASTER ANIMAL of the San people of southern Africa, who depended on it both physically, as a food source, and spiritually, as the San's most important religious symbol, or TOTEM. For the San, an eland contained strong spirit power. When an eland died, a high concentration of supernatural energy was released. By praying, singing, and dancing around the body of the eland, the San could harness this power. A SHAMAN, or healer, would then use the energy to heal the sick, bring RAIN, and perform other acts to reestablish harmony.

Elands have traditionally played significant roles in San rites of passage. A boy was considered to have become a man when he killed his first eland. The eland's skin was stretched out on the ground, and the boy sat on it. Other members of the group danced around the boy and made footprints around the skin, using the eland's hooves. This symbolic gesture meant

A late Stone Age rock painting from Tanzania is a representation of a shamanistic trance dance in which a shaman has a vision of an elephant. (© Werner Forman/Art Resource, NY)

that whatever direction the young man chose, he would move across the path of the eland. The spirits of humans and animals were believed to linger within their footprints.

When a San girl had her first menstruation, she was isolated in a hut, and the women performed a ritual known as the Eland Bull Dance (see also DANCE).

The eland was a favorite animal into which the San Creator, IKAGGEN, transformed himself. According to legend, no human knows where lKaggen is today; only the elands know.

ELEPHANT The African elephant is the largest living land animal. It averages about 10 feet tall at the shoulder and can weigh 6 tons. The ears of an African elephant are huge—up to 5 feet long. The elephant's most distinctive features are its long trunk, which is an extension of its nose, and its curving

ivory tusks. Elephants have strong social bonds and live in family groups headed by a female, called a cow.

Numerous myths are told in Africa about its largest animal. The elephant's very size keeps it safe from all predators except humans, who have the weapons—and the magic—to kill it. The elephant is frequently credited with great wisdom. In African fables, the elephant is always the wise chief who settles disputes among the forest creatures. In a myth of the Fang of Gabon, after the Supreme God, NZAME, had created everything, the other aspects of the triple god—Mebere and Nkwa—asked him who would be the master of the animals and plants of Earth. Together, they appointed three animals to serve jointly: the elephant because of his wisdom, the LEOPARD because of his power and cunning, and the MONKEY because of his malice and suppleness.

The Ashanti of Ghana regarded elephants as human chiefs from the past. When they found a dead elephant in the forest, they gave it a proper chief's burial. In Togo also, if a hunter found a dead elephant, he gave the elephant a funeral and staged a dance in its honor. The Mende of Sierra Leone said that the SPIRITS of dead ANCESTORS became elephants.

Numerous tales exist about elephants that take human form or humans who are transformed into elephants. In a tale from Chad, a hunter found an elephant skin and hid it. Soon afterward, he met a large but lovely young woman who was crying. She told the hunter that she had lost her good clothes. The hunter promised her new clothes and married her. They had many large children. One day, however, the wife found the elephant skin her husband had hidden. She put it on and went back into the bush to live as an elephant. Her sons became the ANCESTORS of a clan whose TOTEM, or clan symbol, was the elephant.

In a tale from South Africa, a girl grew so tall and heavy that no man wanted her for a wife. She was accused of witchcraft and exiled from the village. When she wandered into the bush, she met an elephant who spoke to her politely in the Zulu language. She married the elephant, and together they had many tall, strong sons who became the ancestors of a clan of powerful chiefs.

KHONVOUM, the Supreme God of the Pygmies of Central Africa, contacted humans through a mythical elephant named Gor (The Thunderer). In the mythology of the Yoruba of Nigeria, elephants are companions of the warrior gods, in particular OGUN in his aspect as Chief of Hunters.

ENFANT-TERRIBLE

A classification of stories about fabulous children with great powers. An example is the story of MWINDO, the hero of an EPIC of the Nyanga people of Democratic Republic of the Congo. Mwindo was able to walk and talk from birth; could travel on land, under the ground, underwater, and through the air; had the gift of premonition; and could perform miraculous deeds. Other examples of enfant-terrible tales include those of AKOMA MBA, DENG, DITAOLANE, HLAKANYANA, KEJOK, LIBANZA, and SUDIKA-MBAMBI.

EN-KAI (Sky) *Maasai (Kenya)*

The Supreme God and Creator, who brought the RAIN and was the god of fertility. En-kai was a SKY god and the god of the SUN; his wife, Olapa, was the MOON. Among En-kai's praise names are Parsai (The One Who Is Worshiped) and Emayian (The One Who Blesses). En-kai created NAITERU-KOP, the first man, and sent him and his wife to Earth with cattle, goats, and sheep to hold Earth and its natural resources in trust for coming generations. Naiteru-kop and his family were the ANCESTORS of the Maasai. In a different tale, the first people emerged from a termite hole and settled in the neighborhood of the hole.

In a myth about the gift of cattle to the Maasai, En-kai told the first humans to leave their *kraals*, or animal pens, open one night. Some people did as they were told, but others closed up the *kraals* as usual. The people were awakened during the night by the sound of animals. When they looked out of their huts, they saw cattle, goats, and sheep emerging from a termite hole and going into the open *kraals*. The people who received the gift of livestock became the Maasai; the people who had shut their *kraals* became the Kamba.

In another tale, En-kai told a Dorobo to come to him in the morning. A Maasai overheard this and went to the place before the Dorobo. Thinking the Maasai was the Dorobo, En-kai gave him instructions

to follow and told him to return in three days. After the Maasai carried out the instructions, En-kai told the man to stay in his hut no matter what he heard. Then En-kai lowered a strip of hide from the heavens and sent cattle to Earth along the strip. (See also LINK BETWEEN HEAVEN AND EARTH.) Hearing the noise, the Maasai came out of his hut, which caused the strip of hide to break. No more cattle could descend, but the Maasai was satisfied with those he had received. This tale explains why the Maasai had cattle and the Dorobo had to hunt wild game for their food. (In another version of this tale, Naiteru-kop was responsible for the gift of cattle.)

EPIC

A long, narrative story recounting the deeds of a legendary or historical hero. In African traditions, epics may be told in prose or as dramatic poetry and are usually interspersed with songs. Epics—and episodes within epics—often end with songs of praise about the hero or addressed to him. Performances vary around the continent. In West Africa, there may be a principal narrator, or BARD, and a person who serves as a respondent, making exclamations that provide a rhythmic regularity to the narration. In Central African epic style, the narrative takes second place to dramatic and musical action in the performance. The principal narrator may use a bell or a rattle and be equipped with other objects, such as a spear or a staff, that serve as props. The bard moves about freely, so that the story is conveyed not only through narration and music, but also through dance and mime. Performances of epics typically take place over several nights, with a different episode being presented each night. Almost all surviving epics come from recordings of live performances by African bards and storytellers (griots) charged with remembering and passing along a culture's history and tradition through story and song. (See also ORAL TRADITION.)

The epic hero is often a king or the son of a king, although in some epics the hero is an ordinary hunter. Heroes frequently have supernatural abilities that keep them safe from harm. The birth and childhood of heroes may have fantastic or magical aspects. Epics typically deal with the rise and fall of kingdoms, wars between tribes and clans, the search for equity and justice, and the struggle against evil forces. Epic heroes customarily set off on adventures during which they suffer terrible ordeals and have confrontations with MONSTERS, magical forces, and evil beings. These trials may result from rejection by the hero's father, jealousy between brothers or other family members, competition for an inheritance, or an unjust act. The hero's travels may take him to distant lands, to the SKY world, to the UNDERWORLD, or to the land of the dead. Typically, the hero returns home victorious and receives recognition—sometimes a kingship—for his accomplishments.

Among the Fulbe, or Fulani, people of Sudan, a nobleman customarily set out in quest of adventures accompanied by a singer (*mabo*) who also served as his shield bearer. In this way, the singer served as the witness to the lord's heroic deeds, which he then celebrated in an epic poem called *BAUDI*. A great deal of the epic poetry of the Fulbe has been recorded.

For examples of epics, see ANTAR; *BAUDI*; *DAUSI*; LIONGO; MWINDO; OZIDI; *SON-JARA*; SUNDIATA.

EPIC HERO   See EPIC.

ESHU (ESU) *Yoruba (Nigeria)*   The god of chance, accident, and unpredictability. Eshu was one of the most important and complex deities of the Yoruba PANTHEON (known as the ORISA). Because Eshu was a master of languages, he was the messenger of OLORUN, the SUPREME BEING and SKY god, and carried messages and sacrifices from humans on Earth to Olorun. He reported to Olorun on the actions of both humans and the other divinities. Acting on Olorun's orders, Eshu both rewarded and punished humans. He also investigated and reported on the correctness of worship and sacrifices. Eshu had to be given an offering at the beginning of every ritual, or the ritual would fail.

Eshu was said to lurk at gates and crossroads, where he introduced chance and accident into humans' lives. He also appears in myths as the mediator between opposing forces. He negotiated among the *orisas* and restored balance in their relationships. He is credited with having given humans the Yoruba system of divination—the art or practice of foreseeing or foretelling future events (see *IFA*).

Although Eshu was looked upon as protective and even benevolent, that representation was just one aspect of his nature. He was also feared for the evil he could do, and he sometimes led humans to perform evil deeds. This aspect of his character was that of a divine TRICKSTER. Eshu's penchant for causing mischief is illustrated by a tale in which he set two good friends against each other. The men were farmers with adjoining fields, and each day Eshu walked the path that separated their fields, wearing a black cap. One day he decided to play a trick on the friends. He made a cap in four different colors—black, white, green, and red—in such a way that the cap appeared to be a single color, depending on the side from which it was seen. When he put on the cap, he also stuck his pipe at the back of his neck and hung his walking staff across his back instead of his chest. Then he took his usual daily walk. One farmer remarked to his friend how odd it was that Eshu had walked in the opposite direction from his normal route and had worn a white cap instead of a black one. His friend responded that Eshu had walked in his usual direction but had worn a red cap. They argued about this until the argument became violent, at which point they went to the local king to settle the matter. Eshu appeared there, laughingly showed his four-colored cap, and explained that if someone watched his pipe and staff rather than his feet, they would think he was walking in a direction opposite from his actual movement. It was in his nature to create strife and discord, he admitted. Typically, however, he also owned up to his mischief and made everything right in the end.

Eshu did not restrict his tricks to humans. He also played tricks on his fellow *orisas*—often with terrible consequences, as illustrated in a myth about a visit that OBATALA, the creator of land and humans, paid to SHANGO, the god of THUNDER AND LIGHTNING. ORUNMILA, the god of divination, advised Obatala not to go. When Obatala insisted on making the journey, Orunmila instructed him not to protest or retaliate, regardless of what happened to him. On the way, Obatala met Eshu, who asked Obatala to help him lift a bowl of palm oil onto his head. Obatala helped Eshu lift the bowl, but oil spilled over and soiled his white robe. He returned home, changed his robe, and set off again. Again he met Eshu, who once more asked for help lifting the bowl of oil—with the same consequences. When this happened a third time, Obatala continued on without changing his soiled robe. Soon he saw one of Shango's horses running loose. Actually, Eshu had used his supernatural powers to make the horse appear. Obatala caught the horse, intending to return it to Shango. However, Shango's servants—failing to recognize Obatala because of his soiled clothing—thought he was a horse thief and imprisoned him. Months passed, then years, and Obatala languished in the prison, never protesting. During this time a plague raged through Shango's kingdom, the RAIN stopped falling, and crops failed. When Shango consulted an oracle to determine why disaster had fallen on his realm, the oracle told him that a holy person, innocent of any crime, was in Shango's prison. Only by releasing him would the troubles cease. Shango searched the prison

and immediately recognized Obatala. He fell at Obatala's feet and begged his forgiveness. Rather than retaliate for what had been done to him, Obatala ended the plague and restored the rain.

ETIOLOGICAL MYTH A class of traditional stories that explain the origins of things in nature, such as animal attributes, plants, and weather phenomena, or the origins of tribal customs. Etiological myths are commonly called "just-so stories" or "*pourquoi* tales." For examples, see HARE for a myth that explains why hares have a split upper lip and MOLE for a myth that explains why moles live underground. See JACKAL for an explanation for the odd gait of the HYENA.

FA *Fon (Benin)* In the Fon PANTHEON of lesser deities, the god of divination. (See VODUN.) *Fa* also symbolized the personal fate of human beings. According to Fon tradition, the Creator, MAWU-LISA, sent two men to Earth with the message that all humans had their own *fa*—the sacred word, or writing, that was their destiny. Each day, Mawu-Lisa would give this writing to her assistant, LEGBA. She would tell Legba who would be born or die, what dangers each person would face, and what fortune people would encounter. Legba would then bring each individual his or her *fa*.

FANG CREATION ACCOUNT *Fang (Central African Republic, Gabon, Republic of the Congo)* In the beginning, there were only the Creator, MEBEGE, in the heavens and a SPIDER, Dibobia, that hung below him over the primordial waters that covered the world. Dibobia told Mebege that they had to create the Earth. Mebege took hair from under his right arm, material from his brain, and a smooth pebble from the sea. He blew on these things, and they turned into an egg. (See also COSMIC EGG.) Mebege gave the egg to Dibobia, who lowered it into the sea. When enough time had passed, Mebege went down and put semen on the egg. The egg cracked open and three beings emerged—Zame ye Mebege, who was God; Nyingwan Mebege, the sister of God; and Nlona Mebege, the brother of God, who was evil. Mebege and Dibobia withdrew to the heavens, leaving Zame in control of creation. Zame first created termites and worms. He used their droppings to build up the land, which formed in the sea. Finally, he created human beings.

For a different version of the creation account told by the Fang of Gabon, see NZAME.

FARO *Bambara (Mali)* A female creator figure with a male TWIN, Koni, who was also her husband. In the beginning, the Supreme God, Bemba, created two sets of twins—MUSOKORONI and her brother PEMBA, and Faro and Koni. Through their interactions, the world was created. (See BAMBARA CREATION ACCOUNT.)

In another tradition, Faro had a dual identity as both a SKY and a water god. Although seen as male, he was made pregnant by the rocking of the universe and gave birth to several sets of twins. These became the ancestors of the human race. In his aspect as a CULTURE HERO, Faro brought the RAIN and taught humans language, the use of tools, agriculture, and how to fish. According to tradition, Faro is continually reorganizing the universe. He returns to Earth every 400 years to make certain that everything is still in harmony.

In the MANDE CREATION ACCOUNT, Faro (who was male in this account) was destroyed by the actions of his twin brother, Pemba. Mangala, the Creator, brought Faro back to life and made a human of him. Mangala sent Faro to Earth in an ark accompanied by the original ANCESTORS and the first animals and plants.

Faro is also the name of one of the four aspects of the Supreme God, Bemba. Faro was master of water.

FI See JEN PANTHEON.

FIRE The importance of fire for human survival as a source of heat and light and a means of cooking food—as well as its association with the SUN—has contributed to its prominent place in mythology throughout the world. Many African stories tell how people first acquired fire. Frequently, fire was the gift of the Creator. (See ǂGAO!NA; JOK.)

According to the Uduk of Ethiopia, a TRICKSTER FOX brought fire to the people. The Fjort of Republic of the Congo received fire from a river deity. A DOG was responsible for the gift of fire to the Anuak of Sudan.

The gift of fire frequently began with its theft from the being that possessed its secret. In a myth of the !Kung of Namibia, a man named IKai IKini was the only person in the world who had fire, which he made with fire sticks that he kept hidden. ǂGao!na, the !Kung Creator, discovered IKai IKini's secret and, through trickery, stole the fire sticks from him. ǂGao!na broke the sticks into small pieces and scattered them throughout the world so that everyone could have fire. In a tale told by the Ekoi of Niger and Nigeria, a boy stole fire from the SKY god, OBASSI. In revenge, Obassi crippled the boy. According to a story told by the Zande of Democratic Republic of the Congo and Sudan, TORE, the divine TRICKSTER, stole fire from his uncles, divine blacksmiths.

FLOOD Flood myths are found around the world, and Africa is no exception. Throughout all but the desert areas of Africa there are myths about a primordial flood. (According to the !Kung, who live in the Kalahari Desert and its fringes, the very idea of a flood is ludicrous!) Flood myths are as various as the tribes that tell the stories. Following are a few of them.

Bakongo (Democratic Republic of the Congo) An elderly woman, tired and covered with sores, arrived at a town in a valley. She asked for hospitality but was turned away at every home except the last one she came to. The people there took her in and cared for her until she was well again. When she was ready to leave, she told her hosts to come with her. Because of the other inhabitants' lack of hospitality, the town was cursed, and the Supreme God, Nzambi, would destroy it. The night after they left, heavy RAIN fell, turning the valley into a lake. All of the townspeople were drowned.

Ekoi (Niger, Nigeria) At first there was no water on Earth, so the first man, Etim 'Ne, asked OBASSI Osaw, the god of the SKY, for water. Obassi gave him a calabash (a kind of gourd) that held seven clear stones. When Etim 'Ne put a stone in a hole in the ground, water emerged and formed a lake. When Etim 'Ne's children were grown and married, he gave each household a river or lake of its own. When his grandchildren were grown, he told each of them to take seven stones from their parents' rivers or lakes and plant them at intervals to create new streams. All of Etim 'Ne's grandchildren followed his instructions but one. One grandson collected a basketful of stones and dumped them in one place. This caused a flood that covered his farm and threatened to drown the entire Earth. Etim 'Ne prayed to Obassi, who stopped the flood. However, Obassi let a lake remain where the disobedient grandson's farm had been.

Kwaya (Tanzania) A man and woman had a pot that never ran out of water. They told their new daughter-in-law never to touch the pot. However, the curious young woman could not keep from touching it. The pot shattered, and the resulting flood drowned everything.

Maasai (Kenya) The Supreme God, EN-KAI, resolved to destroy humanity because of its sinfulness. He would save only one righteous man and his family. En-kai told this man—Tumbainot—to build an ark and take his family and animals of every kind into it. Then En-kai sent rains that lasted for many days until the whole world was flooded and all living creatures were drowned. Tumbainot sent out first a dove and then a vulture to find out whether any dry land existed. When it seemed that the flood was receding, Tumbainot grounded the ark. He, his family, and the animals left the ark and repopulated the Earth. (This story has obvious Judeo-Christian influences.)

Mandingo (Côte d'Ivoire) A charitable man gave away everything he had. When the Supreme God, Ouende—disguised—asked him for food, the man gave the god the last of his food. Ouende rewarded the man with three handfuls of flour, which kept renewing itself and brought the man great wealth. Then Ouende told the man to leave the area. The god sent six months of rain that created a flood and destroyed the man's selfish neighbors, who had refused the god's request for food.

Mbuti (Democratic Republic of the Congo) A CHAMELEON, hearing a strange noise in a TREE, cut open its trunk. Water came out in a great flood that spread all over the Earth. The first man and woman emerged with the water. (See also HUMANS, ORIGIN OF.)

Yoruba (Nigeria) According to the YORUBA CREATION ACCOUNT, in the beginning there were only the SKY above, ruled by the Supreme God OLORUN, and the misty, watery domain below, ruled by the goddess OLOKUN. At that time, Olokun was the only ORISA (deity) who lived apart; all the other *orisas* lived in the heavens with Olorun. When OBATALA, the second in command to Olorun, created dry land and people filled the world, Olokun became angry over the loss of so much of her domain. In a fit of rage, she sent a great flood that covered the land, drowning nearly all of the world's inhabitants. Then ORUNMILA, the god of divination, fate, and wisdom, came down to Earth and restored the land.

FON CREATION ACCOUNT *Fon (Benin)*
AIDO-HWEDO, the Cosmic Serpent (see also SNAKE), carried the Creator, MAWU-LISA, in his mouth as she shaped the universe. The Earth's surface—its high places and low places, its curves and other physical features—were created by the serpent's movement. Wherever the serpent and Mawu-Lisa rested, mountains formed from Aido-Hwedo's excrement. When the Creator was finished creating the world, she ordered Aido-Hwedo to coil himself into a circle around and underneath the Earth to hold it in place. When there was an earthquake, it happened because Aido-Hwedo stirred. Aido-Hwedo revolved around the Earth, causing the movement of the heavenly bodies.

Traditionally, the Fon had a four-day week in recognition of the four days in which Mawu-Lisa created the world. On the first day, she gave birth to the gods and goddesses of the VODUN, the Fon PANTHEON of deities, and she made humans out of clay. (See also HUMANS, ORIGIN OF.) On the second day, she made Earth habitable for humans. On the third day, she gave humans speech, sight, and awareness. On the fourth day, she gave humans the skills they needed to survive.

FON PANTHEON See VODUN.

FOX
The wily fox is seen throughout Africa as both a TRICKSTER figure and a CULTURE HERO who made significant contributions to humans. According to a myth told by the Uduk of Ethiopia, the fox brought FIRE to people and taught humans to speak.

FROG
An amphibian that lays its eggs in water and undergoes a metamorphosis, changing from an aquatic, gill-breathing tadpole into a semiaquatic, lung-breathing adult frog. Because of this change in form, frogs represent transformation. For many cultures, frogs symbolized the link between the UNDERWORLD and the spiritual realm and functioned as messengers between humans and the gods.

In a myth told by the Ekoi of Cameroon, the SKY god Osawa sent a frog to deliver the message to people that death was the end of all things. In a myth of the Ambundu of Angola, a frog was instrumental in arranging the marriage of the hero KIMANAUEZE to the daughter of the SUN and the MOON.

In an Efe myth, a TOAD was given a pot containing death and was warned not to let anything happen to it. Tired of carrying the heavy pot, the toad accepted a frog's offer to carry the pot for him. Unfortunately, the frog dropped the pot and it broke, letting death escape. (See also DEATH, ORIGIN OF.)

FULBE BAUDI See BAUDI.

FUNZI (MFUZI) *Fjort (Republic of the Congo)* The
mythical blacksmith of the Fjort. After the Fjort received the gift of FIRE from a river deity, Funzi appeared and taught them how to work in iron and copper. This CULTURE HERO is also credited with creating lightning when his hammer struck sparks from his anvil. (See also THUNDER AND LIGHTNING.)

GA-GORIB (≠GAMA≠GORIB, IHAU-IIGAI≠GAIB, The Thrower Down) *Khoikhoi (South Africa)* A MONSTER that killed many people. Ga-Gorib sat on the edge of a great pit and held a stone to his forehead. He dared people who passed by to take the stone and throw it at his forehead. When they did, the stone bounced back and killed the thrower. He was slain by the legendary hero HEITSI-EIBIB, who distracted him, struck him behind the ear, and pushed him into his own pit.

IIGAMAB (GAUNA, GAUNAB) *Berg Damara (Namibia)* The Supreme God, who lived in a high heaven above the stars. IIGamab was associated with the rising clouds, thunder, and water. (See also THUNDER AND LIGHTNING.) The annual renewal of nature—the cycle of the seasons, the supply of game animals, and the growth of crops—was his work.

Another aspect of IIGamab was as the god of death. (See also DEATH, ORIGIN OF.) He shot arrows at humans from his home in the SKY, and those he struck fell ill and died. After death, the souls of the dead made their way to IIGamab's village and gathered around him.

≠GAO!NA (IIGAUWA, GOHA, HISHE, HUWE, XU) *!Kung (Angola, Namibia)* In some tales, a culture hero with supernatural powers; in other tales, a Creator god. The !Kung are one of the three main subgroups into which the San people are divided. The various subgroups of San speak different dialects of a group of languages known for the characteristic "clicks" that can be heard in their pronunciation. The San SUPREME BEING has many different names and aspects, depending on which group told the story. (See also IKAGGEN; SAN CREATION ACCOUNT.)

≠Gao!na created himself; then he created a lesser god and wives for himself and the lesser god. He named himself Hishe (The One Whom No One Can Command) and gave names to his own wife and to the lesser god and his wife. The Great God created the Earth and the waters of the Earth. He made the SKY—a dome over the Earth—RAIN, the SUN, the MOON, the STARS, and the wind. ≠Gao!na commanded the movements of everything he created. Next, he made all the plants and animals. Finally, he created a man and a woman. He gave humans bows and arrows, digging sticks, and the knowledge of how to make things. From the beginning, humans were mortal. When people died, they became *IIgauwasi*—SPIRITS of the dead—and went to live with ≠Gao!na in the sky. ≠Gao!na and his family lived on the upper floor of a two-story house, and the *IIgauwasi* lived on the lower floor.

The Great God lived in the east where the Sun rises. A single tree grew near the house. This tree was associated with the spirits of the dead, and the !Kung feared it. The tree had no name (or it had a name that could not be spoken). The lesser god lived in the west where the Sun sets. Two trees grew beside his house, and these trees had names.

In a story about the origin of FIRE, only one person in the entire world had fire—IKai IKini. While everyone else in the world had to eat raw food, IKai IKini and his family ate cooked food. One day, ≠Gao!na came upon IKai IKini's home. He saw IKai IKini's children eating cooked food and asked for some. Finding it good, he asked how it had been prepared. The children answered that their father had cooked it. Eager to learn the secret, ≠Gao!na returned the next day and watched unseen as IKai IKini took his fire sticks from their hiding place, used them to make a fire, and cooked food. ≠Gao!na came out of hiding and joined |Kai |Kini's family for the meal. After they ate, ǂGao!na suggested that he and |Kai |Kini play a game. The game involved tossing a feather attached to a nut into the air and striking it with a stick as it fell to prevent it from hitting the ground. ǂGao!na used his ability to control the wind to blow the toy toward the place where the fire sticks were hidden. When they reached this place, ǂGao!na seized the fire sticks and ran off with them. As he ran, ǂGao!na broke the fire sticks into small pieces and scattered them throughout the world. Since that time, every piece of wood contains fire and can be used to cook food. ǂGao!na told |Kai |Kini that it was not right for one man to keep fire for himself, and he changed |Kai |Kini into a bird.

GASSIRE *Soninke (Mauritania)* The hero of an episode of the *DAUSI* EPIC. Gassire was responsible for the first disappearance of the Soninke goddess Wagadu.

||GAUWA   See ǂGAO!NA.

GBADU   See VODUN.

GBONKA   See SHANGO.

GIZO *Hausa (Niger, Nigeria)*   The SPIDER, a TRICKSTER hero. Gizo's exploits contain elements common to tales about other African tricksters, such as the Ashanti spider trickster, ANANSI. Like the Anansi stories, stories about Gizo are folktales told for entertainment and are distinguished from myths. The following typical tale of Gizo's trickery contains a common element in African folklore—the tug-of-war.

There was once a famine, and Gizo and his family had no food to eat. Gizo went to the chief of the land—the ELEPHANT—and told her that the chief of the water—the hippopotamus—had sent him. Gizo said that the hippo wanted 100 baskets of grain, which she would send her young men to fetch. In return, she would give the elephant a great horse. The elephant agreed. During the night, Gizo and his family carried all the grain back to their home. The next day, Gizo went to the hippo and told her that the elephant wanted 100 baskets of fish, which she

would send her young men to fetch. In return, she would give the hippo a great horse. The hippo agreed. During the night, Gizo and his family carried all the fish back to their home.

When the elephant and the hippo asked Gizo where their payment was, he told each that he would return with the horse. Then Gizo tied one end of a long rope to a tree near the elephant's home and its other end to a tree by the riverbank. Separately, he told the two chiefs that the rope was attached to a horse so wild that it would require all their young men to retrieve it. So all the elephant's young men pulled on their end of the rope, and the hippo's young men pulled on their end. When all their efforts met with no success, the elephant sent her people to the hippo to ask about the horse, and the hippo sent her people to the elephant. In this way, Gizo's trickery was revealed. Both the elephant and the hippo resolved to find and punish him.

Gizo hid out until hunger overcame him. Then he disguised himself in an antelope skin and went to find food. When the elephant saw him, she thought he was just a scrawny antelope, and she asked for his help in finding the spider. Gizo told her that she should forget about the spider, because it was the spider who had caused him to waste away to skin and bones. He told the same story to the hippo. Later, when the two chiefs saw Gizo in his own form, out of fear they denied having been looking for him.

GOR   See ELEPHANT; KHONVOUM.

GOROBA-DIKE   See BAUDI.

GRIOT   See BARD.

GU (GUN) *Fon (Benin)*   In the Fon PANTHEON of deities (known as the VODUN), the fifth-born son of the Creator, MAWU-LISA. Gu was the god of iron, war, weapons, and tools. He had no head. Instead, a great sword grew out of his neck. Mawu-Lisa told Gu that he was her strength, which was why he did not need a head. The heavenly blacksmith, Gu was the patron of earthly blacksmiths and the inventor of all crafts. He gave humans tools and taught them how to make iron. In one myth, LISA, the male aspect of Mawu-Lisa, brought Gu down to Earth to help make the world more habitable for humans. Gu cleared trees to make fields, taught humans how to till the soil, and showed them how to make shelters.

GULU (GGULU, MUGULU, Sky, Heaven) *Baganda (Uganda)* In the Baganda PANTHEON of deities (known as the LUBAALE), the SKY god. Gulu was the name of both the sky god and the heavens. He was next in power to the Supreme God, KATONDA. Gulu was the father of WALUMBE, the god of death, and of Nambi, who married the first king of Uganda, KINTU.

GURZIL *Huwwara (Libya)* A SUN god and god of prophecy who was identified with the two-horned Carthaginian god Baal Hammon. (Carthage was an ancient city-state in what is now Tunisia.) His symbol was a bull. Gurzil was seen as a protector who guided humans through his foreknowledge of events. In his aspect as a sun god, he dispelled the darkness and brought light to the world.

ǃGWIKWE CREATION ACCOUNT *ǃGwikwe (Botswana, Namibia)* In the beginning, there was just emptiness except for the Supreme God, Pishiboro. His death resulted in the creation of the world. According to legend, Pishiboro was bitten by a puff adder and died. Blood gushed from his wounds, creating rocks and hills, and the thrashing of his body carved out valleys. Water that poured from his body formed rivers and streams. His hair became the clouds from which life-giving RAIN fell.

After Pishiboro was resurrected, he created humans. However, he was not happy with their hairless appearance. He gave them hair, but then they looked like all the other animals. He then remade them with hair on some parts of their bodies and no hair on other parts. (See also HUMANS, ORIGIN OF.) Pishiboro then proceeded to give the animals he had created different forms, names, and purposes. He decreed that animals that had horns were to be eaten. Humans were not to be eaten. When they died or were killed, they were to be buried.

GXAM *Xhosa (South Africa)* A mythical hero who had an encounter with Death. While seeking work, Gxam was blinded by two so-called friends when they stole food from him. His sight was magically restored by CROWS, which the Xhosa regard as birds of God. Gxam continued on his quest, eventually arriving at the home of Death, Malikophu. Death—the force of evil—tried to destroy Gxam, but Death's daughter—a force of good—helped the hero ward off Death's assaults. In the end, good won out over evil, Death was destroyed, and Gxam married Death's daughter.

HAI-URI See MONSTERS.

HARE Although related to RABBITS, hares differ from them in several ways. The ears and hind legs of rabbits are much shorter than those of hares. At birth, rabbits are hairless and blind, while hares are furred and their eyes are open. There are many varieties of TRICKSTER hares, African ancestors of Br'er Rabbit in the Uncle Remus stories. Based on tales brought to America by African slaves, the first Uncle Remus story—"Story of Mr. Rabbit and Mr. Fox as Told by Uncle Remus"—was written by Joel Chandler Harris and appeared in the Atlanta *Constitution* on July 20, 1879. Harris's tales—told in dialect—became so popular that he collected them in a book published in 1881: *Uncle Remus: His Songs and His Sayings*. The African roots of the stories can be found in folktales of the Bantu-speaking peoples.

KADIMBA was the trickster hare of the southern Bantu-speaking peoples of Angola, Botswana, and Namibia. In one tale, a man named Dikithi repeatedly stole cattle and ate all the meat himself, so the other people had no food. Kadimba placed fireflies on Dikithi's clothes. When Dikithi went to steal cattle, he thought that the fireflies were Kadimba's eyes watching him. Thwarted in his attempted theft night after night, Dikithi finally went away.

In a myth of the Luyi of Zambia, a hare was responsible for the ORIGIN OF DEATH. The Supreme God, NYAMBE, sent a CHAMELEON to tell humans that they would have eternal life. However, a hare arrived first with the message that once dead, humans would remain dead. A hare was also the cause of death in a tale told by the Khoikhoi of South Africa. The MOON sent the hare to humans with the message that as the Moon died and was reborn, humans would also be reborn after they died. The hare became con-fused and inserted the word *not* in the message. It told humans that as the Moon died and was reborn, they would die and not be reborn. When the hare admitted what it had done, the angry Moon struck it in the face, splitting its lip. That is why hares have a split upper lip.

HEALER See SHAMAN.

HEITSI-EIBIB (KABIP) *Khoikhoi (South Africa)* A mythical hero who, although human, had supernatural powers. He was killed on many occasions but was always reborn. Renowned for his hunting ability, Heitsi-Eibib was elevated to the status of god of the hunt.

In one story about his deeds, Heitsi-Eibib was traveling with a large group of people when they were pursued by enemies. They came to a great body of water, and Heitsi-Eibib asked the water to open so that he could pass through. The water parted, and Heitsi-Eibib and his people reached the other side safely. When their enemies tried to follow, the water closed again, drowning them.

One of Heitsi-Eibib's feats was destroying the MONSTER GA-GORIB. It was Ga-Gorib's habit to sit on the edge of a large pit and challenge passersby to throw a stone at his forehead. Whenever anyone took up the challenge, the stone bounced off Ga-Gorib's head and killed the person who had thrown it. The person's body then fell into the pit. To end the deaths, Heitsi-Eibib went to Ga-Gorib, who issued his usual challenge. Heitsi-Eibib refused the challenge. He drew Ga-Gorib's attention to one side, and when the monster turned his head, Heitsi-Eibib hit him behind the ear. Ga-Gorib died and fell into his own pit. Another version of this legend describes how Ga-Gorib chased Heitsi-Eibib around the pit until the hero slipped and fell into the pit. He escaped but had to wrestle with Ga-Gorib for a long time before he finally succeeded in pushing the monster into the pit.

HERO   See CULTURE HERO; EPIC.

HEVIOSO   See VODUN.

HLAKANYANA (UHLAKANYANA)   *Xhosa, Zulu (South Africa)*   One of the most popular African TRICKSTER figures. Hlakanyana's story is an example of the ENFANT-TERRIBLE classification of stories about fabulous children with great powers. Hlakanyana spoke before he was born; in fact, he repeatedly stated his impatience about waiting to enter the world. The following story tells of his early life. All the women of one village had children except for the chief's wife. One day, while the men were slaughtering oxen, the chief's wife heard a voice telling her, "Bear me, mother." The voice kept repeating this until the woman gave birth to Hlakanyana, who was a tiny infant with the face of an old man. He at once went to the cattle *kraal*, or pen, and began to eat a strip of roasting meat. Everyone was amazed by him. When the butchering was finished, Hlakanyana offered to carry all the men's shares of the meat to their huts for them. Instead of doing that, he smeared some blood on the mat in each hut and brought all the meat to his mother's hut. When the men arrived at their huts, they asked Hlakanyana where the meat was. He pointed to the bloody mats and said that he had put the meat there, but the dogs must have eaten it. The men beat their wives and children because they had not guarded the meat from the dogs.

The further adventures of Hlakanyana are primarily involved with his obtaining food through trickery. In one story, he wanted an ox head that was being cooked. He drove the village's cattle into the forest and tied them by their tails to trees. Then he cut himself with a stone so that he was covered with blood. He showed himself to the villagers and told them that enemies had stolen all the cattle. He claimed that the enemies had wounded him when he tried to stop them. The men grabbed their spears and ran off in pursuit of the cattle. While they were gone, Hlakanyana ate all the meat in the pot and filled it with dung.

Hlakanyana's last bit of trickery cost him his life. While out walking, he met a tortoise, which he thought would make a good meal. He asked the tortoise if it was tired and offered to carry it. The tortoise refused the offer, but Hlakanyana picked it up anyway and put it on his back. When he returned home, he told his mother to take the tortoise off his back. However, the tortoise held on so tightly she was unable to remove it. Hlakanyana's mother tried to get the tortoise off by pouring hot oil onto it. The tortoise released its grip so quickly that the oil fell on Hlakanyana. He was burned badly and died as a result.

HUMANS, ORIGIN OF   The creation of human beings is mentioned in many accounts. In some African myths, humans were in existence from the beginning (sometimes in spirit form) and lived in the heavens with the Creator. At some point, the Creator allowed the humans to descend to Earth to live.

In many tales that describe how humans were created, they were made from clay. AREBATI, the Efe and Mbuti Creator, made the first human from clay, covered the clay with skin, and poured blood into the skin to bring the human to life. In the Yoruba tradition, OBATALA, the representative on Earth of OLORUN (the Supreme God), made humans out of clay, and Olorun breathed life into them. AMA, the Creator figure of the Jukun of Nigeria, is described as building humans up bone by bone in the way a potter builds a pot from strips of clay. WOYENGI, the female Creator of the Ijo of Nigeria, created humans from soil.

In some traditions, human life began in or under a TREE. For the Damara and Herero of Namibia, the first humans originated from the *omumboronbonga* tree. A man and a woman were first to emerge, followed by oxen. According to the Nuer of Sudan, humans were created under a tamarind tree. According to the Mbuti of Democratic Republic of the Congo, a CHAMELEON, hearing a strange noise in a tree, cut open its trunk. Water came out in a great FLOOD that spread all over the Earth. The first man and woman emerged with the water. In other emergence myths, people came out of a hole in the ground (see MULUKU; MULUNGU) or a cave (see XHOSA CREATION ACCOUNT).

According to the Shangaan of Zimbabwe, N'WARI, the BIRD god, bored a hole in a reed and laid an egg in the hole. The first human hatched from this egg. In the ZULU CREATION ACCOUNT, people grew on reeds in a primordial swamp. For the Thonga people of Mozambique and South Africa, the first humans also emerged either from a reed or a reedy marsh.

In one of the more unusual stories about human origins, Bumba, the Bushongo Creator, vomited up humans (see BUSHONGO CREATION ACCOUNT). In another unusual tale, told by the Yao of Malawi and Mozambique, a chameleon found the first humans in a fish trap. MUNGU, the Nandi and Swahili Creator, made humans from the light of the SUN, MOON, and STARS.

HUVEANE (HUVE) *Pedi, Venda (South Africa)*
A TRICKSTER figure who was sometimes regarded as the first man (although his parents and other villagers appear in the myths). There are various versions of myths related to Huveane. In one version, he was said to have "had a baby." In another, he modeled a baby from clay and breathed life into it. This may be connected to the idea of his being a creator figure. Huveane kept his child in a hollow tree. Each morning, he stole out early to feed the baby before he had to begin herding his family's sheep and goats. His parents became concerned about his strange behavior, so his father followed him one morning and discovered his secret. After Huveane left, his father brought the baby back to his wife. They hid it among firewood and other items. When Huveane found that his baby was not in the tree, he returned home looking sad. He would not tell his parents what was troubling him. At last, his mother asked him to fetch some firewood for her. Huveane found the baby there, safe and sound. His parents let him keep the child and continue to care for it.

When Huveane's secret came out, the villagers suspected him of sorcery. They could not understand where his child had come from except through magic. Out of fear that he would bewitch the village, the villagers made several attempts to kill Huveane. However, since he had foreknowledge of their plans, all their attempts failed. At last the villagers gave up and decided to leave Huveane alone.

Huveane delighted in playing practical jokes on his father and the other villagers. On one occasion, he led his father to a high rock on which there was a pool of water. Huveane placed pegs in the rock so that they could climb up and get a drink. While his father was drinking, Huveane climbed back down, pulling out the pegs behind him and trapping his father on the rock. He returned home, ate all the food his mother had prepared for the evening meal, and filled the empty pots with cow dung. Then he went back to the rock to replace the pegs and let his father come down. When his father sat down to eat and found that the pots were full of dung, Huveane told him that the food had been changed by magic.

Huveane often pretended to be stupid. One day he found a dead zebra and sat on it while tending his flock. When asked where he had been herding that day, he answered that it was by the striped hill. He repeated this for several days. Curious, some people followed him to discover where the striped hill was. By then the zebra was badly decomposed. The people chided Huveane and told him that if he ever found game like this again, he should cover it with sticks to keep the hyenas away and call the villagers to fetch the meat. The next day, Huveane found a small dead bird. He covered it with sticks and ran to the village with the news that he had found game. Most of the villagers went back with him, carrying large baskets for the meat. When they saw the "game," one of the men mockingly told Huveane that this kind of game should be hung around the neck. Huveane proceeded to hang the bird from his neck, gaining a reputation as a total fool.

HYENA Hyenas are both predators that kill other animals for food and scavengers that live off carrion, or dead meat. Their sloping hindquarters and sparse, spotted or striped fur give hyenas a strange appearance that is matched by their eerie voices, which in the spotted or laughing hyena sounds like maniacal laughter. In myths of the Khoikhoi of South Africa, hyenas are frequently the butt of tricks played on them by a JACKAL. In the following tale, the hyena's moth-eaten coat led to her misfortune.

Jackal saw a wagon loaded with fish and was determined to get some of it. When he could not climb onto the wagon, he ran ahead of it and lay in

Book illustrations of a golden jackal and a hyena
(© Michael Masian Historic Photographs/CORBIS)

the road, pretending to be dead. The driver admired Jackal's beautiful fur, so he threw him into the wagon to bring home to his wife. As the wagon rolled along, Jackal threw fish off the back of it and then jumped off himself to claim his meal. He suggested that

Hyena do the same thing, warning her to lie still no matter what happened. So Hyena lay down in the road in front of a wagon, pretending to be dead. The driver, however, remarked on how ugly Hyena was and kicked her again and again to get her off the road. Poor Hyena moaned to Jackal that it was too bad her fur was not as beautiful as his.

In some accounts, Hyena's nature as a scavenger was responsible for the ORIGIN OF DEATH. In a tale told by the Gogo of Tanzania, humans told Hyena that they wanted to live forever. Hyena responded that this could not be, because hyenas needed dead bodies to eat. Therefore, humans died in order to meet Hyena's wishes. According to the Meru of Kenya, the Supreme God Murungu sent a MOLE to tell humans that people would be reborn after they died. On the way, the mole met a hyena, who asked him where he was going. When the mole explained his mission, the hyena said that if this happened, hyenas would have nothing to eat. It threatened to swallow the mole if it delivered that message. Frightened, the mole told humans that they would die and not come back to life.

In a myth of the Madi of Uganda, a hyena was responsible for severing the LINK BETWEEN HEAVEN AND EARTH. At one time humans could maintain contact with the Creator in the SKY by means of a cowhide rope. Unfortunately, a hungry hyena bit into the cord and severed it. Humans were unable to repair the link to the heavens, so the Creator remained distant. The Nuer of Sudan have a similar myth in which a hyena severed the rope that linked heaven and Earth.

IBEJI *Yoruba (Nigeria)* The term for TWINS and also the name of the god of twins. The birth of twins is exceptionally common among the Yoruba—45 out of 1,000 births are twin births, a rate four times as high as that of the United States. Twins are considered to double everything—they are twice as much trouble as single births and bring twice as much good luck to their parents. According to legend, a competition between the two wives of a tribal chief led to the creation of the first pair of twins. Neither woman had given birth to a son, so both had been going to a shrine to pray for male children. Both women became pregnant, and the elder wife gave birth to a son. The ORISAS, or deities, however, favored the younger wife because the elder wife had mistreated her. They blessed the younger wife with male twins.

According to tradition, it was once the practice to kill twins born to poor people. One day, the children of wealthy parents began to die. When the oracle (see IFA) was consulted, it told the Yoruba rulers that the killing of twins must stop because the practice was upsetting to the god SHANGO. Shango, the god of THUNDER AND LIGHTNING, was considered the supernatural father of twins, who were referred to as Thunderchildren. Twins were sacred to Shango and were under his protection. The oracle instructed mothers of twins to dance to Ibeji, the god of twin infants, every five days. The mothers would be paid for these performances, and their families would grow wealthy.

Ibeji were thought to have special powers to bring good or bad fortune to their families. Parents of twins did everything possible to please the children. Arousing the twins' displeasure might bring misfortune on the family. The god Ibeji might punish the parents with illness or death, cause crops to fail, or inflict some other disaster on the household.

Twins were believed to exist in three different worlds at the same time—the world of humans, the bush (forest and uncultivated land), and the spirit world. The bush, which is the home of wild animals, was also thought to be the home of SPIRITS beyond human control. It was therefore mysterious, dangerous, and filled with supernatural power. Twins were thought to have been sent into the world by MONKEYS and were particularly associated with the colobus monkey, which typically bears twins. With respect to

Ere ibeji—carvings representing twins who had died—were commissioned by Yoruba mothers to commemorate their deceased children. *(© The Hamill Gallery of African Art, Boston, MA)*

the spirit world, twins were thought to bridge the gap between that world and the human world. Twins were also believed to share a common soul.

The death of a twin or twins caused special problems. It upset the balance between the spirit world and the human world. The death of a twin was never spoken of as such. Instead, people said that the deceased child had "gone to Lagos" (the major city in Nigeria) to seek fortune for the family. Songs, dances, and special rituals associated with living twins had to be continued after their death. The mother of a deceased twin would have a wooden image—an *ere ibeji*—carved to commemorate the dead child. If both twins died, a set of two carvings was made. The carving represented the child as an adult, not as a child or an infant. *Ibeji* figures were placed on household altars, given offerings of foods sacred to the god Ibeji, and washed with special herbs. At celebrations, the *ibeji* figures were treated as living beings.

IBON See RAIN.

IFA *Yoruba (Nigeria)* The Yoruba system of divination, the art or practice of foreseeing or foretelling future events. This system consists of tossing 16 cowrie shells or palm nuts onto a sacred tray. There are 256 possible patterns, depending on how the shells or nuts fall. Each pattern is associated with a chapter (*odu*) in *Ifa*, an immense volume of traditions. Each of the 256 *odu* contains 600 to 800 poems known as *Ese Ifa*. Each poem contains instructions for solving a given problem. The person who consults the diviner, or oracle, does not tell his or her problem or question. When the cowries or nuts have been thrown, the diviner consults the related *odu* and recites the verses of the figure that was thrown. The client listens for a verse that deals with a problem or question similar to his or her own.

According to myth, ESHU, the divine TRICKSTER, was responsible for giving the *ifa* oracle to human beings. There was a time when humans failed to make sufficient sacrifices to keep the ORISAS—the Yoruba deities—well fed. Eshu went to YEMAJA, *orisa* of the Ogun River, and her husband, Orungan, for advice about solving this problem. Yemaja told him to give humans something that they would always want. Orungan gave Eshu 16 palm nuts and told him

that if he learned their meaning, he would win humans' good will and they would make sacrifices to the *orisas* again. The MONKEYS told Eshu that if he traveled throughout the world, he would hear 16 sayings for each of the 16 nuts. He could then consult with the other *orisas* and pass this knowledge on to humans. Once humans learned how to consult the palm nuts and foresee future events, they returned to offering sacrifices to the *orisas*, who never again went hungry.

Ifa is also another name for ORUNMILA, the god of divining, fate, and wisdom.

IGBO PANTHEON *Igbo (Nigeria)* Like some other African peoples, the Igbo have a PANTHEON of gods and goddesses ranked according to importance and function. The head of the pantheon is CHUKU, the Supreme God. Other high gods in the pantheon are Anyanu, the SUN; Igwe, the SKY; Amadi-Oha, the lightning; and ALA (Chuku's daughter), the earth goddess and mother of the Igbo people. Lesser divine beings include deities associated with nature and agriculture, such as Aha Njoku, a goddess associated with women's activities and the cultivation of yams (a central ingredient in the Igbo diet); SPIRITS that were counterparts of living humans; and spirits of the Igbo ANCESTORS.

IJAPA (ÀJÀPÁ) *Yoruba (Nigeria)* The TORTOISE, a TRICKSTER hero who appears in countless tales. Like his Ashanti counterpart ANANSI, Ijapa was clever, boastful, greedy, lazy, unreliable, aggressive, self-serving, and ambitious. Because of his weaknesses, such as his inability to keep anything to himself, Ijapa's enemies were often able to turn the tables on him. He also frequently outsmarted himself. One of his greatest strengths was his singing ability. His voice could cast a powerful spell on people, making them forget everything. Many tales end with Ijapa's death, but he was always resurrected for the next adventure.

Ijapa's cleverness is illustrated in a tale about the theft of yams. Being lazy, Ijapa and his wife, Yanrinbo, never tended a garden or stored food for a time of need. When a drought came, food was scarce and no one had any to spare for the shiftless couple. Ijapa decided that they must steal yams from a neighbor. Before they sneaked into the neighbor's storage

This Hausa compound in Nigeria with house and storage house would have been similar to the compound of Yanrinbo and Ijapa. (© Werner Forman/ Art Resource, NY)

house, Ijapa had his wife sit on his shoulders with a basket on her head. They filled the basket with yams and returned home. When the neighbor discovered his loss, he followed footprints leading from his storage house to Ijapa's home. The couple was brought before the chief, to whom they protested their innocence. It was the custom for accused people to be given an herb drink that would make them ill if they lied but would not harm them if they spoke the truth. Ijapa swore that he had never stretched up his hands to steal the neighbor's yams. Yanrinbo swore that she had not used her legs to carry her to the neighbor's storage house. Neither of them became ill, so they were released. They had indeed told the truth—it was Yanrinbo who had stretched up her hands to hold the basket on her head and Ijapa who had walked to the neighbor's storage house with Yanrinbo on his shoulders.

Among Ijapa's weaknesses was a tendency to persist in dangerous schemes long after someone more sensible would have quit. A Yoruba proverb says, "When Ijapa is doing something, he will not stop until disaster falls on him." Both his greed and his persistence—and their results—are illustrated in the following tale:

Too lazy to grow his own food, Ijapa the tortoise wandered from farm to farm looking for the best crops to eat. When he came to a farm on which yams grew plentifully, he decided to stay until he had carried away all the yams. He dug so many that the load was too heavy for him to carry. Ijapa, however, would not give up a single yam. He was still struggling with his load when the farmer arrived in the field and caught him. The farmer raised his knife to strike off Ijapa's head, but the tortoise quickly pulled his head into his shell. The farmer then raised a stone to smash Ijapa's shell. He stopped when Ijapa sang that he could not be killed by a stone but only by being buried under a pile of grain. The farmer poured a basket of millet over Ijapa and covered it with a large pot. The next morning, he found that the tortoise had eaten all the millet and, rather than being dead, was quite contented. While the farmer considered his next move, Ijapa saw a priest from the shrine of Osanyin (the god of medicine) approaching. The wily tortoise sang that the farmer could get rid of him by giving him to a passing stranger. The farmer gave the tortoise to the priest, who carried him to the shrine. Unfortunately for Ijapa, the priest had been gathering items to sacrifice to Osanyin. Osanyin was pleased with the offering of tortoise meat and rewarded the priest and his shrine with good fortune.

IKAKI See TORTOISE.

IMANA (The Creator of Everything) *Banyarwanda, Hutu, Tutsi (Burundi, Rwanda)* The Supreme God, who was the all-powerful ruler of all living things. In the beginning, all living things—humans, animals, and plants—lived in the heavens with Imana. Death was not permanent; if someone died, Imana brought the person back to life in three days. In one myth, a childless woman begged Imana for children. He granted her wish and gave her three children, with the provision that she tell no one where they came from. The woman's sister was also childless. She became jealous when she saw her sister's children and demanded to know where they had come from. Her sister resisted telling her, but she finally gave in. Imana was angry at the first woman's disobedience. To try to assuage his anger, the woman killed her children. The sky opened, and the children fell down to Earth, which was a place of suffering and hardship. The children's lives there were miserable. Their mother and aunt begged Imana for forgiveness. He agreed to bring the children back to the heavens when he felt they had suffered enough.

In one myth about the ORIGIN OF DEATH, Death was a sort of wild animal that Imana hunted. Imana ordered humans to stay indoors when he hunted so that Death would have no hiding place. One woman, however, went to her vegetable garden (or banana grove). Death asked for her protection, and she let him hide under her skirt. As punishment for the woman's disobedience, Imana decreed that Death would remain with humanity.

In a related myth, Death hid under the woman's skirts without her knowledge. He entered the house with her, and she died and was buried. For the woman's daughter-in-law, her death was a great relief. Three days later, though, the daughter-in-law saw that the grave was cracking open. Her mother-in-law had been brought back to life by Imana and was trying to emerge. The woman pounded the soil back down and shouted to her mother-in-law to stay dead. This went on for three days; then the grave remained undisturbed. This made the daughter-in-law happy, but it meant that death would be permanent for all humans.

In yet another tale, Imana told a man that if he did not to go to sleep that night, Imana would bring him long life. However, the man was unable to stay awake. A SNAKE had overheard Imana's message and was waiting when Imana arrived. Thinking that the snake was the man, Imana told it that when it grew old, it would shed its skin and be reborn. The man awakened too late. That is why death is permanent for humans, but snakes (it is believed) have eternal life.

INKOSAZANA See ZULU PANTHEON.

ITHERTHER See BUFFALO.

J

JACKAL A small wild dog that resembles the coyote in habit, size, and general appearance. Jackals prey on small animals and insects but also eat carrion (dead meat), fruit, and seeds. In Khoikhoi tales, the clever jackal is a TRICKSTER figure that often plays tricks on a HYENA.

The following tale explains the odd gait of the hyena. Jackal and Hyena were walking together when they saw a white cloud. Jackal climbed up onto it and began to eat the cloud. When he had eaten enough, he called to Hyena to catch him and break his fall, which she did. Then Hyena climbed onto the cloud and ate her fill. She called to Jackal to catch her and jumped off the cloud. Just as she reached him, Jackal jumped to one side, claiming that he had been pricked by a thorn. Hyena landed painfully on the ground, injuring her legs. This is why hyenas appear to be lame in the hind legs.

JAKUTA See ORISA.

JEN PANTHEON *Jen (Nigeria)* In the Jen PANTHEON of deities, the Supreme God is Fi, who is associated with the SUN. Under Fi are several lesser deities and the *kue*, the SPIRITS of the ANCESTORS. The following are the major deities in the Jen pantheon.

> **Ma** The servant of Fi. Ma made all living things. If he was careless or in a mischievous mood, he created ugly people. Ma received from Fi everything humans needed to live— the fruits of the Earth and rain—and passed them on to humanity.
>
> **Nimbwi** The whirlwind, who attended Umwa.
>
> **Umwa** The god of war.

JINN (DJINN, singular: jinni) *Arab (Western Sahara)* SPIRITS that according to Muslim demonology inhabit the Earth, take various forms, and exercise supernatural power. *Jinni* comes from the Arabic *jinniy*, "demon." Jinn are traditionally viewed as evil and dangerous. Jinn are not pure spirit; they have bodies, and if a jinni is killed, its corpse remains. Among their powers are the ability to appear and disappear, to transform themselves into an animal such as a SNAKE, and even to take human form.

Although not generally friendly toward humans, jinn rewarded kindness. In a tale about the poet Abu Zayd (1332–1406), the poet was riding with other people when they came across a snake that was dying of the heat and thirst. Abu Zayd's friends told him to kill the snake. Instead, he revived it with water. On the return trip, Abu Zayd was riding alone when his camel became too tired to go on. He did not know what to do, when suddenly he heard the voice of a jinni. The jinni explained that it had been the snake whose life Abu Zayd had saved. It gave him a fresh camel, and Abu Zayd was able to reach home safely.

The heroes of Arabic EPICS frequently battled jinn in order to achieve their goals. In one section of the *DAUSI*, the epic of the Soninke people, jinn had stolen the great war drum of the people. It was recovered when the hero Lagarre learned to speak and understand the languages of jinn, animals, and birds.

JOK (JOK ODUDU) *Acholi, Lango (Uganda); Alur (Democratic Republic of the Congo, Uganda); Dinka (Sudan)* The Supreme God and Creator, who was present in all things everywhere. Jok created the heavenly bodies, Earth, everything on Earth, humans, and animals. He taught humans the skill of agriculture and gave them FIRE. As Jok Odudu, Jok was the god of birth and was responsible for all births. He sent the RAIN when it was needed to assure good crops and the dry season so that humans could hunt.

Jok did not act directly. SPIRITS also called *jok* were involved in the everyday life of humans and carried out Jok's wishes. According to Lango tradition, the spirits of the dead merged with Jok. He was, in effect, a plurality of spirits united in a single godhead.

In a myth about the ORIGIN OF DEATH, Jok had planned to give humans the fruit of the Tree of Life so that they would be immortal. However, when he called humans to come to the heavens to receive this gift, they delayed in responding. Angry, Jok gave the fruits of the Tree of Life to the SUN, MOON, and STARS. When the humans finally arrived, there was no fruit left for them. That is why the heavenly bodies are immortal and humans are mortal.

JUOK (JWOK) *Anuak, Shilluk (Sudan)* The Supreme God and Creator, who was androgynous, being at the same time both male and female (but referred to as *he*). Juok gave birth to several children—an ELEPHANT, a BUFFALO, a LION, a CROCODILE, a DOG, and finally the first humans, a boy and a girl. Juok was not pleased with the humans, so he told the dog to get rid of them. Instead, the dog nurtured

the children until they were grown. By then the land had become crowded, so Juok decided to set apart land for his different creatures and give them weapons. He planned to deal with the humans last of all. The dog knew that if this happened, there would be no land or weapons left for the humans; the animals would get it all. He told the man to tell Juok that he was the elephant, buffalo, and lion. When the man did, Juok gave him all the spears. When the animals arrived, there were no spears left for them. Instead, Juok gave the elephant tusks, the buffalo horns, the lion strong claws, and the crocodile sharp teeth. The man used his spears to drive off the animals; then he took the best land for himself.

A myth about the ORIGIN OF DEATH describes how a dog helped people attain long lives. In the beginning, death was not permanent. People remained dead for three days and then came back to life. One day, Juok decided to make death permanent by throwing a rock into the river. The dog urged humans to get together and haul the rock out of the river, but they ignored him. The dog was unable to get the rock out by himself, but he managed to break off a large chunk of it and carry it home. Because of this, humans have longer lives than they might have had.

ǀKAANG See ǀKAGGEN.

KABUNDUNGULU See SUDIKA-MBAMBI.

KADIMBA *Bantu (Angola, Botswana, Namibia)* The TRICKSTER HARE of the southern Bantu-speaking peoples. Kadimba plays a role in Bantu tales that is almost identical to that of ANANSI the SPIDER in Ashanti stories and IJAPA the TORTOISE in Yoruba folklore. Like other tricksters, Kadimba was lazy, clever, mischievous, and greedy. The following tale illustrates several of these characteristics and includes a common element of African folktales—the tug-of-war.

Hare's field needed to be cleared before he could plant a crop. That, however, was more work than Hare wanted to do. He soon came up with a way to get his field cleared without having to do it himself. Hare stretched a long rope across his field and lay in wait in the bushes. Soon an ELEPHANT came along. Hare bet the elephant that he could beat him in a tug-of-war. The elephant laughed at the idea but picked up the rope with his trunk.

Hare scampered across his field and hid behind bushes on the other side. Soon a hippopotamus came by. Hare challenged the hippo to a tug-of-war. The hippo thought the idea was ridiculous, but he picked up the rope with his teeth. Hare then hopped into the bushes and gave the rope a tug.

When the elephant and the hippo felt the tug, each of them began pulling hard. They pulled the rope back and forth all day and into the night. Finally, they gave up, each one wondering how the small Hare could have beaten him. Hare was delighted with the results: Each time the elephant and hippo had dragged the rope back and forth, it had plowed another row in Hare's field.

ǀKAGGEN (CAGN, DXUI, ǂGAO!NA, ǁGAUWA, GOHA, HISHE, HUWE, ǀKAANG, KHO, THORA, XU, Mantis) *San (Botswana, Namibia, South Africa)* The Creator, a remote SKY god who made all things but went away from Earth because humans were stubborn and opposed him. Extensive myths are attached to ǀKaggen, who has many aspects. The many different names for the San SUPREME BEING and variations among myths and legends about him are reflections of the different tribal groups into which the San are divided. The San may represent the oldest surviving African culture. San rock paintings date back about 30,000 years and are found over a large area of southern Africa. Today the San are divided into three main subgroups living in the Kalahari Desert and its fringes: the Auen, Heikum, and !Kung. For myths specific to the !Kung, see ǂGAO!NA. (See also SAN CREATION ACCOUNT.)

ǀKaggen, as a divine TRICKSTER, had both creative and destructive aspects. He created an all-devouring monster—FIRE—that burned and swallowed everything: plants, animals, humans, and even the god himself. There was a second creation, and ǀKaggen's offspring and grandchildren learned how to control fire and use it. In this way the destructive force of the Creator was countered and became the servant of humanity. (In one version of this myth, ǀKaggen destroyed the first people he created with fire because they disobeyed him. He then went to live at the top of the sky.)

ǀKaggen could transform himself into any creature, but his favorite forms were the MANTIS and ELAND. The eland is the MASTER ANIMAL of the San—their major food source—and their most important religious symbol, or TOTEM. The eland symbolizes spiritual and environmental well-being and is believed

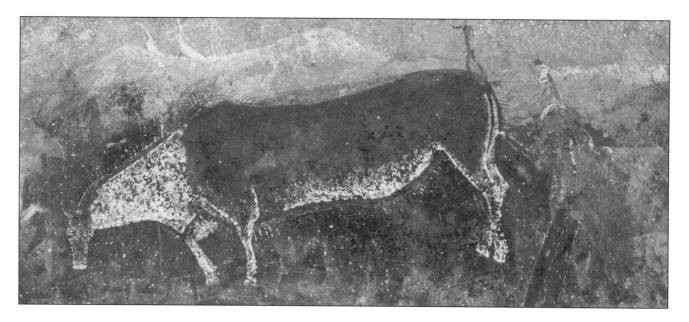

San rock painting of a shaman with an eland (© Anthony Bannister; Gallo Images/CORBIS)

to embody a high degree of supernatural energy. When an eland is killed, the SHAMAN-priest dances around the animal and invites the eland's spirit to enter his body. The harnessed supernatural power is used for such purposes as healing and making RAIN. In San rock art, Mantis (IKaggen) is often depicted as a shaman riding between the two horns of an eland.

Two different versions of the creation of the MOON by IKaggen are given. In one myth, IKaggen was angered when his children killed his beloved eland. He pierced the eland's gall bladder, and the gall blinded him, creating night. Relenting, IKaggen then wiped his eyes with an ostrich feather and threw the feather into the sky, where it became the Moon. According to another myth, IKaggen was walking in the darkness and threw his shoe into the sky. The shoe became the Moon, lighting the way for travelers.

In a story about the ORIGIN OF DEATH, IKaggen—in his aspect as Kho, the Moon—sent an insect to Earth to give humans the message that just as the Moon died and was reborn, so humans would die and be reborn. A HARE overtook the insect and offered to take the message because he was faster. However, the hare delivered the opposite message—that just as the Moon died and perished, so would humans. That is why death is permanent. Angry at what the hare had done, the Moon struck it in the face, cleaving its lip. This is why hares have a split upper lip.

IKAI IKINI   See ╪GAO!NA.

KALUMBA   (SENDWE   MWLABA)   *Luba* (*Democratic Republic of the Congo*) The Supreme God and Creator. In the beginning, Kalumba sent a man and a woman to explore the world. They found the land dark except for the MOON and returned to report this news. Kalumba created the SUN so that the people would have light. The people returned to their new home with a DOG, BIRDS, a FIRE-making stone, iron, and the power to reproduce. The man and woman became the parents of all humanity.

In another tale, humans were living with Kalumba, but they began to quarrel. Kalumba sent them to Earth, where for the first time they experienced hunger, cold, illness, and death. A diviner told the humans that to escape from this world of suffering, they needed to return to the SKY. The people constructed a huge tower that reached to the heavens. When the first humans reached the sky world, they beat drums and played flutes to let people back on Earth know they had arrived. Kalumba was angered by the noise and destroyed the tower so that no more humans could reach him.

In a myth about the ORIGIN OF DEATH, Kalumba knew that both Life and Death would be going along a certain path in order to reach humans. He sent a dog and a goat to guard the path and let Life through—which would assure humans of immortality—but not Death. The dog and goat argued about which of them should stand guard first. The goat insisted that the dog would fall asleep, but he finally left the dog to guard alone. As the goat had predicted, the dog fell asleep, and Death was able to slip past. The next day, not knowing that Death had already passed, the goat stood watch. It did not fall asleep and so caught Life when Life tried to pass by. In this way, Death entered the world.

KALUNGA *Ambundu (Angola); Lunda (Angola, Democratic Republic of the Congo, Zambia)* The Supreme God and Creator, who began as an ancestral god and was elevated to Supreme God—a god of the SKY and of the dead. (See also ANCESTORS.) Kalunga was all-knowing, all-seeing, and a righteous judge.

As god of the dead he was called Kalunga-ngombe. He ruled the UNDERWORLD and was associated with the sea, which was regarded as the realm of death. In the land of the dead, people in effect lived in much the same way they did in the upper, visible world.

See also SUDIKA-MBAMBI.

KAMMAPA See DITAOLANE; MONSTERS.

KANU *Limba (Sierra Leone)* The Supreme God and Creator. Among the different groups of Limba, Kanu had different names. He was called Kanu by the Safroko Limba, Masala by the Sela Limba, and Masaranka by the Tonko Limba. In the beginning, Kanu lived on Earth. Then one creature or element began to attack another, against Kanu's wishes. Despite Kanu's orders, a PYTHON killed and ate a deer. In turn, ants ate the python, FIRE destroyed the ants, and water quenched the fire. Because of these acts, Kanu left Earth and went to live in the SKY.

In a myth about the ORIGIN OF DEATH, Kanu made a MEDICINE that would make humans immortal. He gave the medicine to a SNAKE to bring to humans. However, a TOAD took the medicine instead and spilled it all when he began hopping. Kanu refused to make more medicine, so death came to the Limba.

KAPEPE *Lenje (Zambia)* A mythical hero who went to the heavens to marry the daughter of the Supreme God, LESA.

KATONDA (Creator) *Baganda (Uganda)* In the Baganda PANTHEON of deities (known as the LUBAALE), the Supreme God. The Baganda thought of Katonda as the father of all the gods, just as KINTU, their first king, was thought of as the father of all humans living on Earth. Katonda was regarded as a good deity and a preserver of life who never killed or harmed humans. Traditionally, Katonda was the final judge of humans. He controlled the natural world through *balubaale*, SPIRITS of deified heroes and ANCESTORS and personifications of natural elements.

KEBRA NEGAST (*Book of the Glory of Kings*) See SOLOMONIC DYNASTY, FOUNDING OF.

KEJOK *Dinka (Sudan)* A mythical hero whose life contains elements of tales of the ENFANT-TERRIBLE classification—children with miraculous births and extraordinary powers. A woman named Quay became pregnant without any human agent. After a pregnancy that lasted just a few days, she gave birth to a son who grew to manhood in a few months. Kejok was able to perform miracles, such as restoring the vision of his younger brother's son and bringing a dead cow to life again. He could produce water simply by tapping the ground with his finger. Kejok's younger brother became jealous of his fame and accused him of witchcraft. Kejok declared that he would return to God, his father, and was never seen again.

KHO See IKAGGEN.

KHONVOUM (CHORUM, KHONUUM, KHONVUM, KMVOUM) *Pygmy (Cameroon, Central African Republic, Democratic Republic of the Congo, Gabon, Republic of the Congo)* The Supreme God and Creator, the most important deity in the Pygmy PANTHEON. (See also AREBATI.) Khonvoum was also known as "the great hunter" and was a god of the hunt. He carried a bow made from two SNAKES that appeared to humans as a RAINBOW. Khonvoum made contact with humans through an intermediary animal, either an ELEPHANT named Gor (The Thunderer) or a CHAMELEON.

After he created the world, Khonvoum lowered the first humans—the Pygmies—from the SKY to the

Earth. According to some legends, he created black and white people from black and white clay and the Pygmies from red clay. There are 10 distinct populations of Pygmies: the Aka, Ake, Baka, Benzele, Bongo, Efe, Gyelli, Mbuti, Tikar, and Tswa. They traditionally live as hunter-gatherers in some of the most inhospitable forests of Africa. Khonvoum provided for them all of the animal life and lush vegetation of the forest to sustain their lives.

Khonvoum's nightly task was to renew the SUN so that it could rise again the next day. To do this, he gathered fragments of the STARS and tossed them at the Sun, giving it new energy.

KIBUKA (KIBUUKA) *Baganda (Uganda)* In the Baganda PANTHEON of deities (known as the LUBAALE), the god of war. Humans consulted Kibuka about warfare and matters of defense. In one myth, Kibuka's failure to heed warnings led to his death. Kibuka's brother MUKASA had sent him to Earth to help the Baganda in a war against the Nyoro. Mukasa warned him never to let his enemies know where he was and to have no contact with Nyoro women. During the first day's battle, Kibuka hid himself in a cloud and fired arrows down upon the enemy. The Baganda were successful and captured many of the enemy, including some women. Ignoring his brother's warning, Kibuka had one of the women sent to him. She escaped during the night after having learned Kibuka's secrets and fled back to the Nyoro. The next day, when Kibuka floated over the enemy in his cloud, the Nyoro archers sent a volley of arrows into the cloud. Kibuka was mortally wounded and died.

KIMANAUEZE *Ambundu (Angola)* A CULTURE HERO whose deeds and adventures are featured in a cycle of myths first recorded in the late 19th century. Through Kimanaueze, his son (also named Kimanaueze), and his grandsons, aspects of Ambundu culture can be traced from its beginnings through the colonial occupation of Angola by the Portuguese starting in the 16th century.

The younger Kimanaueze is featured in a myth about his efforts to marry the daughter of the SUN and the MOON. His first obstacle was how to communicate his desire to a goddess who lived in the heavens. He wrote a letter to the Sun and asked several animals and birds to carry it to the SKY world for him, but each one said that it could not. At last, a FROG offered to take the message. In this myth, the frog acts as a mediator between the earthly and divine realms. Frog knew that the heavenly water carriers came down to Earth each day to fetch water from a certain well. He hid in the well. When the water carriers came, he slipped into the water jug. He was carried up to the heavens, where he left the letter, and he returned to Earth by the same means. When Kimanaueze received no response to his letter, he sent Frog with a second one. This time, the Sun sent a letter back saying that he would agree to the marriage if the appropriate gifts were made. Frog continued the negotiations until an agreement was reached.

Kimanaueze then faced the problem of how to bring his bride to Earth. Again, Frog solved the problem. While the young woman was sleeping, he removed her eyes. When she woke and could not see, she told her parents. The Sun sent messengers to a diviner to find out why his daughter had become blind. The diviner told the messengers that she was under a spell. If she did not go to Earth and marry Kimanaueze, she would die. On hearing this, the Sun told the messengers to bring his daughter to Earth. They carried her down and left her at the well. Frog restored her eyes, and she and Kimanaueze were married.

Not long afterward, Kimanaueze's father sent him away on business. While the younger Kimanaueze was away, MONSTERS attacked the family's home and killed everyone but Kimanaueze's new wife, whose divine status protected her. That was the end of the older Kimanaueze. In time, the young couple had TWIN sons—a miraculous child named SUDIKA-MBAMBI and his brother, Kabundungulu.

KINTU *Baganda (Uganda)* The legendary first king of the Baganda. In the early 20th century, the royal family of Uganda traced its lineage back more than 1,000 years to Kintu. Kintu was credited with uniting the isolated clans of the region into a nation. A cycle of legends grew around him. One of these legends explains the ORIGIN OF DEATH.

When Kintu first arrived in Uganda, there were no sources of food in the land. He brought with him one cow, and he lived off what she could provide. Nambi, the daughter of the SKY god GULU, fell in love with Kintu and wanted to marry him. Gulu set a series of tests for Kintu before he would permit the marriage. As the first test, Gulu stole Kintu's cow. The hero would have starved to death without his cow, but Nambi showed him how to find edible herbs and other plants. Kintu passed this test and others. For a final test, Gulu told Kintu that he could marry Nambi if he could pick his own cow out of Gulu's herd. Nambi sent a bee that told Kintu to choose the cow on whose horns it landed; that was Kintu's cow.

Kintu and Nambi were married and went to Earth. Gulu warned them never to return to the heavens. If they did, Nambi's brother WALUMBE (Death) would follow them back to Earth. The couple brought many things with them from the heavens, among them goats, sheep, and chickens. Nambi realized that they had forgotten grain to feed the chickens. Despite Kintu's efforts to stop her, she insisted on returning to the heavens for the grain. Walumbe followed her home. He began asking for the couple's children, but Nambi and Kintu refused to give them up. They begged Gulu for help, so he sent Nambi's brother Kaikuzi to confront Walumbe. The brothers fought. In the end, Walumbe escaped and fled into the ground, where he became ruler of the UNDERWORLD. Since that time, Death has lived on Earth.

KISRA *Bargu (Benin)* A mythic hero who originally lived in Mecca but was driven out and eventually settled with his followers in Benin. In one account, Kisra had preached a new religion, which angered the Muslims. In another account, he was the leader of a small clan and had refused to accept the teachings of the prophet Muhammad. According to tradition, Kisra and his followers crossed into Africa and migrated across the continent to the Niger River. The Yoruba people may have been a part of Kisra's clan; tradition connects him to the Yoruba migration. After Kisra chose a place in which to settle, the clan split up into separate groups, each of which founded a different town. Kisra founded the kingdom of Busa and became its first king.

KITAKA See LUBAALE.

KIUMBI *Asu, Pare (Tanzania)* The Supreme God and Creator, who lived in the SKY. As is the case with many African deities, Kiumbi had once been close to the humans he had created. However, when humans disobeyed his orders, Kiumbi withdrew to a great distance. The only way people could reach him was through the ANCESTORS, who served as the mediators between the god and humanity.

In an attempt to reach Kiumbi and restore their former closeness with the Supreme God, people tried to build a tower to the sky. The higher they built the tower, the farther away Kiumbi went. Angered by the people's attempts to reach him, Kiumbi sent a famine to Earth. Everyone died except a young boy and girl who became the new parents of the human race.

KIWANUKA See LUBAALE.

KONGO COSMOLOGY *Kongo (Angola, Democratic Republic of the Congo)* According to the COSMOLOGY of the Kongo people, Earth was once two mountains, opposed at their bases and separated by an ocean that was the realm of the dead, Mpemba. The ocean was both a barrier between the world of the living and the world of the dead and a means of access between them.

In Mpemba, the SUN rose and set just as it did on Earth. The living and the dead exchanged day and night at sunset and dawn. The Sun's setting symbolized death, and its rising symbolized rebirth. The Sun itself was a symbol of the continuity of life. Just as the Sun rose and set in an endless cycle, life was an endless cycle. Death was merely a transitional stage in the process of change.

KONO CREATION ACCOUNT *Kono (Guinea)* In the beginning, the world was dark and empty except for a man named Sa, his wife, and their daughter. When the Supreme God, Alatangana, saw Sa's situation, he was horrified. Alatangana made the world more habitable, although it was still in darkness. Alatangana wanted to marry Sa's daughter. When Sa refused, Alatangana married her anyway and took her away with him. They had 14 children, seven boys and seven girls, each of whom spoke a different language and was a different color. Alatangana could not understand his children, so he went to Sa for advice. Sa instructed him to send the children to the far parts of the world; this accounts for the origin of the different races and languages of humans. (See also HUMANS, ORIGIN OF.)

Alatangana's children asked him to do something about the lack of light in the world. Alatangana sent two BIRDS to Sa to ask him for advice on this problem. Sa gave the birds the ability to sing, and their voices called light into the world. In return for this favor and because Alatangana had taken Sa's daughter away, Sa asked the god to send him one of his own children whenever requested. This was how death came to the world. (See also DEATH, ORIGIN OF.)

KORAU (fl. mid-13th century) *Hausa (Niger, Nigeria)* A hero who, according to tradition, defeated the last chief of the Katsina dynasty of Hausa kings and established a new dynasty. The Katsina dynasty was founded by a grandson of the legendary hero BAYAJIDA. Its last king was Sanau. Both Sanau and Korau were renowned for their wrestling ability. Korau knew that the secret of Sanau's strength was a charm he wore. (See also AMULETS AND TALISMANS.) Korau persuaded Sanau's wife to steal the charm. Then he challenged Sanau to a wrestling match. Because he was bound by honor, Sanau could not refuse the challenge, even though his charm was gone. Korau easily defeated Sanau. While the king lay on the ground, Korau slew him with his sword. The sword Korau used to kill Sanau has been preserved among the royal insignia of the Katsina.

KUDU See TORTOISE.

KWASI BENEFO *Ashanti (Ghana)* A mythical hero who made a journey to ASAMANDO, the land of the dead. Kwasi Benefo had many cattle and flourishing fields. In time, he chose for his wife a woman who pleased him. Unfortunately, she fell ill and died not long afterward. He grieved for her, but after a while he married a second woman, who became pregnant and died before she could give birth. Sad as he was, Kwasi Benefo married a third woman. After bearing him a son, however, she was killed by a falling tree. Despairing, Kwasi Benefo took his son and went into the forest to live apart from other people. After some

years, he emerged from the forest and went to a distant village where no one knew him. He married for a fourth time, but yet again, he lost his wife.

This time, Kwasi Benefo resolved to travel to the land of the dead to see the four young women who had been his wives. He made the long, difficult journey to the UNDERWORLD. Eventually he came to the bank of a deep, swiftly flowing river. AMOKYE, the woman who welcomed the souls of dead women to Asamando, appeared before him and asked why he had come. When he explained his purpose, she let him cross the river but warned him that his wives would be invisible to him. He came to the house where his wives lived, and although he could not see them, he could hear their voices. They sang a song of welcome, praised him as a husband, and told him that he should marry again. This time, they said, his wife would not die. Kwasi Benefo returned to his village and took up his old life. He married for the fifth time, and he and his wife had children and lived on happily.

KWOTH *Nuer (Sudan)* The Supreme God and Creator, who was without form and had no fixed abode. As Kwoth Nhial (Spirit Who Is in the Sky), Kwoth was associated with—and said to reveal himself through—everything related to the SKY: the SUN, MOON, STARS, and natural phenomena. He was spoken of as falling in the RAIN, blowing in the wind, and being in THUNDER AND LIGHTNING. The RAINBOW was called "God's necklace."

As in the mythologies of other African cultures, in Nuer tradition there was once a LINK BETWEEN HEAVEN AND EARTH. A rope joined the two realms. At that time, death did not exist. When people grew old, they would climb the rope to heaven. There, Kwoth would make them young again and return them to Earth. One day, a HYENA climbed up the rope and entered heaven. Kwoth told the sky SPIRITS to keep a close watch on the hyena and prevent it from returning to Earth, where it would cause problems. However, the hyena managed to escape and climb down the rope. When it was near Earth, the hyena cut the rope. Humans were no longer able to climb to heaven to be rejuvenated, so death entered the world. (See also DEATH, ORIGIN OF.)

LAGARRE *Soninke (Mauritania)* The hero of an episode of the *DAUSI* EPIC. Lagarre was responsible for the rediscovery of the Soninke goddess Wagadu.

LÉBÉ *Dogon (Burkina Faso, Mali)* The first ANCESTOR to die. Lébé was extremely old and had grown tired of life. He called on AMMA, the Supreme God, to release him from his worn-out body. Lébé died, but because death was unknown, his relatives thought he was only sleeping. At last, when Lébé's body began to decompose, they buried him. Some years later, the Dogon decided to move to another land, and they wanted to take Lébé's remains with them. When they opened the grave, however, instead of Lébé's bones they found a SNAKE. The snake followed the Dogon on their migration, convincing them that it was the incarnation of Lébé.

LE-EYO See NAITERU-KOP.

LEGBA *Fon (Benin)* In the Fon PANTHEON of deities (known as the VODUN), the seventh-born and last son of the Creator, MAWU-LISA. After Mawu-Lisa had divided the realms of the universe among her first six children, there was no realm left for Legba, so she made him her messenger. It was Legba's task to visit the realms of the other deities and report back to Mawu-Lisa. Legba was given the gift of languages so that if anyone—divine or human—wanted to communicate with Mawu-Lisa, the message had to go through him. He held the key to the gate separating the world of humans from that of the gods. He was an important figure in determining the fate of humans.

Legba was intelligent and cunning; one of his aspects was as a divine TRICKSTER. On one occasion, Mawu-Lisa sent Legba to Earth to see how SAGBATA, the Earth god, was doing. Sagbata reported that

Hevioso (SOGBO) was withholding the RAIN. Legba promised to consult with Mawu-Lisa about the problem. He would then send a BIRD named Wututu to tell Sagbata what to do. Wututu brought Sagbata the message that he was to build a fire so great that its smoke would reach the heavens. Sagbata kindled a great fire, and the smoke rose up into the sky. Legba went to Mawu-Lisa with the news that Earth was burning up, and heaven itself was in danger of being consumed by fire. Mawu-Lisa at once gave the order that Hevioso was to release the rain. Legba had, in fact, created the original problem. He had told Mawu-Lisa that there was not enough water in heaven, so the Creator had ordered Hevioso to withhold the rain. Legba had never consulted with Mawu-Lisa about the problem on Earth; building a fire had been his idea.

LEOPARD A large cat with a distinctively dark-spotted yellow coat, found throughout Africa. Leopards are distinguished by their athletic ability and are excellent tree climbers and swimmers. They range from 3 to 5 feet in length, not counting the tail, and weigh as much as 200 pounds. Throughout Africa the leopard symbolizes skill, cunning, and physical strength. The leopard is also used to indicate royal, political, and spiritual power.

In some traditions, a leopard was the symbol of ritual power. The leopard represents the spiritual aspect of the kingdom of Benin. According to legend, the founder of the Aladahonu dynasty of rulers of Dahomey (now Benin), King Adjahuto, was the son of a leopard. In the legend, a leopard came out of a river and mated with one of the wives of the king of Adja. She later gave birth to three sons—Adjahuto, Agasu, and Te Agbanli—children of the leopard. The king knew what had happened and shared his knowledge with his principal wife, who was childless. She spread the word about the leopard's children in order to turn people against them. The brothers fled to Allada, where they ruled together until they quarreled and separated. Adjahuto stayed in Allada, Agasu went north, and Te Agbanli went south. The descendants of Agasu ruled ancient Dahomey, Adja, Allada, and many other kingdoms.

In a myth of the Fang of Gabon, after the Supreme God, NZAME, had created everything, the other aspects of the triple god—Mebere and Nkwa—asked him who would be the master of the animals and plants of Earth. Together, they appointed three animals to serve jointly: the ELEPHANT because of his wisdom, the leopard because of his power and cunning, and the MONKEY because of his malice and suppleness.

For many African cultures, the leopard is a cult and TOTEM animal and an attribute of the storm god. The Igbo of Nigeria revere the leopard and associate it with fertility.

LESA *Lamba (Zambia)* The Supreme God and Creator of all things. The Lamba conceived of Lesa as living in a village so large that its ends could not be seen. Lesa spent each day on a metal throne, sitting in judgment on the affairs of the people who lived in his village.

The Lamba have two different myths about the ORIGIN OF DEATH. In one, the chief of Earth sent messengers to ask Lesa for seeds to plant. Lesa gave the messengers several tied-up bundles and warned them not to open the bundles themselves but to deliver them to the chief. On the way back to Earth, however, curiosity overcame the messengers, and they began to undo the bundles. One of the bundles contained death. When it was opened, death escaped into the world. The second myth follows the "failed message" theme, in which the Supreme God sent two animals to humans with messages of eternal life and death. Lesa first sent a CHAMELEON with the message that when people died they would return again. The chameleon took so long on his journey that Lesa sent a second messenger—a LIZARD—with the message that when people died they would be dead forever. The lizard overtook and passed the chameleon, reaching Earth first with its message of the perma-

nence of death. When the chameleon finally arrived, the people were so angry about its delay that they killed it.

LEVE   See NGEWO.

LEZA (Rain) *Ila, Kaonde (Zambia)* The Supreme God, who was closely related to nature. In one myth of the Kaonde, Leza gave a honey bird three sealed calabashes (a kind of gourd) to take to the first humans. The bird was to tell the humans that they could open the first two gourds, which contained seeds, but not the third one. They could open that only after Leza went down to Earth and taught them about its contents. On the way, however, the curious honey bird opened all three calabashes. The first two held seeds, but in the third one were all the evils of the world—death, disease, poisonous reptiles, and beasts of prey. Leza was unable to recapture these evils, and so they remained in the world. (See also DEATH, ORIGIN OF.)

LIBANZA *Boloki (Central African Republic)* The hero of a cycle of myths in the ENFANT-TERRIBLE category—stories of miraculous children with supernatural powers. Libanza's mother gave birth to the ELEPHANTS, other animals, and insects. Then she told Libanza to come out and be born. First he threw out spears, a shield, and a chair covered with brass nails; then he himself emerged. As soon as he was born, he asked his mother how his father had died. When told his father had been killed, Libanza set out to find and punish his father's murderer. After several attempts, he was eventually successful.

On his further adventures, Libanza was accompanied by his sister, Nsongo. Libanza had the ability to change himself into anything, including inanimate objects. On his journey with his sister, he changed himself into a sickly looking boy covered with sores. He and his sister were enslaved twice, first by a hunter and then by a sugarcane farmer. In each instance, Libanza freed himself and his sister by using his secret strength. Among the things Libanza did was climb a palm tree that grew higher and higher until it reached the heavens, where he stayed for a while. (See also LINK BETWEEN HEAVEN AND EARTH.) He also slew a MONSTER that had been devouring people.

LIGHTNING See THUNDER AND LIGHTNING.

LINK BETWEEN HEAVEN AND EARTH

Throughout African mythology, in the beginning there was a link between heaven—the home of the gods—and Earth—the home of humanity. Along this link, humans moved back and forth between heaven and Earth and the gods came down to Earth. Gods and humans remained fairly close to each other. The nature of the link varied considerably from culture to culture. The severing of the cord separated heaven and Earth, and as a result, God became distant from humanity. The severing of the link also often meant that humans would, for the first time, experience death. (See ARUM.) Following are some of the links between heaven and Earth that appear in African myths.

Chain OBATALA, the deputy of the Yoruba Supreme God, had a gold chain made on which he descended to the water-covered world in order to create dry land. WULBARI, the Supreme God of the Krachi of Togo, sent the first humans down to Earth on a chain.

Rope For the Abua of Nigeria (see ABUA), the Dinka of Sudan (see ABUK; NHIALIC), the Nuer of Sudan (see KWOTH), and the Sara of Chad and Sudan (see WANTU SU), the link was a rope.

Spider Web For many African tribes, such as the Ambundu of Angola, a SPIDER web was the connecting link between Earth and the heavens. NYAMBE, the Supreme God of the Rotse of Zimbabwe, ascended to the heavens from Earth on a thread of spider web.

String In a myth of the Thonga and Tsonga of Mozambique, South Africa, and Zimbabwe, a young woman climbed a string to reach heaven, the home of the Supreme God, TILO.

Strip of Leather EN-KAI, the Supreme God of the Maasai of Kenya and Tanzania, lowered cattle to the Maasai along a strip of leather. In a tale told by the Madi of Uganda, at one time, humans could maintain contact with the Creator by means of a strip of cowhide. Unfortunately, a hungry HYENA bit into the cord and severed it. Humans were unable to repair the link to the heavens, so the Creator remained distant.

Umbilical Cord In the creation account of the Bambara of Mali, the creator figures MUSOKORONI and her twin brother PEMBA descended to Earth on an umbilical cord, which they then severed.

World Tree According to the Uduk of Ethiopia, the *birapinya* tree linked heaven and Earth until an angry woman cut it down. A tree was also the link between heaven and Earth in myths of the Holoholo and Yombe of Democratic Republic of the Congo and Tanzania, the Ovimbundu of Angola, the Nuer of Sudan, and the Boloki of Central African Republic.

LION A large member of the cat family that lives on the grassy plains, or savannas, of Africa. An adult lion can be up to 6 feet long and weigh more than 400 pounds. Lions live in permanent social groups called prides that can number as many as 25 individuals. The males, with their flowing manes, are majestic animals traditionally regarded as "king of the beasts"—although the females do most of the hunting.

In many traditions, the lion is a symbol of ritual power and is associated with royalty. Mari-Jata, the founder of the Mali empire, was called the "Lion of Mali." Similarly, Haile Selassie (1891–1975), the last emperor of Ethiopia, was called the "Lion of Judah." The Azande people of Democratic Republic of the Congo believed that people became various animals when they died; dead rulers became lions. The Maasai of Kenya and Tanzania, who hunted lions, wore scars inflicted by a lion as a badge of courage.

Powerful and regal though they are, lions are frequently portrayed in folktales as gullible, not very bright, and easily tricked. The tale that follows, from the Lamba people of Zambia, is an example.

A lion was caught by the leg in the noose of a spring trap. The harder he struggled, the more tightly the trap held him. As the days passed, he grew weak from hunger and thirst. At last, a warthog family came by. The lion begged the warthogs to set him free, which out of kindness they did. The lion then demanded one of the warthog piglets to eat. Although weakened by his ordeal, the lion was still stronger than the warthogs. The father warthog agreed to give the lion a piglet, but first said he wanted to hear all about the trap. The warthog asked many questions of the lion, such as where the trap

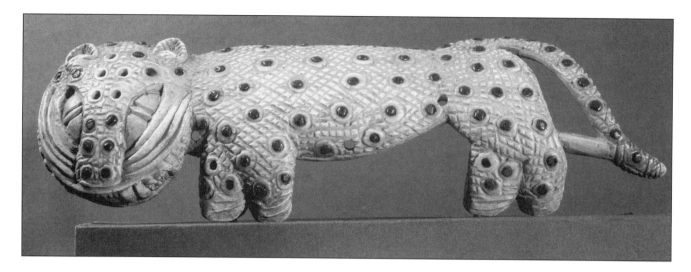

The figure of a lion is represented in an ivory and copper arm jewel from Benin. (© Werner Forman/Art Resource)

was lying, how it was set, and how the trap had caught him. Eager for his promised meal, the lion decided to shorten the questioning by showing how he had been trapped—and was caught once more. The warthog family went on their way, leaving the lion to free himself—if he could.

LIONGO (fl. 1100s) *Swahili (Kenya)* The semihistorical, semimythical hero of an EPIC poem. Liongo was a member of the royal family of Shaka, a small principality that was founded by colonists from Persia (now Iran). Liongo was famous for his great height and strength, courage, skill with the bow, and talent as a poet. Although he was the eldest son, he could not succeed his father as shah, or ruler, because his mother was one of the shah's lesser wives. Instead, his half-brother Mringwari became shah following their father's death.

Made bitter by what he saw as injustice, Liongo behaved in a high-handed way and treated the people of Shaka oppressively. He became hated. His quarrel with Mringwari reached the point that Liongo made an attempt on his brother's life. He was captured and imprisoned. While in prison, Liongo composed and sang many beautiful songs, to the delight of everyone who heard them. When Liongo was told that his brother had sentenced him to death, he made plans to escape. With his mother's help, he was able to do so. He then led the life of an outlaw, raiding towns and attacking travelers.

Mringwari wanted to have Liongo killed, but it had been discovered that no spear or arrow could harm him. Mringwari convinced Liongo's nephew (or in one version of the epic, his son) to find out the secret of Liongo's charmed life. Liongo told the boy that he knew why he had come and that the boy would regret what he was doing. Then he explained that the only way to kill him was to drive a copper needle into his navel.

The boy reported back to Mringwari, who had a copper needle made. He then sent the boy back with orders to kill Liongo.

One night, when Liongo was in a deep sleep, his nephew stabbed him in the navel with the copper needle. The pain woke Liongo up. He gathered up his bow and arrows and left the house. Halfway to the well where people got their water, his strength failed him and he fell to his knees. He fitted an arrow to the bowstring and died. The people saw him kneeling there, but they did not know he was dead, so they were afraid to go for water. After several days, they asked Liongo's mother to go speak to him. When she touched Liongo, she knew that he was dead. The people buried Liongo; according to tradition, his grave can still be seen at Ozi. Instead of giving Liongo's nephew the wife and wealth he had been promised, the people killed him for his treachery.

LISA (LESA, LEZA) *Fon (Benin)* In the Fon PANTHEON of deities (known as the VODUN), the male half of the Great God and Creator MAWU-LISA, who had a dual female-male nature. Lisa was associated with the SKY, the east, the daytime, and the SUN. He created RAIN and wind; according to one tale, it thundered when he beat his rugs.

LIZARD   Many different types of lizards live throughout Africa, but in myths they are most frequently referred to only as "a lizard." In some traditions, lizards were held to be unlucky; for one to enter a Zulu hut was a terrible omen. In many myths about the ORIGIN OF DEATH, two messengers were sent to humanity. One carried the message that humans would die but would be reborn; the other carried the message that death would be permanent. Lizards frequently carried the message of the permanence of death. (See CHIUTA; LESA; TILO; UMVELINQANGI; UNKULUNKULU; ZIMU.) In some myths, lizards exhibited a spiteful maliciousness and deliberately changed the message of life into one of death. (See QAMATHA.) In a myth of the Uduk of Ethiopia, the MOON spat and told the lizard to swallow the spittle, but the lizard refused. The Moon cursed the lizard—and humans along with it—by declaring that when the lizard and humans died, they would not be reborn.

According to the Ngombe of Democratic Republic of the Congo, the SKY was supported by two beings holding poles. If they grew tired and let the sky tilt, all human beings would turn into lizards.

LOA   See SPIRITS.

LOMA   *Bongo (Sudan)*   The SUPREME BEING and Creator, an androgynous god with two aspects: Loma, the male aspect, and Ma Loma, the female aspect. Together, Loma and Ma Loma created the Earth and humans. Loma was said to be present in every object and living creature in the world and to make his presence felt through them.

Loma also created many other Loma that were his reflections. The most important of these with respect to the everyday lives of the Bongo was Loma Gubu, a creator figure who was lord of the forest. Loma Gubu made the mountains, rivers, trees, and the animals that lived in the forest, which were his property. He determined whether hunting expeditions would be successful, and he sat in judgment over people's treat-

ment of animals. People who mistreated animals or did not respect them were likely to die suddenly.

As with many African deities, Loma was close to his creations in the beginning. Because of people's disobedience, however, he withdrew, and humans could no longer approach him directly. Loma had permitted humans to use just one grain of millet to prepare food. This grain would multiply until there was sufficient millet for everyone. One woman, however, took two grains to use. As punishment, Loma decreed that the millet would no longer multiply; people would have to find or grow their own food. Then Loma retreated to his village in the east.

LUBAALE   *Baganda (Uganda)*   The name for the PANTHEON of deities of the Baganda people. *Lubaale* refers to beings from Olubaale, the dome of the SKY, and contains about 70 divinities. KATONDA was the Supreme God and Creator. He exercised his control over the natural world by means of SPIRITS called *balubaale*. Some *balubaale* were personifications of natural elements. Others were heroes or ANCESTORS who had been elevated to divine status. The following list presents the attributes of some of the other deities in the Baganda pantheon.

Gulu   The sky god, who was next to Katonda in power. GULU, meaning "sky" or "heaven," was the name of both the sky god and the heavens.

Kibuka   The god of war. Humans consulted KIBUKA about warfare and matters of defense.

Kitaka   Mother Earth, who was consulted about agricultural matters in order to assure abundant crops.

Kiwanuka   "Something that descends at a great speed," the god of thunder and lightning. He was also a god of fertility; couples wanting a child prayed to Kiwanuka.

Mukasa   The god of plenty, who gave humans food, cattle, and children. MUKASA was a deified hero—a human who was raised to divine status because of his generosity and goodness.

Musisi   "Earthquake," the son of Wanga. People prayed to Musisi during natural catastrophes such as earthquakes.

Nambi   The daughter of Gulu, who married KINTU, the first king of Uganda.

Walumbe The god of death. Originally, WALUMBE lived in the sky with his father, Gulu. Following battles with his brother Kaikuzi, Walumbe escaped into the Earth, where he ruled the underworld.

Wanema The father of the gods Kibuka and Mukasa.

Wanga One of the oldest of the deified heroes of the Baganda. WANGA had the gift of foretelling ways to avoid common problems and was also consulted on matters of illness and disease.

LWANDA MAGERE *Luo (Uganda)* A mythic hero who led the Luo to victory over their enemies. According to legend, in ancient times the Luo were at war with the Lango and the Nandi. Time and again the Luo were defeated, until the hero Lwanda Magere emerged. His courage and skill at warfare changed the course of the war. The Luo defeated the Lango and Nandi every time they met in battle.

The Lango elders discussed ways to overcome Magere. At last they came up with a plan. Pretending to desire peace, the Lango offered Magere a beautiful Lango princess as a wife. Her true purpose was to discover the secret of Magere's power. The Luo elders suspected trickery on the part of the Lango and warned Magere against accepting the woman. Ignoring their advice, he took her as his wife. In time, she learned his secret: He could be harmed only by means of his shadow. Spears aimed at his body could not harm him, but if a spear struck his shadow, he would die. For this reason, he fought only at night.

The woman reported back to her people. The Lango challenged Magere to a daytime battle. The Luo elders warned him not to go, but Magere's pride was too great to allow him to refuse the challenge. During the battle, the Lango aimed their spears at Magere's shadow rather than his body. The shadow was struck, Magere died on the battlefield, and the Luo were defeated.

MA   See JEN PANTHEON.

MAKEDA   See SOLOMONIC DYNASTY, FOUNDING OF.

MAKONI CREATION ACCOUNT *Makoni* (*Zimbabwe*)   In the beginning, Maori, the Supreme God and Creator, made the first man and called him Mwuetsi, "MOON." Maori placed Mwuetsi at the bottom of a lake (the sea in one version of the legend) and gave him a *ngona* horn (an antelope horn symbolic of the crescent Moon) filled with *ngona* oil. Mwuetsi begged Maori to let him live on Earth. Maori allowed him to do so but warned him that he would regret it—the end would be his death.

At that time Earth was cold and empty—there were no trees, plants of any kind, or animals. When Mwuetsi complained about this condition, Maori gave him a maiden to be his wife for two years—Massassi, the Morning Star (the morning phase of the planet VENUS). Massassi made a FIRE with fire-making tools Maori had given her. Then she and Mwuetsi lay down to sleep. Mwuetsi did not know why Maori had given him this woman. He touched the *ngona* oil with his finger and then touched Massassi with the same finger, symbolically anointing her. The next morning, Massassi began to give birth to grasses, bushes, other plants, and trees until they covered the entire Earth.

After two years, Maori took Massassi back. Mwuetsi mourned her so bitterly that Maori gave him another woman to be his wife for two years—Morongo, the Evening Star (the evening phase of the planet Venus). Morongo would not let Mwuetsi simply touch her with his finger; she demanded that he have intercourse with her. Each time that Mwuetsi lay with Morongo, she gave birth the next day. The first day, she gave birth to chickens, sheep, and goats;

the second, to ELAND and cattle; the third, to human children who were fully grown by nightfall. On the fourth night, Maori sent a thunderstorm and spoke through it to the couple, warning them to stop what they were doing. Morongo told Mwuetsi to make a door for their home so that Maori could not see them. The next day, she gave birth to dangerous creatures—LIONS, LEOPARDS, SNAKES, and scorpions.

When Mwuetsi wanted to lie with Morongo again, she told him to have relations with his daughters instead. The daughters gave birth to children who were fully grown in just a day. Mwuetsi became the *mambo*, or leader, of all the people. Mwuetsi still wanted to lie with Morongo, but she had coupled with a snake that was still in her bed. When Mwuetsi lay down, the snake bit him, and he fell ill. Following this, the RAIN ceased falling, rivers and lakes dried up, plants withered, and people and animals began to die. Mwuetsi's children consulted the oracle to find out what could be done. They were told that Mwuetsi had to be sent back to the primordial lake (or sea). So Mwuetsi's children killed him. As Maori had warned, death was the end.

MAMLAMBO   See ZULU PANTHEON.

MANDE CREATION ACCOUNT *Mande* (*Mali*)   Mangala, the Creator, created an egg containing a pair of TWINS, PEMBA and his brother FARO (see also COSMIC EGG). Pemba was a rebel who left the egg ahead of time, carrying part of his placenta with him. This became the Earth. Pemba then mated with the Earth, causing it to become impure. Pemba's actions destroyed his brother Faro, whose placenta became Earth's trees. Mangala restored Faro to life and turned him into a human being. He sent Faro to Earth in an ark made out of the placenta. Along with

Masks from *(top row, left to right)* western Nigeria (Ibibio), Benin (Fon), Gabon (Fang), Democratic Republic of the Congo (Luba) *(© Werner Forman, © Seattle Art Museum, © Seattle Art Museum, © Christie's Images/CORBIS); (bottom row, left to right)* Angola (Chokwe), western Cameroon (Bamileke), Côte d'Ivoire (Baule), and Cameroon (Mambila) *(National Museum of African Art/Smithsonian Institution, © Réunion des Musées Nationaux/Art Resource, NY, © The Hamill Gallery, Boston, MA, © Réunion des Musées Nationaux/Art Resource, NY).*

Faro, Mangala sent the first ANCESTORS and the first animals and plants. After the ark landed, a blacksmith who was on board struck a rock with his hammer, and the first RAIN fell. Faro and his people planted the Earth with seeds, and humanity flourished. However, Faro's struggle with his evil brother Pemba continued.

For another creation account involving Pemba and Faro, see BAMBARA CREATION ACCOUNT.

MANGALA   See MANDE CREATION ACCOUNT.

MANTIS   *San (Botswana, Namibia, South Africa)*   A large, carnivorous insect that in some species reaches 6 inches in length. Mantises' powerful, spiny forelegs are held in an attitude of prayer, which gives the insect its common name, "praying mantis." This, coupled with the insect's wedge-shaped head and large, protruding eyes, gives the mantis a striking appearance. A unique characteristic of the mantis is that the female kills and eats the male after he has impregnated her. In myth, Mantis personifies the concept that creation is not only birth but death as well and that through death, life is renewed.

Myths about Mantis often reveal him as a shapeshifter. Mantis is the most beloved incarnation of the San Creator god IKAGGEN. IKaggen could transform himself into any animal form, but the forms of the mantis and the ELAND (a type of antelope) were his favorite. In one myth, Eland was the well-loved first son of Mantis, who wept when Eland was killed. This myth taught the San to honor the death of an eland, their MASTER ANIMAL.

MAORI   See MAKONI CREATION ACCOUNT.

MASALA   See KANU.

MASARANKA   See KANU.

MASK   In many parts of the world, especially where people live close to the forces of nature—as in Africa—masks are worn during ceremonies as a way of appealing to forces that seem beyond human control. The first Africans to wear masks may have been hunters who disguised themselves in order to stalk their prey. Over time, people began to wear masks for many purposes: to entertain the community, to represent SPIRITS, and to celebrate important occasions. Masks are worn during rites of initiation, ceremonies of secret societies, and DANCES performed on a wide variety of occasions.

Masks not only conceal or disguise—they transform. In many African traditions, people believe that masks and their related costumes transform the person wearing them into the spirit of what the mask represents. Accompanied and aided by music and dance, the mask-wearer bridges the gap between the visible world and the spirit world and communicates with the powers that are believed to control people's fate. The mask-wearer speaks with the spirit's voice. Masked dancers sometimes enter into a trance, or dreamlike state, when the spirits possess them.

The Dogon of Burkina Faso and Mali are renowned for their mask-making skills. Dressed in masks and magnificently crafted costumes, members of the Awa mask society perform elaborate funeral dances to honor the dead. These dances dramatize the conflict between life and death.

Elephant societies of the Bamileke of Cameroon (to which men pay to belong) sponsor performances to honor the king and other members of royalty. Groups of dancers wear richly beaded elephant masks with dangling cloth trunks.

MASSASSI   See MAKONI CREATION ACCOUNT.

MASTER ANIMAL   Where hunting was the way of life, the master animal—the primary source of food for a people—was revered. In traditional hunting societies, people believed that if animals' deaths were honored, the animals would appear and offer themselves willingly. By killing the animal, the hunter enabled it to enter the spirit world, from which it would return to nourish humanity. When the master animal was not treated properly, the consequences could be terrible for the people who depended on it. See BUFFALO for a Baronga tale in which the mistreatment and death of their master animal had a devastating effect. See ELAND for information about the master animal of the San.

MASUPA   *Efe (Democratic Republic of the Congo)* The Supreme God and Creator, who never showed himself. Masupa created three children—two sons and a daughter—whom he gave everything they needed. They lived happily and comfortably without having to labor or struggle. Masupa's only commandment to his children was that they should never try to see him. However, his daughter could not overcome her curiosity. Her daily task was to bring water to Masupa's house and leave it outside the door. One day, after she placed the water pot in front of the door, she hid, hoping to get a glimpse of her father. All she saw was his arm as he reached out for the pot, but that was enough to anger Masupa. He told his children that from that time on they would have to live without him.

Masupa gave his children weapons, tools, and the knowledge they would need to survive on their own. His daughter's special punishment was to bring forth children in pain and to work hard all her life. Masupa then left his children. From that time on, people had to labor for everything that Masupa had once given them freely. With the birth of the first child, death came into the world—the child died two days after being born. (See also DEATH, ORIGIN OF.)

MAWU   *Fon (Benin)* In the Fon PANTHEON of deities (known as the VODUN), the female half of the Great God and Creator MAWU-LISA, who had a dual female-male nature. She is associated with aspects of the world that relate to the Earth, the west, the MOON, and night.

MAWU-LISA (Continuer of Creation) *Fon (Benin)* The Great God of the Fon PANTHEON (see VODUN). Mawu-Lisa was a complex and androgynous deity of whom the deities MAWU (who was female) and LISA (who was male) were two aspects. Mawu-Lisa symbolized opposing aspects of human life. Mawu-Lisa is described as one person with two faces. One face—the face of Mawu—is that of a woman whose eyes are the MOON. The other face—the face of Lisa—is that of a man whose eyes are the SUN. The aspect called Mawu directed the night. The aspect called Lisa directed the day. Mawu-Lisa created the universe (see FON CREATION ACCOUNT) and gave birth to the gods and goddesses of the Fon pantheon. She divided up the realms of the universe among her children. Only her youngest son, LEGBA, could communicate directly with Mawu-Lisa. Deities and humans alike had to speak to her through Legba.

MBABA MWANA WARESA (Lady Rainbow) *Zulu (South Africa)* The goddess of the RAINBOW, RAIN, harvest, and agriculture. She was especially loved by the Zulu for bringing them the gift of beer.

The tale of the goddess's search for a husband is well known. Although Mbaba Mwana Waresa lived in the SKY in a beautiful house made of rainbow arches, she was lonely and unhappy. She was unable to find a husband among the gods, who were too warlike, so she decided to search among mortals. In a simple village, she found the cattle herder Thandiwe, who sang of his true love for the land. Hearing his song, Mbaba Mwana Waresa knew that she had found the perfect partner.

MBUMBA See RAINBOW.

MBUYU See NYAMBE.

MDALI *Xhosa (South Africa)* The Supreme God and Creator of humanity. The original name of the Xhosa Creator was Mdali. Over time, he was called by other names—QAMATHA and Thixo (or Tiko). This change probably came about after the Xhosa

migrated into the lands of the Khoikhoi and San, and the myths and legends of these people merged. This accounts for inconsistencies in Xhosa accounts of the creation of humans. (See also HUMANS, ORIGIN OF.) According to one myth, Mdali emerged from a cave in the east called *Daliwe*, which means "creator." In one version of the XHOSA CREATION ACCOUNT, humans and animals also emerged from this cave (called Uhlanga in this version). In the creation account associated with Mdali, he created the first humans by splitting a reed, out of which a man and two women emerged.

A Xhosa tale about the ORIGIN OF DEATH is an example of the "failed message" theme. Mdali sent a CHAMELEON to humans with the message that they would live forever. After the chameleon left, however, Mdali had second thoughts. He sent a salamander—an animal known for its speed—to overtake the chameleon and give humans the message that they would die. The salamander arrived first, which is why humans die.

MEBEGE *Fang, Pahouin (Central African Republic, Gabon, Republic of the Congo)* The Supreme God, who in the beginning was alone with only Dibobia, a SPIDER, hanging below him. Mebege was lonely, so Dibobia told him they must create the Earth. Mebege took hair from under his right arm, material from his brain, and a smooth pebble from the sea. He blew on these things, and they turned into an egg. (See also COSMIC EGG.) Mebege gave the egg to Dibobia, who lowered it into the sea. When enough time had passed, Mebege went down and put semen on the egg. The egg cracked open and three beings emerged—Zame ye Mebege, who was God; Nyingwan Mebege, the sister of God; and Nlona Mebege, the brother of God, who was evil. Mebege and Dibobia withdrew to the heavens, leaving Zame in control of the rest of creation. See also FANG CREATION ACCOUNT.

MEBERE See NZAME.

MEDICINE The power possessed by people, things, and actions. Medicine can be used for good purposes, such as healing, controlling game and the weather, and seeing into the future. It can also be used for evil purposes such as witchcraft or sorcery. People (usually healers, medicine people, or SHAMANS) acquire medicine from SPIRITS, ANIMALS, or objects that have power.

MEDICINE MAN OR WOMAN See SHAMAN.

MENELIK See SOLOMONIC DYNASTY, FOUNDING OF.

MILKY WAY The river of light in the night sky, the great spiral galaxy composed of billions of stars, and the home of our solar system. Our home system of Sun and planets is about two thirds of the way out from the galaxy's center. Tales about the origin of the Milky Way are abundant in African mythology. According to the San, it was created when a young girl in ancient times threw the ashes of a cooking fire into the sky. The Pokomo said that it was created by smoke from the campfires of the "ancient people." To the Sotho and Tswana, the Milky Way was Molalatladi, the place where lightning rested. It kept the sky from collapsing.

MODIMO *Sotho (Lesotho, South Africa)* The Supreme God, Creator, and head of the SOTHO PANTHEON of gods. As in the case of many other African deities, Modimo was a god with dual aspects. He was viewed as both father and mother of humanity, as being in the SKY and also in the Earth. When a lightning bolt appeared to enter the Earth, it was said that Modimo was returning to himself. Modimo was a powerful god, feared for his vengefulness and his control of FIRE, but at the same time he was seen as remote, intangible, and unknowable.

According to one myth, Modimo lived in a hole in the ground that was also the home of the dead. People had both their beginning and their end within the Earth.

MOLE A burrowing, short-furred animal with a short tail and spadelike forefeet adapted for digging. Moles live mostly underground and feed on earthworms and insects. A tale of the Meru of Kenya explains both the ORIGIN OF DEATH and the reason moles live underground. The Supreme God, Murungu, sent a mole to tell humans that people would be reborn after they died. On the way, the mole met a HYENA, who asked him where he was going. When the mole explained his mission, the hyena said that if this happened, hyenas would have nothing to eat. It threatened to swallow the mole if it delivered that message. Frightened, the mole told humans that they would die and not be reborn after death. The mole returned to Murungu and told him what had happened. To punish the mole, Murungu told it that from that time on it would live underground, far from God. That is why the mole lives in a hole in the ground and comes out only at night when no one can see it.

MONKEY Any of a wide variety of highly intelligent primates found in tropical and subtropical forests and jungles. Most monkeys are tree-dwellers, although some—such as baboons—are ground-dwellers. All monkeys are excellent climbers with grasping hands. The clever and mischievous monkey appears in numerous tales of tribes in areas where monkeys are found.

In a myth of the Fang of Gabon, after the Supreme God, NZAME, had created everything, the other aspects of the triple god—Mebere and Nkwa—asked who would be the master of the animals and plants of Earth. Together, they appointed three animals to serve jointly: the ELEPHANT for his wisdom, the LEOPARD for his power and cunning, and the monkey for his malice and suppleness.

In an account of the Makua of Malawi and Mozambique, monkeys became the first humans. The Creator, MULUKU, first made a man and a woman who did not obey his instructions about how to survive on Earth. He then called on a pair of monkeys and gave them the same instructions. The monkeys obeyed every command. Pleased with their behavior, Muluku cut off the monkeys' tails and told them that from then on they would be humans. He stuck the tails onto the humans, and told them that they would be monkeys. (See also HUMANS, ORIGIN OF.)

According to the Yoruba of Nigeria, TWINS were thought to have been sent into the world by monkeys. Twins were particularly associated with the colobus monkey, which typically bears twins. (See also *IBEJI*.)

MONSTERS Life on the African continent was filled with very real dangers: natural catastrophes such as earthquakes and floods, violent weather that included tornadoes and thunderstorms, dangerous beasts that preyed on humans and other animals, and poisonous plants and reptiles. Is it any wonder that Africans believed in supernatural monsters that preyed on and devoured humans? In African mythology, monsters come in all sizes and shapes and frequently can shift shapes at will. Descriptions of some of the monsters in African myths follow.

Aigamuxa Man-eating monsters that the Khoikhoi of South Africa said were sometimes encountered in the dunes. An unusual feature of these creatures was the location of their eyes—on their insteps. When the *aigamuxa* wanted to see what was happening, they had to get down on their hands and knees and hold up one foot.

Ga-Gorib "The Thrower Down" in the Khoikhoi tradition, a monster that killed many people. GA-GORIB sat on the edge of a great pit and held a stone to his forehead. He dared people who passed by to take the stone and throw it at his forehead. When they did, the stone bounced back and killed the thrower. He was slain by the legendary hero HEITSI-EIBIB, who distracted him, struck him behind the ear, and pushed him into his own pit.

Hai-uri A semi-invisible, man-eating monster of the Khoikhoi tradition. Hai-uri had just one side, one leg, and one arm. Despite this seeming handicap, it was quite agile when pursuing human prey and could jump over bushes.

Kammapa A giant beast in the myths of the Sotho of Lesotho that devoured all of humanity except one pregnant woman who had managed to hide from it. Her son, the hero DITAOLANE, slew the monster and released all the people and animals it had swallowed.

Makishi (singular: *kishi*) Many-headed monsters that killed the CULTURE HERO KIMANAUEZE, according to the Ambundu of Angola.

Mukunga M'bura The mythical RAINBOW, a predatory monster that lived in water, according to the Kikuyu of Kenya. At night, the monster came out of the water to steal and eat cattle.

Tikdoshe An evil dwarf in the mythology of the Zulu of South Africa. It was like Hai-uri of the Khoikhoi tradition, having just one side, one leg, and one arm. Tikdoshe fought humans, killing those it defeated but rewarding human victors with magical secrets.

Yehwe Zogbanu A 30-horned, forest-dwelling giant in the tradition of the Fon of Benin that was a constant threat to hunters.

MOON Earth's satellite. The changes in the Moon's appearance over a 29-day period have fascinated people around the world. As the Moon circles Earth, we see differing amounts of its sunlit side. During these phases, the side of the Moon visible from Earth first waxes (grows in size) and then wanes (shrinks in size). The Moon's cycle is divided into quarters. The cycle begins with the new Moon, when the Moon is between Earth and the Sun. The side facing Earth is unlit and cannot be seen. As the Moon moves around Earth, a little sunlight creeps around its edge, and we see a crescent. When the Moon is one-quarter of the way around its orbit, we see half of it lit up; this phase is called "first quarter." When the Moon is exactly opposite the Sun, all the sunlight falls on its Earth-facing side, and the Moon is full. Then the phases reverse from full to last quarter and new Moon.

For many African cultures, the Moon's phases symbolized the constant cycle of death and renewal as the Moon died and was reborn again each month. In a Nandi legend about the ORIGIN OF DEATH, a DOG told humans that all people would die as the Moon did. Unlike the Moon, he said, they would not be reborn unless they gave him milk from a gourd and beer to drink through a straw. The people laughed and gave the dog milk and beer on a stool. The dog became angry because they had not served him in the same way as a human. He decreed that all people would die and only the Moon would return to life. The Zande of Sudan also have a myth related to the Moon and death. The corpses of a man and the Moon were lying next to a grave. A FROG and a TOAD were told that if they jumped over the grave carrying a corpse, it would never die again. The frog successfully jumped over the grave with the corpse of the Moon. The toad did not succeed; it fell into the grave with the man's corpse. This is why the Moon's life is renewed each month, but people die forever.

In a San legend about the phases of the Moon, the Moon was a man who had angered the SUN. Whenever the Moon became full and prosperous, the Sun cut away pieces of him with a knife until finally only a small piece was left. The Moon pleaded with the Sun to leave this tiny piece for his children. It was from this piece that the Moon was able to grow and become full again. The Jukun of Nigeria saw the Moon as a young boy who waned as he aged. Then he went away and rested, returning to youth.

The brilliant planet VENUS appears part of the time as an evening star and part of the time as a morning star. A myth told by tribes in Gabon relates these two appearances of Venus to the Moon's phases. The Morning Star and the Evening Star were two wives of the Moon. The Morning Star, Chekechani, met with her husband in the morning. Because she never prepared meals for him, he lost weight and became thinner. At the time of the new Moon, when his hunger became too great, he left to visit his other wife. Puikani, the Evening Star, fed her husband well, and he began to put on weight again.

In most African traditions, the SUPREME BEING created the Moon as well as the Sun and other heavenly bodies. A few tales describe the Moon's origin in other ways. In an Ekoi tale, Sheep and Antelope were farmers who shared their produce with other animals. Antelope, however, refused to give food to Crocodile, whereas Sheep was generous. Crocodile shared the food Sheep gave him with PYTHON. When the food was gone, Python took a shining stone from his head and gave it to Crocodile to buy more food with. Crocodile walked back to the farm in the darkness, with the stone lighting his way. Entranced by the light, Sheep sold his farm to Crocodile in exchange for the stone. With no farm now, Sheep had no food. Antelope refused to share his food with Sheep because Sheep had been so foolish to give up his farm for a stone. Sheep went off in search of food and met Effion Obassi, the Supreme God. Effion Obassi shared his food with Sheep, so Sheep gave him the shining stone. Effion Obassi took the stone into the heavens, where it became the Moon. In the San tradition, IKAGGEN, the Supreme Being, was having trouble seeing as he walked one night, so he threw his shoe into the sky, and it became the Moon. From then on the Moon walked through the sky at night, lighting

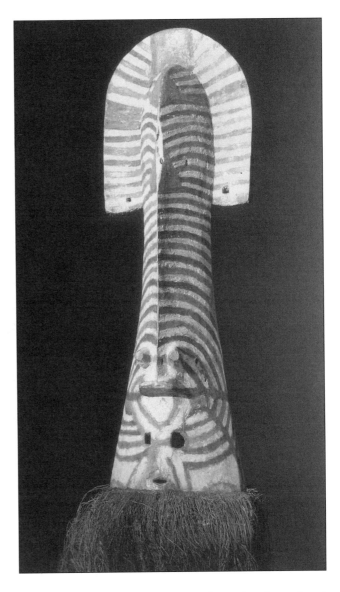

In the dance of the new Moon performed at funeral and wedding celebrations by the Tetela of Democratic Republic of the Congo, dancers wore helmet masks like the one shown. (© Werner Forman/Art Resource, NY)

the way for travelers. In a Hamba EPIC about a hero's search for his father, the hero—Okangate—brought home many things after each quest, one of which was the Moon.

In many African traditions, the Supreme Being combines both masculine and feminine elements. Typically, the Sun represents the deity's masculine element, and the Moon represents the feminine element. In some African societies, these gender roles are reversed, and the Moon is the masculine element of God.

Snow-covered Mount Kilimanjaro in Tanzania is the highest mountain in Africa, with two peaks of 19,340 feet and 16,896 feet joined by a broad saddle. (© *John Dominis/Index Stock Imagery, Inc.*)

Among some groups—such as the Sotho, Tswana, and Venda—disease was associated with the Moon. If the horns of the waxing crescent Moon pointed up when the new crescent was first sighted, it was said to be holding up various diseases. When the horns were tipped downward, the Moon poured disease onto the world.

In an Uduk tale, the Moon was directly responsible for the origin of death. The Moon spat and told a LIZARD to swallow the spittle. When the lizard refused, the Moon decreed that when the lizard died, he would not be reborn. Death would also be permanent for humans.

According to the Soko of Democratic Republic of the Congo, the Moon and a toad created the first humans. The Moon planned to make the humans, but the toad argued that because he was a creature of the Earth, he should create them. The Moon warned the toad that his creations would be inferior to the Moon's and would die after just one of the Moon's trips around the Earth. Later, the Moon relented and decided to give humans longer life and greater intelligence. First, though, he killed the toad.

MORONGO   See MAKONI CREATION ACCOUNT.

MOTHER EARTH AND FATHER SKY To the Ewe of West Africa, the rainy season represents a marriage between Mother Earth and Father Sky, when the RAINS cause plants to grow.

MOUNTAINS, SACRED   The great African mountains, such as Mount Kilimanjaro and Mount Kenya, are seen as sacred by the people who live near them. People make sacrifices and offerings, perform rituals, and offer prayers to deities at these places.

Mount Kenya is called Kere-Nyaga (Something That Possesses Brightness) by the Kikuyu of Kenya.

According to legend, it is the final resting place of the Supreme God, NGAI. The Kikuyu address Ngai in prayers and sacrifices as Mwene-Nyaga (Possessor of Brightness). They face in the direction of Kere-Nyaga when they pray.

MUBILA *Lega (Democratic Republic of the Congo)* A mythic hero whose story is an example of the ENFANT-TERRIBLE genre—tales of children with miraculous births and supernatural powers. Mubila spoke before he was born, chose his own name, and was born holding a spear, knife, shield, necklace, whistle, and belt. He had greater than human strength, possessed the power of prophecy, and could fly. Although Mubila could be killed, he was always resurrected.

As is typical universally with the pattern of hero myths, Mubila undertook a quest to determine the killer of his father (he first accused one of his brothers) and encountered and overcame many obstacles. Having been killed and resurrected, he went in search of his own murderers. He had many battles with human enemies, supernatural beings, and animals. In the end, Mubila surmounted all obstacles, returned to his home village, which he purified, and was honored by his people.

MUJAJI (MODHADJE, MODJADJI, Ruler of the Day) *Lovedu (South Africa)* A RAIN goddess and transformer of the clouds. *Mujaji* was also the honorary title of the queen of the Lovedu people. The queen's control over the rain—central to the agricultural cycle—provided the justification for the queen to rule. During life, she was not only the being who brought rain from the clouds, she guaranteed the coming of the rainy season. When the queen died, it was believed that this caused the seasons to fall out of harmony, with inevitable drought. Even the emotions of the queen were thought to affect the rain. If she was upset or angry, this could affect the natural cycle of the seasons.

MUKASA *Baganda (Uganda)* In the PANTHEON of deities of the Baganda people (known as the LUBAALE), a deified hero who became a god of plenty. Mukasa gave people cattle, food, and children and was the deity to whom people turned with concerns about health and fertility. While still a child, Mukasa disappeared without a trace. He finally reappeared on an island in a lake, sitting under a large tree. The people who found him knew that he must be superhuman, and they were uncertain what to do with him. They built him a house in which to live and found that he would eat only the heart, liver, and blood of animals. The man who found him became his chief priest. According to some myths, Mukasa died and was buried on the island. Other stories say that he simply disappeared again.

MUKUNGA M'BURA See MONSTERS.

MUKURU *Herero (Namibia)* The ANCESTOR-god and Creator of the Herero people. Mukuru was considered a benevolent god who brought life-giving RAIN, healed the sick, and supported the elderly. When people died it was because they were called home by Mukuru. The Herero viewed their tribal chief as the incarnation of Mukuru and believed that he continued Mukuru's task as a bringer of culture.

MULINDWA See CHWEZI.

MULUKU *Makua (Malawi, Mozambique)* The Supreme God and Creator, who made the Earth and created the first humans. According to myth, after he created Earth, Muluku dug two holes. A man emerged from one hole and a woman from the second. He gave them land and the tools they needed to live and instructed them in how to cultivate crops, care for the land, and use what the Earth gave them. However, instead of working the land, the people went into the forest to live off what they could find there. Muluku then summoned two MONKEYS and gave them the same tools and instructions. The monkeys followed his instructions and pleased him. He cut off the monkeys' tails and attached them to the humans, saying that from that time on the humans would be monkeys, and the monkeys would be humans.

MULUNGU (MLUNGU, MUNGU, MURUNGU) *Eastern Africa* The widely spread name of the Supreme God and Creator; many peoples worshiped him as a SKY god whose voice was thunder. (See also

THUNDER AND LIGHTNING.) In a CREATION ACCOUNT of the Kamba of Kenya, the first man and woman emerged from a termite hole, and a second pair—along with a cow, goat, and sheep—were thrown down from the heavens by Mulungu. From these four people and their children came the clans of the Kamba, Kikuyu, and Maasai.

According to the Nyamwezi people of Tanzania, Mulungu could not be reached by worship. Communication could take place only through a hierarchy of SPIRITS that served as intermediaries between humans and the Supreme God. The first people rejected a MEDICINE that would have given them immortality because the first woman advised them that following death they would return to the spirit world. The Nyamwezi did not associate death with Mulungu. Instead, an evil spirit was believed to bring death and misfortune to humans.

In a myth of the Yao of Malawi and Mozambique, a CHAMELEON found the first humans in its fish trap and reported this find to Mulungu. Mulungu told the chameleon to wait to see what the humans would do. The man made FIRE, which sent all the animals fleeing. At this time, Mulungu lived on Earth, so he also was forced to flee to evade the fire. A SPIDER spun a thread to the sky so that Mulungu could escape. (See also LINK BETWEEN HEAVEN AND EARTH.) Mulungu then retreated to the sky and decreed that when humans died, they would join him in the sky.

In another Yao myth, a man named Ntembe had a SNAKE twisted around his head that killed everyone who passed by. Mulungu complained to Ntembe about his actions. Ntembe told Mulungu to take the humans to live with him, which he did. Ntembe remained where he was and became a mountain.

MUNGU *Nandi, Swahili (Kenya, Tanzania)* The Creator, who made the heavens and Earth. In the beginning, Earth and SKY were the same, until Mungu placed the sky above the Earth. He created the Earth's waters and the RAIN. Then Mungu created FIRE and the SUN, MOON, and STARS. From the light that these created, Mungu made human beings. When he placed humans on Earth, the harmony of their lives was linked to the movements of the heavenly bodies. This harmony was sometimes disrupted

when a SNAKE approached the Moon and swallowed it. (See also ECLIPSE.) It was the responsibility of people on Earth to intervene with the snake on behalf of the Moon and force the snake to vomit up the Moon.

MUSIKAVANHU See SHONA CREATION ACCOUNT.

MUSISI See LUBAALE.

MUSOKORONI *Bambara (Mali)* In the BAMBARA CREATION ACCOUNT, the female half of a primordial pair of TWINS; the goddess of disorder. Musokoroni and her brother, PEMBA, descended to Earth on an umbilical cord and lived recklessly. In one account, the Supreme God sent a FLOOD to cleanse the Earth, and Musokoroni died in the flood. In another account, Musokoroni wandered Earth creating discontent and unhappiness and bringing illness and death to humanity.

MVELINQANGI See UMVELINQANGI.

MWARI *Shona (Zimbabwe)* The SUPREME BEING and giver of RAIN; an androgynous god who was at the same time both male and female. Mwari was also known as Dzivaguru (The Great Pool). In addition to his dual aspect as a male-female deity, Mwari was also simultaneously the god of darkness and of light, of the SKY and of Earth. According to the SHONA CREATION ACCOUNT, Mwari created the first human and dropped him from the sky onto Earth. The dreams of the first man, Musikavanhu, created the animals and birds. The first woman also appeared to the man in a dream and came to life when he touched her.

In time, humans became proud and declared that God was dead. Mwari warned humans about the dangers of their pride, but they ignored him. He cursed the Earth, sent both drought and FLOOD, created dangerous animals, and caused people to make war against each other.

MWINDO *Nyanga (Democratic Republic of the Congo)* The hero of an EPIC story of the ENFANT-TERRIBLE genre—stories of miraculous children with supernatural powers. The Mwindo epic is more a per-formance than a narration. It contains many different literary forms: prose, poetry, songs, prayers, blessings, proverbs, riddles, and asides made by the narrator. BARDS who narrated the Mwindo epic believed that its performance gave the narrator protection against disease and death. As with the epics of other cultures, the Mwindo epic is a record of the culture and beliefs of the Nyanga people.

Mwindo was the son of Shemwindo, the chief of Tubondo, and his favorite wife. Mwindo could walk and talk from birth and possessed amazing powers, such as the ability to move on land, under the ground, underwater, and in the air. He had the gift of premonition, could destroy evil forces, and was born with a magical scepter. Another of his powers was the ability to ally himself with powerful superhuman beings and natural elements, such as lightning (see THUNDER AND LIGHTNING), BATS, and SPIDERS.

Mwindo's father did not want any of his wives to bear sons, because he feared that sons would compete with him. So when Mwindo was born, his father tried to kill him. However, because of Mwindo's powers, all of Shemwindo's attempts to slay him failed. Shemwindo finally had his councilors seal Mwindo inside a drum and throw the drum into a river. Still in the drum, Mwindo traveled down the river in search of his father's sister, Iyangura, who was married to Mkuti, the great water serpent. (See also SNAKE.) Iyangura freed Mwindo from the drum.

Mwindo was determined to return home to fight his father, and he and Iyangura set out together. That evening, they reached the home of Mwindo's mater-nal uncles, the Baniyana. The Baniyana dressed Mwindo in garments made of iron and told him they would go to Tubondo with him. All the uncles were killed in the first attempt to take Tubondo. Mwindo called down lightning that destroyed the entire town, but his father escaped by descending into the UNDER-WORLD. Mwindo brought his uncles back to life and then followed his father underground. He underwent trials and performed many tasks while in the subter-ranean world, until finally the beings that lived there turned his father over to him. After returning to the surface world with his father, Mwindo restored to life all the people of Tubondo. The kingdom was then divided into two parts, one ruled by Mwindo and the other ruled by his father.

Some time later, some of Mwindo's followers were swallowed by a dragon while they were out hunting. Mwindo slew the dragon and freed his people. Light-ning, a friend and ally of both Mwindo and the dragon, was upset that Mwindo had killed the dragon. To teach Mwindo a lesson, Lightning took him into the SKY world to undergo suffering in the realm of the sky gods. Lightning brought Mwindo to the realms of MOON, SUN, STARS, RAIN, and Hail, where he endured many ordeals and gained new wisdom. Before Mwindo was allowed to return to Earth, the gods instructed him never again to kill an animal. Back on Earth, Mwindo passed on to his people the command that all beings were sacred in the eyes of the gods and that humans had no right to determine any being's fate. He gave his people laws for living in harmony, and he ruled as a great chief.

MWUETSI   See MAKONI CREATION ACCOUNT.

NAITERU-KOP (NEITEROGOB, NEIT-
EROKOP) *Maasai (Kenya)* Depending on the
myth, Naiteru-kop was the first man or a CULTURE
HERO (or minor god) who was responsible for the gift
of cattle to the Maasai. In some tales, Naiteru-kop
was a mediator between the Supreme God, EN-KAI,
and humans. According to one myth, in the beginning En-kai created Naiteru-kop and a woman to be
his partner. En-kai sent the couple to Earth with 100
head each of cattle, goats, and sheep. The couple
found that Earth was rich in natural resources—
rivers, lakes, forests, plains, minerals, and wildlife. En-
kai gave them control over these resources on the
condition that they be good custodians and hold all
of creation in trust for coming generations. Naiteru-
kop and his wife had three sons and three daughters.
The first son was given a bow and arrows and became
a hunter. The second son was given a hoe and
became a farmer. The third son was given a rod with
which to herd his father's cattle when he inherited
them. Naiteru-kop's third son was believed to be the
immediate ANCESTOR of the Maasai people. The
myth explains the Maasai's reverence for nature and
their spiritual attachment to livestock—particularly
cattle—as a source of food and wealth.

The following story explains how the Maasai got
their cattle. In the beginning, only the Dorobo
people had cattle. One day, a Maasai named Le-eyo
heard the god Naiteru-kop tell a Dorobo to meet him
at a certain place the next morning. Le-eyo made a
point of reaching that place before the Dorobo.
Naiteru-kop asked Le-eyo where the Dorobo was, and
Le-eyo responded that he did not know. Then
Naiteru-kop started to lower cattle down from the
SKY until there were many of them on Earth. The
cattle wandered off and mixed with the cattle of the
Dorobo. Because the Dorobo could not tell which
cattle were theirs, they lost all of them to the Maasai.

This is how the Maasai came to own all the cattle
and the Dorobo had to hunt wild game for their food.
(In another version of this legend, En-kai is credited
with the gift of cattle to the Maasai.)

In a myth about the ORIGIN OF DEATH, Naiteru-
kop told Le-eyo that if a child died, Le-eyo was to say,
"Man, die and come back again; MOON, die and
remain away." However, because the next child that
died was not one of Le-Eyo's, he said, "Man, die and
remain away; Moon, die and return." When one of
his own children died, Le-eyo spoke the original message that Naiteru-kop had given him. However,
Naiteru-kop told him that it was too late. Because Le-
eyo had spoken the wrong words when the first child
died, death was now permanent for humans, and the
Moon would always be reborn.

NAMBI See KINTU; LUBAALE.

NANA-BULUKU (Original Creator) *Fon
(Benin)* The SUPREME BEING who ruled over everything as the creator of the beginnings of the universe.
At the same time both MALE and FEMALE, Nana-
Buluku was the parent of MAWU and LISA, the female
and male aspects of the Great God MAWU-LISA. (See
also VODUN.) Nana-Buluku established the structure
of the universe and left the task of completing it to
Mawu-Lisa.

NANGABAN *Habbe (Mali)* A mythic hunter
who helped lead the Habbe people on their migration
to the land they presently occupy. Originally a forest
people, the Habbe were defeated by enemies and
driven out of their homeland. According to legend,
when they came to the Niger River, CROCODILES
came out of the river and carried all the people across
it on their backs. The Habbe suffered hunger and
thirst in a barren land but finally they arrived at the

cliffs and mountains that were to become their new home. Nangaban went ahead to scout the land. Another encounter with crocodiles reassured him that this was the place where the Habbe were meant to settle. He and his dogs came to a pool of water filled with crocodiles. Nangaban was ready to defend himself, but his dogs went into the water and began to drink, unbothered by the crocodiles. Nangaban drank as well, and then he went back to lead the people up into the mountains. The Habbe built houses on the cliff tops and ledges, intermarried with the cave-dwellers they found living there, and established a new homeland.

NASILELE　See NYAMBE.

NDAHURA　See CHWEZI.

NGAI (GITHUKU, MAAGU, MUGAI, MUIKUMBANIA, MURUNGU, MWENENYAGA) *Akamba, Embu, Kikuyu (Kenya); Maasai (Kenya, Tanzania)* The Supreme God and Creator of all things. As with many African deities, Ngai was remote from humans and took little interest in their everyday activities. He lived in the SKY but had temporary homes on Earth on the tops of mountains, where he rested during his visits to Earth. Ngai's powers were manifested in the SUN, MOON, STARS, RAIN, RAINBOW, and THUNDER AND LIGHTNING.

In a myth about the ORIGIN OF DEATH, Ngai sent a CHAMELEON to tell humans that they would never die. However, shortly after the chameleon left on its mission, Ngai changed his mind. He sent a second messenger—a BIRD—to tell humans that they would die and not be reborn. The chameleon was just beginning to stammer out its message of immortality when the bird arrived. The bird quickly gave its message of the permanence of death before the chameleon could finish.

NGANAMBA FASA　See DAUSI.

NGEWO *Mende (Sierra Leone)* The Supreme God, a SKY god who was remote from the affairs of humans. The SUPREME BEING of the Mende was once Leve, a female deity. She was supplanted by the male god, Ngewo, and the two were blended into a single deity.

According to one myth, there was a time when people forgot Ngewo, stopped praying to him, and neglected to make offerings to the ancestral SPIRITS. (See also ANCESTORS.) Because of this, the people's lives changed for the worse, and illness and death came among them. One night, the people heard the voice of Leve telling them that they had to pray to Ngewo again and make offerings to the ancestors. When the people did so, their lives improved.

In a myth about the ORIGIN OF DEATH, Ngewo sent a DOG and a TOAD to humans to carry messages of life and death. The dog carried the message that people would not die, and the toad carried the message that death would come. Although both started out at the same time, the dog stopped in hope of getting some food from a woman, and the toad continued on. The toad arrived first, saying that death had come. The dog arrived too late; humans had accepted the toad's message of death.

NGOMA-LUNGUNDU　See DRUMS AND DRUMMING.

NGUN *Bari, Fajulu (Sudan)* The Supreme God, who, as is the case with many African gods, had two aspects: Ngun Lo Ki and Ngun Lo Kak. Ngun Lo Ki was the SKY god and was associated with RAIN. Ngun Lo Kak was the god below the earth and was associated with agriculture. Ngun Lo Ki created humans and maintained their life force; Ngun Lo Kak brought death.

Myths about Ngun contain another common theme in African mythology—a rope as the LINK BETWEEN HEAVEN AND EARTH. The severing of the rope broke the connection between humans and the sky god, making it more difficult to reach him. Communication with the Supreme God required the intercession of a rain chief, or SHAMAN.

NHIALIC (ACEK, JOK, NYALICH, In the Above) *Dinka (Sudan)* The Supreme God, who was associated with the heavens. Nhialic created the Earth and established the order of the universe. He was closely linked with DENG, the god of RAIN and fertility. In some regions, Deng was regarded as the SUPREME BEING and Nhialic was not mentioned; in other regions, they were considered the same spirit.

According to myth, Nhialic created the first man (Garang) and woman (ABUK) out of clay. He made them quite tiny and placed them in a pot, which he then covered. When he uncovered the pot, Garang and Abuk were fully grown.

In the beginning, Earth and the SKY were close to each other and were connected by a rope. (See also LINK BETWEEN HEAVEN AND EARTH.) People who wanted to reach Nhialic could climb up the rope to the heavens. Nhialic told the first woman and man, Abuk and Garang, that they could plant and grind just one grain of millet a day for their food; this would be enough for them. One day, however, Abuk decided to plant more than one grain. When she took a long-handled hoe and began to prepare the soil, she accidentally hit Nhialic. Offended by this treatment, Nhialic withdrew far from Earth. He sent a BIRD to sever the rope that linked heaven and Earth, so that humans could no longer reach him. Before that time, there was no death. Since then, humans have had to work hard for food, and illness and death came into the world. (See also DEATH, ORIGIN OF.)

NIMBWE   See JEN PANTHEON.

NJAMBE   *Boloki (Central African Republic)*   The Supreme God. In a tale about the ORIGIN OF DEATH, Njambe allowed people to choose between having immortality and having personal possessions. One day, a man carrying two bundles appeared in a village and offered humans a choice between the bundles. One was large and contained beads, cloth, knives, mirrors, and other desirable objects. The smaller bundle, the man said, contained everlasting life. The women dressed themselves in the beads and cloth and greedily carried away the large bundle. The man—who was really the god Njambe—disappeared with the smaller bundle, and people lost their chance at immortality.

NKWA   See NZAME.

NTIKUMA   See ANANSI.

NWABI   See CHAMELEON; MDALI.

N'WARI   See SHANGAAN CREATION ACCOUNT.

NYALITCH   See NHIALIC.

NYAMBE (NYAMBI)   *Lozi, Luyi (Zambia); Rotse (Zimbabwe)*   The Supreme God and Creator of all things, all-knowing and all-powerful. There are three parts to the divinity in Lozi religious belief: Nyambe; the SPIRITS of the ANCESTORS; and the shadows, or spirits. Nyambe controlled the universe, including the lives and fates of humans. According to tradition, members of the Lozi royal family were descended from Mbuyu, Nyambe's daughter. It was said that Nyambe and his wife, Nasilele, once lived on Earth. However, people were aggressive and persisted in imitating Nyambe. He could not find a place on Earth where he felt safe, so he fled to the heavens by climbing a thread spun for him by a SPIDER. After that, the SUN came to be regarded as his symbol, and prayers to him were always made at sunrise. The MOON was Nasilele's symbol. According to the Rotse, after Nyambe left Earth, humans tried to construct a tower tall enough to reach him in the heavens, but it collapsed.

In a Lozi story about the ORIGIN OF DEATH, the first man—Kamunu (or Kamonu)—began to kill and eat animals against Nyambe's commands. Each time Kamunu killed an animal, Nyambe punished him by taking away one of his possessions. In the end, Nyambe took Kamunu's son, and so death came into the world because of Kamunu's disobedience.

According to a Luyi story, Nyambe wanted people to return to life after they had died, but Nasilele insisted that they should remain dead. When Nyambe's favorite dog died, he wanted to restore it to life. Nasilele objected because she had not liked the dog. When Nasilele's mother died, she wanted Nyambe to restore her to life. Nyambe reminded Nasilele that she would not let him bring his dog back to life. In the end, Nyambe gave in and began to revive his mother-in-law. His attempt failed when Nasilele, out of curiosity, interfered with the ritual. Nyambe then became determined to grant humans eternal life. He sent a CHAMELEON to Earth with the message that humans would die but be reborn. However, Nasilele convinced Nyambe to accept her position, so he sent a HARE to overtake the chameleon with the message that death would be permanent. In keeping with the "failed message" theme, the hare

In this idealized scene of Ashanti village life, a woman pounds grain in her mortar with a long-handled pestle like the one that annoyed the god Nyame and caused him to leave Earth to live in the sky. (© Bettmann/CORBIS)

arrived first, and humans accepted its message, not the chameleon's.

NYAME (ONYAME, The Shining One) *Ashanti (Ghana)* The all-knowing, all-powerful Supreme God, Creator of the universe, and head of the Ashanti PANTHEON of gods and goddesses (known as the ABOSOM). As with many African gods, Nyame was remote from humans and unconcerned about their daily activities. In some traditions, Nyame was considered to be male, in others to be female, and in still others to be androgynous—at the same time both male and female.

Nyame was one part of a triune deity, or triad, which consisted of Nyame, NYANKOPON, and ODOMANKOMA. Nyame represented the natural universe; Nyankopon represented its *kra*, or life-giving power; and Odomankoma represented the creative force that made the visible world. Not all Akan-speaking people make these distinctions among the three

names of the deity. Those who distinguish between Nyame and Nyankopon identify Nyame as the female element, symbolized by the MOON, and Nyankopon as the male element, symbolized by the SUN.

In some traditions, after Nyame created the Earth and peopled it with humans, he lived on Earth among people. In one tale, this situation ended when a woman bumped Nyame with her pestle as she pounded grain in her mortar. Angry, the god went away to the SKY. In a different version of the myth, Nyame was watching a group of women pounding grain. The women asked him to leave. When he did not move, they rushed at him and struck him with their pestles until he left Earth for the sky.

According to one myth, in the beginning people could not reproduce. Nyame sent a PYTHON down to Earth to teach people how to mate. After that, children were born.

In one tale about the ORIGIN OF DEATH, Nyame sent his servant—a goat—to give humans the message that although death would come to them, they would not remain dead. They would come to live with Nyame in the heavens. On the way, the goat stopped to eat some grass. Annoyed by this delay, Nyame sent a sheep with the same message. Unfortunately, the sheep got the message wrong; it told people that death would be the end. When the goat finally arrived, the people told it that they had accepted the sheep's message. In this way, death came into the world. In a different myth, people had grown tired of dying, so they sent a sheep to take a message to Nyame asking him to let them continue to live. To make certain the message got to Nyame, they also sent a DOG. Being faster than the sheep—which had stopped to eat grass—the dog reached Nyame first. However, he gave the wrong message. He told Nyame that people wished to remain dead rather than join Nyame in the heavens. Nyame agreed to this, and when the sheep arrived with the correct message, Nyame could not reverse his decision.

Nyame's goat was also responsible for thwarting Nyame's plans with respect to his sons, Bia and TANO. Nyame planned to give Bia, his favorite, the most fertile and beautiful parts of the country of Ashanti (now Ghana). Tano would receive the barren coastal lands (now the Côte d'Ivoire). Nyame sent the goat to tell his sons to come to him for their inheritance the next day. The goat preferred Tano to Bia, so it instructed Tano to disguise himself as Bia and go to Nyame very early in the morning. Deceived, Nyame gave Tano the land intended for Bia. When Bia arrived, Nyame realized what had happened, but it was too late to correct the error.

In some myths, Nyame appears as the father of the TRICKSTER-hero ANANSI the SPIDER.

NYANKOPON (ONYANKOPON) *Ashanti (Ghana)* One aspect of the triple god NYAME. (The third aspect was ODOMANKOMA.) Nyame represented the natural universe; Nyankopon, its *kra*, or life-giving power; and Odomankoma, the creative force that made the visible world. Not all Akan-speaking people make these distinctions among the three names of the deity. Those who distinguish between Nyame and Nyankopon identify Nyame as the female element, symbolized by the MOON, and Nyankopon as the male element, symbolized by the SUN. See also ABOSOM.

NYIKANG (NYAKANG) *Shilluk (Sudan)* The mythic ANCESTOR of the Shilluk, who led them on their migration to their present homeland during the heroic age. Nyikang or his spirit was believed to be in all Shilluk kings. As an immortal being, Nyikang personified the timeless and changeless institution of the kingship. According to Shilluk belief, it was not the individual human who reigned as king; it was the spirit of Nyikang in the king. Nyikang was the intermediary between humans and the SUPREME BEING, JUOK. He was believed to be a part of the Supreme God in much the same way as he was a part of the king. It was said that Nyikang did not die but disappeared in a whirlwind.

NYOHWÈ ANANU See DA ZODJI; VODUN.

NZAME *Fang (Gabon)* A triad or trinity—a god with three aspects: Nzame, Mebere, and Nkwa. Nzame represented the transcendent aspect of the deity—the god of the heavens. Mebere and Nkwa represented the male and female aspects of creation respectively. It was Nzame who created the universe—heaven, SUN, MOON, STARS, the Earth, animals, and plants—and blew life into it.

When Nzame was finished, he showed Mebere and Nkwa his creation. They suggested that Earth needed a chief to rule over everything. At first, they appointed three animals to serve jointly: the ELEPHANT because of his wisdom, the LEOPARD because of his power and cunning, and the MONKEY because of his malice and suppleness. This did not satisfy Nzame, so the gods created a being in their own image to rule the world. Nzame gave him strength, Mebere gave him leadership, and Nkwa gave him beauty. They named him Fam, which means "power." Fam's power soon went to his head. He became arrogant, mistreated the animals, and decided he had no need to worship Nzame. In punishment, Nzame called on THUNDER AND LIGHTNING, which destroyed everything in the world. Only Fam survived, because he had been promised eternal life. Fam disappeared, but he was still alive somewhere, and he could emerge from hiding at any time to cause harm.

Nzame, Mebere, and Nkwa created all the plants and animals of the Earth all over again. Nzame then created a new man in the image of the gods, but this time he made the man mortal. The new man, Sekume, was the ANCESTOR of the Fang. Not wanting to leave Sekume alone on Earth, Nzame gave him permission to make a woman from a TREE. Sekume and his wife, Mbongwe, lived happily and had many children.

OBASSI *Ekoi (Niger, Nigeria)* The Supreme God and Creator. As with many African gods, Obassi had a dual nature and was effectively two gods: Obassi Osaw and Obassi Nsi. Obassi Osaw was the god of the SKY, and Obassi Nsi was the earth god. Between them they created everything that exists. In the beginning, the two gods were together, but they decided to separate. After Obassi Nsi went to live on Earth, his powers grew. When a child was born it fell to Earth, and when people died they returned to the earth from which all things sprang. These events strengthened Obassi Nsi.

In a story about the origin of FIRE, a chief sent a boy to ask Obassi Osaw to give fire to humans. The request made Obassi angry, and he sent the boy back to Earth. The chief then went to Obassi himself to beg forgiveness, but Obassi would not pardon him. When the boy saw that even the chief could not get fire, he decided to steal it. He went back to the home of Obassi, where he made himself useful. Obassi came to trust the boy and gave him tasks to do. One day, Obassi sent him to get a lamp from one of his wives. The boy saw that this wife was the keeper of fire. She let him light the lamp with a brand from the fire. Secretly, the boy wrapped the smoldering brand in leaves and hid it. When he could sneak away, he laid the brand in dry wood and blew on it until the wood caught fire. Then he set off for home with the glowing wood. For the first time there was fire on Earth. However, Obassi saw the smoke rising from the fire. As punishment for the theft, he crippled the boy who had stolen the fire.

OBATALA (OBTALA, OLUFON, King of the White Cloth) *Yoruba (Nigeria)* In some accounts the second in command in the Yoruba PANTHEON of deities (known as the ORISA). As the deputy of the SUPREME BEING, OLORUN, Obatala was Olorun's representative on Earth. In some accounts, Obatala was regarded as the founder of the first Yoruba city, Ife.

In the YORUBA CREATION ACCOUNT, Obatala created land, vegetation, and humans. (See also HUMANS, ORIGIN OF.) According to the Yoruba, in the beginning Earth was just a vast expanse of water and marshes. Obatala suggested to Olorun that Earth would be improved if there were solid land on which *orisas* and other forms of life could live. Olorun agreed, so Obatala said that he would undertake the task. He went to ORUNMILA, the god of divination, who could divine the best way to proceed with any undertaking, and asked him how to begin. Following Orunmila's instructions, Obatala descended to Earth on a golden chain and poured sand on the waters. He then placed a hen and a pigeon on the sand. The birds scratched at the sand, scattering it in all directions. Where the sand fell, the waters turned into dry land. Obatala stepped down onto the land, which he named Ife. He planted a palm tree that created many more palm trees. When Olorun sent his servant, the CHAMELEON AGEMO, to Earth to ask how Obatala was doing, Obatala said that things would be improved with more light. So Olorun created the SUN.

After a while, Obatala decided that things would be better if there were people on Earth. He shaped human figures out of clay and called on Olorun to breathe life into them. However, while Obatala was forming the humans, he had become thirsty and had drunk too much palm wine (the TRICKSTER ESHU was said to have tempted him with the wine). Obatala's drunkenness caused him to misshape some of the figures. When Obatala sobered up, he saw that some of his creations had twisted limbs, hunched backs, and other deformities. He was filled with remorse and resolved to be the special protector of all humans with disabilities. Obatala then gave people the tools they needed for life, and humanity flourished and grew. Obatala ruled Ife for many years. Eventually he became homesick, ascended the golden chain, and returned to the SKY.

According to Ife tradition, while Obatala was sleeping off the effects of the palm wine, Olorun saw that he had left his work undone. Olorun sent ODUDUWA (the first king of Ife) to complete the task of creation. Oduduwa created his own humans and went on to rule Ife.

ODOMANKOMA *Ashanti (Ghana)* One aspect of the triple god NYAME. (The third aspect was Nyankopon.) Nyame represented the natural universe; Nyankopon, its *kra,* or life-giving power; and Odomankoma, the creative force that made the visible world. Not all Akan-speaking people, however, make these distinctions among the three names of the deity. Odomankoma was revered as god of the Earth and its physical features. Some Akan said that Odomankoma created Earth by carving it from an inert substance that had no *kra.* In other traditions, Odomankoma was said to have first made the ocean; he then created the Earth and the SKY by pressing the Earth down and raising the sky up. After that he made all the things of the world, animals, and humans. (See also HUMANS, ORIGIN OF.) In some traditions, Odomankoma created Death, and Death killed him. (See also DEATH, ORIGIN OF.) After Odomankoma died, he either lived on in a different form or was resurrected, depending on the traditional account.

ODUDUWA (ODUDUA, ODUWA) *Yoruba (Nigeria)* One of the members of the Yoruba PANTHEON of deities (known as the ORISA). According to traditions held in the city of Ife, Oduduwa was the first ruler of that city; he was called the Father of Ife and, by many, considered father of all the Yoruba people. In Ife, Oduduwa was regarded as the *orisa* who created dry land and performed feats that in other areas were attributed to OBATALA. In one account, while Obatala was forming human figures from clay, he became incapacitated by drinking palm wine and

fell asleep. OLORUN, the supreme *orisa,* sent Oduduwa to Earth to finish the work Obatala had left undone. (See also YORUBA CREATION ACCOUNT.)

OGBE BABA AKINYELURE *Yoruba (Nigeria)* A famous warrior hero who, when his son was killed in a battle, refused to return home because of his guilt. Ogbe was so renowned as a warrior that when he went into battle, only the greatest warriors faced him. As suited a great warrior, he had many wives and many children. His favorite was a son named Akinyelure. Ogbe showed his affection for the boy by calling himself Ogbe Baba Akinyelure—Ogbe, Father of Akinyelure.

One morning, after Ogbe and the other warriors had spent days—and nights—celebrating their victories with palm wine, a messenger arrived with news that an enemy force was on its way. As the weary warriors prepared to go into battle, Akinyelure approached his father and said that he wanted to go with him. Ogbe agreed, saying that they would fight side by side. In the heat of the battle, however, Ogbe lost track of where Akinyelure was. Only after the enemy had fled did he discover that Akinyelure had been killed. Wracked with guilt over having failed to protect his son, Ogbe insisted on staying where he was. He took root and became an *iroko* tree. From that time on, people made sacrifices in his memory each year at the foot of the *iroko* tree.

OGBOINBA   See WOYENGI.

OGHENE (OGHENU-KPABE) *Isoko, Urhobo (Nigeria)* The Supreme God and Creator, who was associated with the SKY and existed at the junction of Earth and sky. Oghene was seen as a benevolent god. He provided each newborn child with a personal spirit, or *emema,* that was responsible for the child's welfare. After death, the *emema* left the world and went to the UNDERWORLD, where life continued much as before.

Oghene's original intention had been for people to live forever. When people became elderly, they shed their aging skin like a snake and became young again. However, since no one died, Earth became overpopulated. People and animals argued about what to do to solve this problem. The DOG—which was loyal to people—argued that Oghene should make the world larger to accommodate the increased numbers of people. The TOAD—which was not friendly toward people—argued that death would be the solution. The people sent both animals to take their arguments to Oghene. With Oghene's approval, the point of view of the animal that arrived first would become the natural order. The dog ran far ahead of the toad. Assured of his victory, he went in search of food, overate, and fell asleep. The toad arrived first, with the result that death came into the world. (See also DEATH, ORIGIN OF.)

OGUN (OGUM) *Yoruba (Nigeria)* In the Yoruba PANTHEON of deities (known as the ORISA), the god of iron, knives, the forge, and war. Because of these associations, Ogun was the guardian divinity of anyone whose work involved metal: warriors, hunters, artisans, blacksmiths, goldsmiths, and ironworkers of all kinds. He ruled over oaths and the cementing of pacts. DOGS and the truth were sacred to him. One aspect of Ogun was as Chief of Hunters; in this role he married Red Buffalo Woman, an aspect of the goddess OYA.

Ogun was responsible for the gift of iron and knowledge of the forge to other *orisas* and humans. When some of the *orisas* wanted to live on Earth, they found their way blocked by a dense forest. They had only tools made of wood, stone, or soft metal. One after another, the *orisas* tried to cut down the trees and failed. Their machetes were not strong enough to cut through the hard wood. At last Ogun came with his iron machete and swiftly felled the trees and cleared the land. Amazed, the other *orisas* asked Ogun what material had such strength. He told them that it was iron, a secret he had learned from ORUNMILA, the god of divination.

Ogun built a forge and made other iron implements for himself—an iron spear, a knife, and weapons—but he would not share his knowledge with anyone. The *orisas* realized that begging Ogun for the secret of iron would never work. At last, they asked him to become their ruler and, in exchange for their loyalty and service, to teach them how to make iron. After careful consideration, Ogun agreed. He became the ruler of Ire and surrounding areas, and he built

forges and taught both humans and *orisas* how to make iron.

According to tradition, just as Ogun cleared away the trees for the *orisas*, he assisted humans in the same way. His machete could clear a path for them and open the way to wealth, health, and prosperity. However, if neglected, he punished people with accidents and warfare. In this way, he was both a creator and a destroyer.

OKANGATE　See MOON.

OLODUMARE　See OLORUN.

OLOKUN (Owner of the Sea) *Yoruba (Nigeria)* In the Yoruba PANTHEON of deities (known as the ORISA), the goddess of the sea, who lived in a world of sea, marshes, and mist. (In some traditions, Olokun was male.) According to the YORUBA CREATION ACCOUNT, in the beginning there were only

A 13th-century Yoruba bronze head. Thought to be a portrait of an Ife king, it is also identified with Olokun, *orisa* of the sea. (© *Werner Forman/Art Resource, NY*)

the SKY above, ruled by the Supreme God, OLORUN, and the misty, watery domain below, ruled by Olokun. At that time Olokun was the only *orisa* who lived apart; all the other *orisas* lived in the heavens with Olorun. When OBATALA, the second in command to Olorun, created dry land and people filled the world, Olokun became angry over the loss of so much of her domain. In a fit of rage, she sent a great FLOOD that covered the land, drowning nearly all the world's inhabitants. ORUNMILA, the god of divination, fate, and wisdom, came down to Earth and restored the land.

Olokun could do nothing more about the loss of her realm, but she resisted accepting Olorun as the head of the *orisas*. Olokun's chief skill was weaving and dyeing cloth, and she believed that this skill made her superior to all the *orisas*, including Olorun. Olokun challenged Olorun to a contest to determine which of them was more skilled at making cloth. Olorun sent his servant, AGEMO the CHAMELEON, to Olokun with the message that if her cloth were as magnificent as she claimed, he would enter the contest. He asked Olokun to show the best examples of her weaving to Agemo, who could then report back to Olorun on their quality. One by one, Olokun brought out pieces of cloth dyed in brilliant colors. As she showed each cloth to Agemo, his skin turned the exact color of the cloth. Finally, Olokun brought out a cloth that had a multicolored pattern. When Agemo's skin reproduced the colors and pattern perfectly, Olokun felt defeated. If a mere messenger could duplicate her creations, she thought that Olorun's abilities must be even greater. Olokun instructed Agemo to return to Olorun with the message that she acknowledged his supremacy.

OLORUN (Owner of the Sky) *Yoruba (Nigeria)* The Supreme God and head of the Yoruba PANTHEON of deities (known as the ORISA). Olorun was also known as Olodumare (Owner of Endless Space). (Strictly speaking, in the Yoruba religion Olodumare was the SUPREME BEING; he was supplanted by Olorun and came to be identified with him.) Olorun was the ruler of the SKY and the father of the other deities of the Yoruba pantheon. He was associated with peace, harmony, justice, and purity. In some traditions Olorun had an androgynous

nature—being both male and female at the same time; sometimes he appeared as a female deity. Many praise names were given to Olorun: Olofin-Orun (Lord of Heaven), Oba-Orun (King of the Sky), Eleda (Creator), Oluwa (Lord), and Orisha-Oke (Sky God).

Although Olorun was transcendent—beyond the limits of human experience and knowledge—he was not removed from humanity but could be called on at any time. The *orisa* ESHU served as the intermediary between humans and the Supreme God, carrying sacrifices up to Olorun and the god's commands down to humans. Olorun's servant AGEMO the CHAMELEON carried messages between Olorun and the other *orisas*. Only Olorun had the power to create life. When OBATALA, Olorun's second in command, created the first humans from clay, he called on Olorun to give them the breath of life. See also OLOKUN; YORUBA CREATION ACCOUNT.

OLU-IGBO See ORISA.

OMBWIRI See ANCESTORS; SPIRITS.

OMUMBOROMBONGA See TREES.

ONYANKOPON See NYANKOPON.

ORAL TRADITION Although some African cultures had a written language from ancient times, most Africans were primarily oral record-keepers. Cultural beliefs, traditions, histories, myths, legends, and rules for living were passed down from generation to generation by word of mouth. In contrast to written literature, African narratives were orally composed and transmitted. As a result, even traditional oral "texts" were not static or unchanging. Oral narratives constantly evolved and changed across time, cultures, places, regional style, storytellers, and audiences. As scholars and recorders learned, even the same African storyteller did not simply memorize and repeat the same story the same way each time. BARDS (known in West Africa by the French term *griots*) created, embellished, and adapted narratives to the needs and interests of particular audiences, alternating between text and improvisation. This dynamic tradition serves to explain the different accounts of

San storytellers, such as the woman shown, carry on the oral tradition—a major source of education for the young. (© Peter Johnson/CORBIS)

tales recorded at different times in the history of a culture or from different bards.

ORIGIN OF DEATH   See DEATH, ORIGIN OF.

ORIGIN OF HUMANS   See HUMANS, ORIGIN OF.

ORION   The Hunter, a familiar constellation that is characterized by three closely spaced STARS that mark his belt and three fainter stars suspended at an angle from the belt to form his sword. These six stars found places in the starlore of various African tribes. For the Tswana of Botswana and South Africa, the stars of Orion's sword were three dogs chasing the three warthogs of the belt. Warthogs—which frequently have litters of three young—have their litters

during the period when Orion is prominent in the sky. The Maasai of Kenya called the three stars of the sword "The Old Men." Three other stars that pursue them from the left are called "The Widows." According to the Maasai, the Widows are chasing the Old Men in order to marry them.

ORISA (ORISHA) *Yoruba (Nigeria)*   The name for the PANTHEON—the term for all the gods of a particular people taken together—of the Yoruba, as well as for the members of the pantheon themselves. The Yoruba have an elaborate hierarchy of deities, each with his or her own attributes, duties, and functions. At the top of the pantheon is OLORUN (also known as Olodumare), the Supreme God. (Strictly speaking, in the Yoruba religion Olodumare was the SUPREME BEING; he was supplanted by Olorun and came to be identified with him.) Next come his associates, lesser deities—numbering 400 or more—who are ranked in order of the importance of the function they oversee. A dozen or so greater *orisas* were active in earthly affairs and are universal in Yoruba belief. Some of these, such as OBATALA, played roles in creating and ordering the Earth and human life. Others, such as Yansan, the god of the wind, were personifications of natural forces and phenomena such as thunder, lightning, fire, and tornadoes. The minor *orisas* were called on to perform a wide variety of services: to protect people against their enemies, to ensure good crops and fertility, and to maintain health. The lesser *orisas* were usually localized deities worshiped in relatively small areas. Lowest in the pantheon are the SPIRITS of ANCESTORS and of ordinary dead people. Some *orisas* were originally humans who performed great deeds or who were the rulers of ancient city-kingdoms. They were deified, or elevated to the status of gods, after their death. For example, a woman named Moremi was deified after she saved the city of Ife from raiders.

The Yoruba religion is a living religion in Nigeria, Cuba, Brazil, Haiti, and some areas of the United States. The Yoruba pantheon can be confusing because of different traditions in different areas. Accounts told in Ife might be different from those told in Oyo or Lagos because of differing interpretations of ancient events. An *orisa* may have one name in one area and a totally different name in another—

and also have different genders. For example, the sea goddess OLOKUN was male in some traditions. Sometimes there were also differences as to which *orisa* performed a given feat—in some traditions Obatala created land; in the Ife tradition it was ODUDUWA. The following list presents the attributes of some of the deities in the Yoruba pantheon.

Aja A forest goddess who taught the uses of medicinal herbs.

Eshu The god of chance, accident, and unpredictability. A master of languages, ESHU was charged with carrying messages and sacrifices from Earth to the gods in the sky. Eshu had both good and evil qualities and frequently appears in myths as a TRICKSTER.

Ibeji The god of TWINS. (See also *IBEJI*.)

Jakuta (The One Who Hurls Stones) An *orisa* associated with Shango and considered a coworker with Shango in the creation of thunder and lightning. In some traditions, *Jakuta* is simply another name for Shango.

Obatala (King of the White Cloth) Second in command and deputy of Olorun. OBATALA created land over the water beneath the sky and founded the first Yoruba city, Ife. He created humans and served as Olorun's representative on Earth.

Oduduwa A deified ancestor; according to Ife tradition, the first ruler of the city of Ife. In one myth, ODUDUWA was credited with taking over from Obatala the task of creating the Earth and its inhabitants. Oduduwa was sometimes seen as female and the wife of Obatala. Obatala and Oduduwa also represented the male and female aspects of a single androgynous divinity.

Ogun The god of iron and war, and consequently the guardian divinity of humans whose work involved iron, such as barbers, blacksmiths, butchers, hunters, and warriors. (See also OGUN.)

Olokun (Owner of the Sea) The goddess of the sea and marshes. She reigned over the watery swamps that existed before land was created. In some traditions, OLOKUN was male.

Olorun (Owner of the Sky) The Supreme God; also known as Olodumare (Owner of Endless Space). OLORUN was acknowledged as the owner of everything and the highest authority in all matters. In some traditions Olorun was androgynous, being at the same time both male and female.

Olu-Igbo (Owner of the Bush) The *orisa* of the bush and jungle.

Orisa-nla The first god, who existed before the other *orisas* and from whom all the *orisas* came. (See also ORISA-NLA.)

Orisha-Oko The *orisa* of agriculture and patron of farmers.

Orunmila (The Sky Knows Who Will Prosper) The god of divination, fate, and wisdom; the oldest son of Olorun. ORUNMILA possessed special knowledge of future events and had the authority to speak to humans for Olorun.

Osanyin The *orisa* of medicine and divining.

Shango The god of THUNDER AND LIGHTNING, whose servants were the wind and the RAINBOW. SHANGO was said to have been the fourth ruler of the city of Oyo and was deified after his death. His wives were Obba, *orisa* of the Obba River; OSHUN, *orisa* of the Oshun River; and OYA, *orisa* of the Niger River.

Yansan The *orisa* of the wind.

Yemaja The *orisa* of the Ogun River and the mother goddess from whose body 15 gods sprang forth, among them Ogun and Shango. In some accounts YEMAJA is identified as a wife of Ogun.

See also AGEMO; YORUBA CREATION ACCOUNT.

ORISA-NLA (ORISANLA, ORISHANLA)
Yoruba (Nigeria) The first god, who existed before the gods and goddesses of the Yoruba PANTHEON (known as the *ORISA*) came into being. In the beginning, there was just formless space in which Orisa-nla lived with his slave, Atunda. One day, while Orisa-nla worked in a hillside garden, Atunda became rebellious. He rolled a huge boulder down the hill. The boulder smashed into Orisa-nla with such force that

he shattered into hundreds of pieces. These fragments of the godhead became the deities of the Yoruba pantheon.

ORISHA-OKO See ORISA.

ORUNMILA (ORUNMILLA, The Sky Knows Who Will Prosper) *Yoruba (Nigeria)* In the Yoruba PANTHEON of deities (known as the ORISA), the god of divination, fate, and wisdom and the eldest son of OLORUN, the Supreme God. Orunmila possessed special wisdom and knowledge of future events. People who wanted to know the future consulted Orunmila through his priests. He was widely known by the name IFA, the word that designates divining. He had the authority to speak to humans for Olorun.

In the YORUBA CREATION ACCOUNT, Orunmila instructed OBATALA about how to create land and guided him during the process. After land had been created, OLOKUN, the goddess of the sea, was angry at the loss of so much of her domain. She caused a great FLOOD that covered the land, inundated the fields, and drowned many people. The survivors begged ESHU—the messenger of Olorun—to carry their plea for help to Obatala. Obatala went to Orunmila for advice. After casting the palm nuts to divine the future, Orunmila said that he would go to Earth and turn the water back. After he restored the land, the people begged him to stay and protect them. Not wanting to stay on Earth, Orunmila instead decided to share his knowledge with humans. He taught various people how to divine the future and control invisible forces. Then he returned to the SKY.

OSANYIN See IJAPA; ORISA.

OSAWA See DEATH, ORIGIN OF.

OSEBULUWA See CHUKU.

OSHUN *Yoruba (Nigeria)* In the Yoruba PANTHEON of deities (known as the ORISA), the *orisa*, or goddess, of love, pleasure, beauty, and diplomacy and of the Oshun River. Oshun was considered to be generous and benign. She was one of the wives of SHANGO, the god of THUNDER AND LIGHTNING.

OWUO (Death) *Krachi (Togo)* A cannibalistic giant. A young man in search of food came across the giant and asked him for food. The giant agreed to give him some, on the condition that in payment the youth would work for him. The food the giant gave him was like nothing he had ever eaten. After some time, the young man wanted to return to his home village. The giant said that he could go if he sent a boy to take his place. The young man sent his brother. When he got hungry for the giant's food again, the young man returned. Once again, the giant agreed to give him food in return for work. When the young man asked where his brother was, the giant told the youth that his brother was away on an errand. When the young man wanted to return home again, the giant told him to send back a woman to be his wife. The young man sent his sister and her maid. Not long afterward, the young man wanted more of the giant's food, so he returned again. He saw no sign of his brother, his sister, or her maid. While he was eating, he suddenly realized that the bone he gnawed was his sister's. The meat the giant had served him earlier had been from his brother.

The young man fled back to his home village and told his people what had happened. He led the people to the giant, and they set him on fire. When the giant was dead, the people discovered MEDICINE hidden in his hair. They sprinkled the medicine on the bones and meat in the giant's house, and those he had killed came back to life. The young man dropped some of the medicine into the dead giant's eye—and the eye opened. According to the myth, every time the giant shuts his eye, someone dies. He is still lying on the ground winking and blinking. See also DEATH, ORIGIN OF.

OYA (AWYA) *Yoruba (Nigeria)* In the Yoruba PANTHEON of deities (known as the ORISA), the *orisa*, or goddess, of the Niger River and one of the wives of SHANGO, the god of THUNDER AND LIGHTNING. People greatly feared her anger; when Oya became angry, she sent tornadoes and hurricanes to strike down buildings. According to tradition, Oya served as guardian of the gates of death.

One aspect of Oya was as Red Buffalo Woman. In Yoruba culture, there was a strong association between the BUFFALO and the goddess, in part because a buffalo's horns are shaped like a crescent MOON, another symbol associated with female deities. The buffalo was a symbol of female reproduction and was therefore linked to the goddess's power to restore and renew. Marrying Red Buffalo Woman was the goal of the god OGUN, Chief of Hunters. Each night he went hunting, searching for her. One night, as he lay on his tree platform, a buffalo cow came walking toward his hiding place. She paused next to a termite mound and, as Chief of Hunters watched in amazement, began to remove her hide. As she did so, she changed into a beautiful woman. She then hid her buffalo hide in the termite mound and walked off toward the village market. Chief of Hunters removed the hidden hide and brought it to his home. Then he went to the market where, by trickery, he induced Red Buffalo Woman to go to his home. When she returned to the termite mound later that night, she discovered that her hide was missing. She concluded that Chief of Hunters must have seen her transforming herself and taken the hide, so she returned to his home and confronted him. He told her that he would give back the hide only if she married him. She agreed, but she made him promise that he would never tell his other wives who she really was. Years passed, and Chief of Hunters kept his promise despite the curiosity of his other wives. One night, though, his wives got him drunk on wine and tricked him into betraying the newest wife's secret. When they taunted Red Buffalo Woman for being an animal, she donned her hide and transformed herself into a buffalo again. Then she killed each of the other wives. She spared Chief of Hunters when he praised her and reminded her how he had cared for her. Before Red Buffalo Woman left, she told Chief of Hunters that he could call on her for help if he used her true name—Oya.

OZIDI *Ijo (Nigeria)* The hero of an EPIC of the Ijo people. According to Ijo legend, the high priest of the god of the Tarakiri clan was worshiping when he fell into a trance and the story of Ozidi was revealed to him in a vision. The high priest began to enact the story and took it from town to town until it spread throughout all the lands of the Ijo. Traditionally, the telling of the Ozidi saga takes place in the open, where the audience participates in the songs, dances, and commentary that accompany the telling. Performances occur over a period of seven nights. The BARD who narrates the story wears a white robe that is associated with Ozidi.

The Ozidi saga follows the pattern of other epics: A child is born following the death of his father. He embarks on a quest, during which he has a string of adventures, undergoes tests, and performs great feats of magic and strength. With the assistance of a female relative, he is triumphant and establishes his people. Ozidi was the son of a general who died before Ozidi was born, murdered by treacherous colleagues. The Ijo believe that a violent, unhappy death such as that prevents a dead man from joining his ANCESTORS. It is the obligation of his heirs to restore the man's honor. This was Ozidi's quest: to call home his father from the place where the murdered man's body was unceremoniously dumped and to restore him to his proper place.

On his quest, Ozidi was guided by his grandmother, Oreame, a supernatural being who was in charge of his fate. In keeping with the adventures of epic heroes, Ozidi engaged in battle with all manner of humans and MONSTERS, always triumphant because the gods—including the Supreme God, Tamara—were with him. Before each battle, Ozidi vomited up his sword and battle outfit. Accompanying him into battle were his grandmother, musician-assistants, and animals. Ozidi, however, eventually overstepped the natural bounds set to his quest. He went too far, killing his uncle and both an innocent woman and her newborn son. The Smallpox King came to take Ozidi's life as punishment, but his mother intervened and saved him. The manner of Ozidi's rescue showed that although not even the Supreme God or the supernatural powers of his grandmother could save the hero, the innocence and love of his mortal mother had the power to purify and restore him. Following his recovery, Ozidi gave up his battle sword for good.

PANTHEON The term for all the gods and goddesses of a particular people taken together. Many African cultures center on the worship of a multitude of deities. At the head of the pantheon is the Creator, or SUPREME BEING. The Creator is usually not involved with the everyday affairs of human beings; such duties are handled by lesser gods and goddesses. These figures are still divine, but they lack the power of the Creator. They manage the world of humans, and it is to them that humans appeal when they are in need. Customarily, each lesser god or goddess has a specific function or responsibility for a given force of nature. Among African pantheons are the following:

ABOSOM	The Ashanti pantheon
LUBAALE	The Baganda pantheon
ORISA	The Yoruba pantheon
VODUN	The Fon pantheon

See also CHWEZI; IGBO PANTHEON; JEN PANTHEON; SOTHO PANTHEON; ZULU PANTHEON.

PEMBA *Bambara, Mande (Mali)* In the BAMBARA CREATION ACCOUNT, the male half of a primordial pair of TWINS. Pemba and his sister, MUSOKORONI, descended to Earth on an umbilical cord and began to live reckless lives. In one account, the Supreme God sent a FLOOD to cleanse the Earth, and Musokoroni died in the flood. In another account, Musokoroni planted Pemba in the ground and left to wander the Earth, causing discord and unhappiness.

In the MANDE CREATION ACCOUNT, Pemba was a rebel. The Supreme God, MANGALA, created an egg containing a pair of twins, Pemba and his twin brother FARO (see also COSMIC EGG). Pemba left the egg ahead of time, carrying with him part of his placenta, which became the Earth. Pemba then mated with the Earth, which made it impure. Pemba's actions caused the death of Faro, who was restored to life by Mangala.

PISHIBORO See IGWIKWE CREATION ACCOUNT.

PLEIADES A cluster of STARS in the constellation Taurus the Bull. Familiarly called the Seven Sisters, the cluster actually consists of between 300 and 500 stars, although only six are visible to the unaided eye. (Various theories have been presented about why, if only six stars are visible, ancient legends around the world always refer to seven. The missing seventh may be a variable star that has dimmed to invisibility.) Because they are so conspicuous, the Pleiades' place in starlore is universal.

In the Southern Hemisphere, the constellation Taurus—home of the Pleiades—moves through the night sky from November through March. Throughout Africa, the Pleiades were used as a marker of the growing season. The Khoikhoi call the Pleiades Khuseti or Khunuseh, "the rainstars." Their appearance in the east signals the beginning of the rainy season. For the Xhosa, the Pleiades are *isiLimela*, the "digging stars"—a sign that it is time to begin tilling the soil. The Maasai call these stars *'n-Gokwa*, and—as for other tribes—their appearance and disappearance signal the beginning and end of the rainy season.

PRAYING MANTIS See MANTIS.

PYTHON Any of a species of SNAKES that kills by constricting, or squeezing, its prey until it can no longer breathe. The African rock python can reach a length of 28 feet and may weigh more than 250 pounds! The python's upper and lower jaws are attached with stretchy ligaments, which enable the snake to open its mouth extremely wide to swallow large animals. Full-grown adults can consume animals as large as antelopes. Pythons also feed on pigs, jackals, baboons, and monkeys. Although mostly terrestrial, the python also enters lakes and rivers and sometimes climbs trees. Pythons are a frequent subject of African myths.

Through the shedding of their skins, pythons and other snakes symbolize renewal and rebirth and are regarded as immortal. According to a myth told by the Fipa of Tanzania, the Supreme God, Leza, came to Earth one night and asked who did not wish to die. Humans and all the animals were asleep, but the python was awake and quickly answered Leza. That is why humans and other animals die, but pythons die only when they are killed. Pythons shed their skin each year and are renewed.

In a myth of the Ekoi of Nigeria, the Supreme God, Effion Obassi, created the MOON from a shining stone taken from a python's head. In some traditions, the RAINBOW was believed to be the belched-out breath of a python. According to an Ashanti myth, in the beginning people could not reproduce. After the Supreme God, NYAME, sent a python down to Earth to teach people how to mate, children began to be born. A python named THARU was responsible for the origin of the Venda people.

The Baga of Guinea have a tradition of snake worship; they regard pythons as reincarnations of their ANCESTORS and treat them with respect.

This brass plaque representing a python decorated the palace of the *obas* (rulers) of Benin. Pythons were regarded as messengers of Olokun, the Yoruba *orisa* of the sea. *(© Werner Forman/Art Resource, NY)*

QAMATHA (QUAMTA, QUMATHA) *Xhosa (South Africa)* One of three names by which the Xhosa Supreme God is known; the others are MDALI and Thixo. Some tales, however, are associated with Qamatha rather than with Mdali or Thixo. These were probably inherited from the Khoikhoi and San, groups that settled in southern Africa long before the Xhosa. Qamatha created and controlled all things; he was addressed through the SPIRITS of the ANCESTORS, which provided a link between God and humanity.

In a myth about the ORIGIN OF DEATH, Qamatha sent a CHAMELEON to Earth to tell people they would never die. On the way, the chameleon became tired and stopped to rest. A curious LIZARD saw the chameleon and asked where it was going. Upon hearing the chameleon's message, the malicious lizard raced ahead and gave people the opposite message— that they would die. When the chameleon finally arrived, the people did not believe its message, so death became permanent.

RABBIT For the Ama and Nyimang of Sudan, rabbits were associated with death. According to the traditions of both groups, there was once a time when neither people nor animals died. However, humans and rabbits did not get along together—in fact, they tried to destroy each other. One day, a rabbit gave poisonous roots to a man. Unsuspecting, the man ate the roots, fell into a coma, and died. That was how death came into the world.

In another tale about the ORIGIN OF DEATH, whenever someone died, ABRADI, the Supreme God, told the people that the person would come back to life the next morning if they just set the corpse aside. However, on one occasion when a man died, a rabbit reached the people before Abradi arrived. The rabbit told the people that Abradi would destroy them if they did not bury the man, so that is what they did. When Abradi discovered that the people had buried the man, he was so angry that he decreed that from then on death would be permanent.

RAIN Rain, which is so essential to agriculture and therefore to survival, has a prominent place in African religion and mythology. When it rained, according to various tribes, God was weeping or God's blessings were falling. Rain was viewed as a divine gift that fell on Earth. When it failed to rain, people wondered what they had done wrong and tried to find a way to set the matter right.

Many SUPREME BEINGS—who were almost universally SKY gods—were also rain gods credited with bringing the life-giving rain. The Dinka name for the Supreme God—DENG—literally means "rain." (For examples of deities associated with rain, see CHIDO; CHIUTA; CHUKU; DZIVAGURU; EN-KAI; JOK; LESA; LISA; MUKURU; MWARI; NGUN; NHIALIC; WAGA; XU.)

Rain goddesses include MBABA MWANA WARESA, the Zulu goddess of the RAINBOW and the rain, and MUJAJI, the rain goddess of the Lovedu of South Africa.

The rain chief of the Bari and Fajulu of Sudan intercedes with the Supreme God to bless his people with rain. The rain chief does not claim to bring the rain himself. The Supreme God gave his ANCESTORS sacred rain-stones and rainmaking power; it is through these ancestors that the rain chief reaches God. It is the rain chief's duty to combat evil forces that bring strong sunlight and drought to destroy the crops.

For the Lotuko of Sudan, the spiritual and earthly head of every community is the rainmaker. The first rainmaker was a mythical being called Ibon, who came to Earth in the form of water and left behind rain-stones. SPIRITS of the dead intercede with the Lotuko Supreme God, AJOK, for rain.

SNAKES were frequently associated with the rain. BUNZI, the cosmic serpent of the Woyo of Democratic Republic of the Congo, was a rainmaker and creator of the RAINBOW.

RAINBOW The rainbow appears as a SPIRIT or as a male or female deity in many African traditions. The Supreme God—who was most often a SKY and weather god—frequently manifested himself as a rainbow (see NGAI; WAGA). MBABA MWANA WARESA (Lady Rainbow) was the rainbow goddess of the Zulu of South Africa.

SNAKES—usually referred to as rainbow serpents—were often associated with the rainbow. For the Yombe of Zaire, the rainbow was a water snake named Mbumba who worked his way from Earth to the sky by climbing through trees. Cosmic serpents that were seen as the rainbow were AIDO-HWEDO and BUNZI. Although Thingo—the name by which the Zulu of South Africa called the rainbow—was not a snake, it lived with one in a pool of water. Thingo was a fabulous animal that either resembled a sheep or, in some tales, was a sheep.

Rainbows were often symbols of deities. KHON-VOUM, the Supreme God of the Pygmies of Central Africa, carried a bow made of two snakes that appeared to humans as a rainbow. The Nuer of Sudan called the rainbow "God's necklace."

A rainbow named Oshumare was the servant of SHANGO, the Yoruba god of THUNDER AND LIGHT-NING. Oshumare served as Shango's water carrier.

In a few tales, the rainbow was a MONSTER. In a tale from the Kikuyu of Kenya, Mukunga M'bura, the rainbow, lived in the water and emerged at night to steal and eat cattle.

RED BUFFALO WOMAN See OYA.

RUHANGA See DEATH, ORIGIN OF.

S

SA See KONO CREATION ACCOUNT.

SAGBATA (AI, AZÕ, King of the Earth, Owner of the Soil) *Fon (Benin)* In the Fon PANTHEON of deities (known as the VODUN), the general name given to the Earth Pantheon as well as the name of the first earth god. The first children of the Creator, MAWU-LISA, were DA ZODJI and his TWIN sister–wife Nyohwè Anuna, who were themselves the parents of the Sagbata gods of the Earth Pantheon. Sagbata was one of their sons. He went to live on Earth, taking his parents' riches with him. The one thing he could not bring with him was the RAIN, which remained under the control of his brother Hevioso (SOGBO). Therefore, Hevioso was able to withhold rain from Earth whenever he was angry with his brother.

In a myth that explains how Sagbata's control of Earth was stabilized, Hevioso had withheld the rain, causing a great drought. Mawu-Lisa sent LEGBA, her youngest son and messenger, to Sagbata to discover how well he was doing on Earth. Sagbata reported that Hevioso was withholding the rain. Legba promised to send a BIRD named Wututu to tell Sagbata what Mawu-Lisa decided to do about the problem. Wututu came to Sagbata with the message that Sagbata was to build a fire so great that its smoke would reach the heavens. What actually had happened was that Legba—a TRICKSTER—had told Mawu-Lisa that there was not enough water in heaven, and the Creator had ordered Hevioso to withhold the rain. After Sagbata kindled the great fire and the smoke rose up, Legba went to Mawu-Lisa with the news that Earth was burning up, and heaven itself was in danger of being consumed by fire. Mawu-Lisa at once gave the order that Hevioso was to release the rain. She also decreed that since Earth was in danger from fire, rain would be regulated from

Earth, not the heavens. She sent Wututu to live on Earth, where the bird could signal when rain was needed.

SALAMANDER See MDALI.

SA NA DUNIYA *Hausa (Niger, Nigeria)* The Bull of the World. In the COSMOLOGY, or worldview, of the Hausa, Earth was supported on one of the horns of Sa Na Duniya. When he got tired holding the Earth on one horn, he tossed it onto the other. This explains earthquakes.

SANAU See KORAU.

SAN CREATION ACCOUNT *San (Botswana, Namibia, South Africa)* There is a great hole in the Marootze country. According to San tradition, the first people emerged from this hole. The tracks of their feet can be seen in the surrounding rocks. Cattle and all the rest of the animals followed the people out of the hole. One man went back into the hole and is still there.

SANGBWA TURE See TURE.

SASABONSAM See MONSTERS.

SE See VODUN.

SEGBO See VODUN.

SERPENT See SNAKE.

SHAMAN Originally a term given to medicine men or exorcists by the Tungus of Siberia, *shaman* has been extended to other cultures to refer to individuals

97

A Ndebele shaman wearing an *isiba* headdress with porcupine quills divines the setting Sun. (© *Lindsay Hebberd/ CORBIS*)

with similar responsibilities and powers. A shaman is a ritual leader who aids people in matters of health and well-being and whose skill traditionally depends on supernatural powers. Shamans are variously referred to as medicine men or women, healers, herbalists, or witch doctors. They treat patients' physical problems with healing herbs and medications and also attempt to heal the underlying spiritual causes of illness. In traditional African thought, illness was always caused by supernatural forces such as magic, witchcraft, or SORCERY. The cause of the illness could be determined by consulting oracles or through divination. Once the cause was identified, the healer could plan a course of treatment.

The shaman gained access to the spirit world and to the source of the power to be used in healing through a trance state, often achieved through dance. The trance dancer entered another level of consciousness through which he or she reached the source of supernatural energy and was transformed by it. The shaman could then use this energy for heal-

ing, rainmaking, or reestablishing harmony in the community.

SHANGAAN CREATION ACCOUNT
Shangaan (Zimbabwe) One day, N'wari, the BIRD god, flew down from the mountains to the edge of a river. It bored a hole in a reed and laid an egg in the hole. From this egg the first man hatched. He built himself a hut and, in time, married a woman. (The myth does not say where the woman came from.) The two produced many children, who in turn produced more children who became the Shangaan people (who were at first called the Tsonga).

SHANGO (CHANGO, SANGO) *Yoruba (Nigeria)* In the Yoruba pantheon of deities (known as the ORISA), the god of thunder and lightning. As a weather or storm god, Shango was closely associated with natural elements. His wives were the *orisas*, or goddesses, of the rivers Niger (see OYA), Oshun (see OSHUN), and Obba (or Oba). Shango is typically por-

trayed with a double ax—the symbol of the thunder-bolt—on his head, six eyes, and sometimes three heads. His symbolic animal was the ram, whose bellowing resembles the sound of thunder. His servants were Afefe, the wind, and Oshumare, the RAINBOW. Oshumare's duty was to carry water from Earth to Shango's palace in the SKY.

According to myth, Shango created thunder and lightning by throwing thunderstones down to Earth. Wherever lightning struck, priests of Shango searched the surrounding area for the thunderstone. The Yoruba believed these stones had special powers and enshrined them in temples to the god.

Shango was said to have ruled over the city-kingdom of Oyo in ancient times as its fourth king. He was raised to the status of a divinity after his death. According to tradition, the historical Shango was tyrannical, powerful, and greatly feared by his subjects. It was said that when he spoke, fire and smoke burst forth from his mouth. In one account, when Shango discovered a charm (see AMULETS AND TALISMANS) that enabled him to call down lightning from the heavens, he unintentionally destroyed his own palace with it. Most of his wives and children were killed. Shango was so devastated by his loss that he went into the forest and hanged himself from an *ayan* tree, whose wood was used to make ax handles.

In another account of Shango's leaving, Shango had become jealous when his subjects praised two of his warlords—named Timi and Gbonka—more highly than they did him. Shango resolved to get rid of these heroes. He sent Timi to conquer the city of Ede, feeling certain that Timi would be defeated. To the contrary, Timi's army defeated the Ede warriors, and Timi took over rule of the city. Under his rule, Ede grew strong and famous. Jealous of Timi's success, Shango ordered Gbonka to challenge Timi in battle. Gbonka defeated Timi and brought him back to Oyo, where Shango ordered the two to fight to the death. Again Gbonka defeated Timi, but he refused to kill his friend. Shango again ordered Gbonka to fight Timi. Gbonka warned Shango that if he defeated Timi again, the contest would be between Shango and him, and one of them would have to leave Oyo forever. Gbonka felled Timi and cut off his head, which he threw contemptuously into Shango's lap. Enraged, Shango condemned Gbonka to death by

fire. However, the flames could not harm Gbonka. He walked out of the fire and told Shango to leave Oyo and never return. Shango left and hanged himself from an *ayan* tree. During a great storm that fell on Oyo, Shango's voice came from the sky declaring that he had not died but had returned to his place in the sky. It was believed that Shango continued to keep watch on Oyo and punish people who spoke against him by striking them with lightning.

A representation of Shango, the Yoruba *orisa* of thunder and lightning, tops this wooden staff used by devotees of the deity. On his head is a double-headed ax—the symbol of the thunderbolt. (*© Werner Forman/Art Resource, NY*)

SHONA CREATION ACCOUNT *Shona (Zimbabwe)* The Supreme God and Creator, MWARI, made the first man, Musikavanhu, in the heavens. He put the man to sleep and dropped him down to Earth. As Musikavanhu was falling, he woke up and saw a stone falling near him. Mwari told him to step onto the stone. Water gushed from the place where the stone landed with Musikavanhu, and it became a sacred place for the Shona.

Musikavanhu had a dream of birds and animals. When he woke, his dream had come true—birds flew through the skies and animals roamed the Earth. Mwari then instructed Musikavanhu about how he was to live: He could eat vegetables and fruits, but he must not harm the animals. Mwari also commanded the animals not to eat each other. A woman appeared, and when Musikavanhu touched her, she came to life and became his wife. Musikavanhu instructed their children in the ways in which they were to live; then he and his wife went to the heavens to live with Mwari.

SIRAT ANTAR   See ANTAR.

SKY Almost universally, the sky has been seen as the home of the divinities, and African traditions are no exception. Out of reach, the sky gods could not be manipulated by humans, but the gods could still exert an influence on Earth and its inhabitants. Stories of cosmic order are stories associated with the sky because the sky is where that order is seen. For people of most cultures, the cosmos was controlled by all-seeing, all-knowing, all-powerful gods whose business was to make the rules of the cosmos and enforce them.

Because of the relationship between the sky and the weather, sky gods were often viewed as weather gods as well, with power over the RAIN and THUNDER AND LIGHTNING.

SNAKE The snake is a potent symbol in African cultures throughout the continent. It is associated with healing, fertility, RAIN and the RAINBOW, and the knowledge of secret things. Snakes are often associated with flashes of lightning and feared for their speed and power. (See also THUNDER AND LIGHTNING.) Through the shedding of their skins, snakes also symbolize renewal and rebirth and are frequently regarded as immortal. The Baga of Guinea have a tradition of snake worship; they regard PYTHONS as reincarnations of their ANCESTORS and treat them with respect.

Snakes, or serpents, play various roles in the mythologies of different African cultures. AIDO-HWEDO, the rainbow serpent of the Fon of Benin, carried the Creator, MAWU-LISA, in his mouth as the Creator made the world. He then coiled himself around and under the world where he continues to support it and all the heavenly bodies. Other rainbow serpents include BUNZI (or Woyo) and MBUMBA (or Yombe). In some areas, the rainbow was believed to be the breath of a giant python. CHINAWEZI, the cosmic serpent of the Lunda, was considered the mother of all things; she controlled the waters and made rivers swell when she heard thunder. According to Swahili tradition, a lunar ECLIPSE occurs when a snake swallows the MOON.

In a Fipa tale about the ORIGIN OF DEATH, the Creator, Leza, came to Earth and asked who did not wish to die. Only the serpent was awake. Humans and all the other animals were asleep. So only the serpent answered Leza. That is why humans and other animals die, but the serpent has eternal life. It changes its skin each year and is renewed.

SNO-NYSOA (God the Creator) *Kru (Liberia)* The Creator, who lived in the heavens and had four sons of whom he was extremely fond. Sno-Nysoa gave each of his sons a necklace of LEOPARD teeth for protection and sent them to visit Earth. When he wanted them to return, they refused because life on Earth was so pleasant. Earth begged Sno-Nysoa to let his sons remain. However, Sno-Nysoa said that he would get his sons back. The next morning, the eldest failed to wake up. Earth went up to the heavens, where Sno-Nysoa explained that he had taken his son back. He showed his son to Earth and told Earth to bury the body that had been left behind. The same thing happened to each of the remaining sons. When the fourth son failed to wake up, Earth found that he could not go up to the heavens to see the young man. Sno-Nysoa had closed the way. From that time on, Sno-Nysoa used his power to take people from Earth, and no one could ever see them again.

SOGBO (HEVIOSO, SO) *Fon (Benin)* In the Fon PANTHEON of deities (known as the VODUN), the second-born of the Great God and Creator, MAWU-LISA. Sogbo was the chief of the Thunder Pantheon. He was androgynous—at the same time both female and male—and gave birth to the gods of the Thunder Pantheon. Sogbo lived in the SKY and was associated with THUNDER AND LIGHTNING and FIRE. He was represented as a ram with lightning coming from its mouth and two axes standing by its side. Sogbo was also called *Hevioso,* a popular general term for the Thunder Pantheon. His messenger was a BIRD named Wututu.

Sogbo sent his children to Earth to inhabit the sea. The Thunder and Sea Pantheons are thus linked, with Sogbo as the thunder god and his children as rulers of the sea. Sogbo's children had a wide variety of functions. They guarded the sea's treasures, controlled the RAIN, and created storms. One was exiled because he sank boats. The youngest of Sogbo's children was Gbade, a TRICKSTER who did whatever he pleased and whose voice was heard in the thunder.

SOLOMONIC DYNASTY, FOUNDING OF

Amhara (Ethiopia) A great EPIC presents the legend of the founding of the Solomonic dynasty of Ethiopian kings. According to legend, the first king, Menelik I, was the son of the biblical King Solomon and the Queen of Sheba. Present-day Ethiopia was first settled around the sixth or seventh century B.C. by Sabaeans, a Semitic people who migrated from the land of Saba, or Sheba, in southern Arabia. *Saba* means "the land of the south," and the Sabaeans gave this name to their new home. Around the third century B.C., one group of Sabaeans—the Habashat—established a kingdom centered on the city of Axum. The Axumite empire flourished until about the fifth century A.D. and gradually declined until the eighth and ninth centuries. Its end is recorded as coming soon after A.D. 800.

The story of the Solomonic dynasty mixes myth and legend, history, and Old Testament fragments. Over the centuries, later generations came to believe that the land ruled by the Axumite kings was the original Sheba. When the Sabaeans settled in Africa, they brought with them a written language with an alphabet related to one developed by the Phoenicians. The history of the Sabaeans and of the Axumite kings was recorded, at first on stone and later on parchment. The *Kebra Negast (Book of the Glory of Kings)* records the history of the Ethiopian rulers beginning with the first king, Menelik I.

According to the legend, the land that is now Ethiopia was ruled by a giant serpent named Arwe. (See also SNAKE.) The serpent was described as being as long as a river and having teeth as long as a man's arm. His appetite was so enormous that he ate everything the people grew, their livestock, and their daughters as well. Out of fear, the people met the serpent's demands for food. When angered, Arwe thrashed his body, causing powerful earthquakes that destroyed entire villages.

One day a stranger arrived in the land and questioned the people's obedience to the serpent. He told them that he would destroy Arwe for them. The man asked the people to bring him a perfect white lamb and a bowl filled with the juice of a euphorbia tree. He then brought these as offerings to the serpent. After Arwe swallowed the lamb, the man offered him the bowl of milky white euphorbia juice, saying that it was milk to quench the serpent's thirst. Arwe drank down the poisonous juice and fell dead. Out of gratitude, the people asked the stranger to stay and rule over them, which he did. When he grew old, he asked the people to accept his daughter, Makeda, as their ruler. Following his death, Makeda became the Queen of Sheba.

There are many variants of the legend, but the basic ingredients are the same. A trader from the north told Makeda about Solomon, a powerful and wise king whose capital was Jerusalem. The trader's stories aroused Makeda's interest, filling her with a desire to visit Jerusalem and meet the great king. She assembled a caravan bearing gifts for Solomon and in time arrived in Jerusalem. Solomon was pleased not only with the gifts Makeda had brought but with the lovely queen as well. Makeda became pregnant by Solomon and returned to Axum, where she gave birth to a son, Menelik.

When Menelik was grown, the people realized that one day he would succeed Makeda. However, they refused to accept him as their king because he had no father. Makeda told Menelik that he did have a father—Solomon, the great king in Jerusalem—who could help him gain acceptance as Axum's ruler. Menelik journeyed to Jerusalem, where Solomon eventually recognized him as his son. When the time came for Menelik to return to Axum, Solomon presented him with a wealth of gifts. Menelik also asked for the firstborn son of every family to go with him as his army. Before leaving Jerusalem, Menelik managed to steal the Ark of the Covenant from the temple, replacing the true Ark with a false one. (The Ark contained the stone tablets that Moses had brought down from the mountain with the Ten Commandments on them.) Menelik was welcomed in Axum with great celebrations, and he became King Menelik I. Emperor Haile Selassie of Ethiopia (1891–1975) was considered the 110th descendant of Menelik.

SONINKE DAUSI See *DAUSI*.

SON-JARA *Mande, or Mandinka (Mali)* The national EPIC of the Mande people; a record of the events that led to the foundation of the Mali empire. Mali was a powerful West African trading empire that emerged in the 12th century and was absorbed into the Songhai empire around 1450. The founding of the Mali empire is attributed to Son-Jara Keita (perhaps better known as SUNDIATA or Sunjata), whose life and exploits are the subject of the *Son-Jara*. Actual details of Son-Jara's life are unknown. The epic transforms him into a figure of myth and legend. It consists of seven episodes, which are traditionally performed over a seven-day period. An oral recitation of the complete epic, with musical accompaniment, can last almost 60 hours.

According to the ORAL TRADITION, Son-Jara's father was descended from Bilal, an Islamic hero and one of the companions of the prophet Muhammad, the founder of Islam. Son-Jara's quest involved an attempt to bring together the two halves of his nature. His father, Fata Magan, had brought Islamic law to his kingdom. Son-Jara's mother and grandmother represented traditional African religion and magic; his grandmother—the Buffalo Woman of Do—could transform herself into a BUFFALO.

Just before Son-Jara was born, his father's first wife gave birth to a son, Dankaran Tuman. However, the news of Son-Jara's birth reached Fata Magan first,

so he named Son-Jara his heir. Son-Jara had been cursed at birth; he was crippled and weak and could not walk for nine years. A magical staff from a custard apple tree enabled him to walk. Once he overcame his disability, Son-Jara grew strong and powerful.

Dankaran Tuman's mother plotted to gain the kingdom for her son. She succeeded in having Son-Jara, his mother, and his sister and brother exiled. Tuman became the Mandinka king. At that time, Sumanguru (also written as Samanguru or Sumamuru), the last king of Ghana, was attempting to reestablish the Ghana empire by recovering its lands, including those of the Mandinka. Trying to please Sumanguru, Tuman sent his firstborn daughter to be one of Sumanguru's wives. Sumanguru attacked anyway, defeated Tuman's forces, and drove him into exile.

In the meantime, no one would take in Son-Jara and his family. The nine Queens of Darkness (divinities of the dead) finally gave them refuge. Learning of this, Sumanguru sent a red bull to the Queens of Darkness as a bribe for them to kill Son-Jara. One of the queens warned Son-Jara. He turned himself into a lion and caught nine water buffalo as gifts for the nine queens. They sent back Sumanguru's bribe. Son-Jara and his family then went to Mema, where his mother died. Son-Jara won the support of Prince Birama of Mema and returned to his own land with an army to confront Sumanguru.

Son-Jara fought three battles against Sumanguru and was driven off each time. In order to help her brother, Son-Jara's sister, Sugulun Kulunkan, offered herself to Sumanguru. During the night he described to her the ritual that could be used to defeat him. Kulunkan gave this information to Son-Jara. Sumanguru's mother scolded her son for having revealed his secrets to a woman. In return, Sumanguru cut off his mother's breasts and disowned her. He then demanded the wife of his nephew and chief lieutenant, Fa-Koli. Angered by such treatment, Fa-Koli deserted to Son-Jara. He offered to perform the magic ritual that would defeat Sumanguru. This was the turning point in the conflict between Son-Jara and Sumanguru. Sumanguru was defeated. The epic ends with the kingdom united under Son-Jara.

SORCERY The use of power gained from the assistance or control of SPIRITS, especially for divining.

Sorcerers were living humans who possessed special knowledge that allowed them to use spiritual powers normally the preserve of the ANCESTORS. Depending on the nature of the spirits that assisted the sorcerer, sorcerers could use their power for good or evil purposes.

SOTHO PANTHEON *Sotho (Lesotho, South Africa)*

As is true of many African cultures, the Sotho had a PANTHEON of deities, each of which had a specific responsibility. The Supreme God, Creator, and head of the pantheon is MODIMO, a god with dual aspects. Modimo was viewed as both father and mother of humanity, as being in the SKY and also in the Earth. Some of the other Sotho deities are the following:

Lotiloe   God of the dance.
Ramaepa   God of the field. He prevented enemies from crossing the boundaries into Sotho territory.
Ramochasoa   God of water, who lived on the bottom of bodies of water.
Toona   God of revenge.

SPIDER

The eight-legged, web-weaving arachnid appears in countless African tales as a TRICKSTER and frequently as a CULTURE HERO as well. The Ashanti and related Akan-speaking peoples of Ghana have ANANSI, who figures in a vast body of folktales called ANANSASEM, or spider stories. Anansi is preoccupied with outwitting animals, human beings, and even the deities. However, he is also credited with bringing RAIN, teaching humans to sow grain, and performing other acts associated with culture heroes. GIZO, the spider trickster of the Hausa of Niger and Nigeria, has numerous adventures common to the tales of other African tricksters. He sometimes appears as a villain. WAC, the spider trickster of the Jo Luo of Sudan, is often outrageous in his actions but on occasion performs positive deeds, such as saving humans. The spider hero of the Fiote and Fjorte of Republic of the Congo was responsible for the gift of FIRE.

The spider's web-weaving ability plays a role in tales that involve a LINK BETWEEN HEAVEN AND EARTH. Frequently, the link is a strand of spider web. When the SUPREME BEING of the Yao of Malawi and

The spiders decorating the rim of this Bamum bowl from Cameroon are associated with divination. Throughout the region, spiders represent wisdom. *(National Museum of African Art, Smithsonian Institution)*

Mozambique, MULUNGU, was forced to leave Earth, he asked a spider for help. The spider spun a thread that reached to the SKY, and Mulungu went up it to the heavens. NYAMBE, the Supreme Being of the Rotse of Zimbabwe, also ascended from Earth to the heavens on a spider web.

In a tale told by the Fang and Pahouin of Central African Republic, Gabon, and Republic of the Congo, a spider named Dibobia initiated the creation of the Earth. The Creator, MEBEGE, was lonely in his home in the sky, with just Dibobia hanging beneath him above the primordial waters. Dibobia told Mebege that they must create the Earth. (See FANG CREATION ACCOUNT.)

SPIRITS

Spirits play important roles in the religions and mythologies of Africa. Although invisible, spirits were believed to be everywhere. There were guardian spirits, spirits of ANCESTORS, spirits of the dead, and evil spirits. Spirits were powerful forces and needed to be treated with care. For this reason, numerous rituals and taboos were associated with spirits.

The spirits of ancestors and of departed heroes were usually seen as spiritual guardians that protected the community against enemies. People expected ancestral spirits to continually guard the living. For example, the Zulu of South Africa invoked the help of the spirit world by calling on the *amadlozi*, the ancestors of the Zulu people. Guardian spirits were also thought to reside in natural objects, such as mountains, trees, and rivers, and to protect the areas in which they lived. According to the Isoko and Urhobo of Nigeria, the SUPREME BEING, OGHENE, provided each newborn child with a personal spirit, or *emema*, that was responsible for the child's welfare. At death, the *emema* left the world and went to the UNDERWORLD, where life continued much as it had on Earth.

Spirits of dead people who were not considered ancestors—who were ordinary members of the community—were also part of the spirit world. Although not revered as ancestors were, the spirits of the dead were respected and acknowledged in ritual observances. In some traditions, however, spirits of the dead were hostile to humans. The *badimo*, the spirits of the dead in the tradition of the Tswana of Botswana and South Africa, were not merely hostile; they undid the acts of the Supreme God, perverted his purposes, and turned humans away from him. In other traditions, such as that of the Lango, the spirits of the dead returned to the godhead, merging with the Supreme Being (see JOK).

Because spirits had more contact with human beings than did the Supreme God, they were able to keep the deity in touch with human activities. Spirits frequently were seen as mediators between the Supreme God and humans. The *mizhimo*—the ancestral spirits of the Ila and Kaonde of Zambia—mediated between humans and the Supreme God, LEZA. For the Kipsigis and Nandi of Kenya, the *oiik*—spirits of the dead—stood between humans and the Supreme God, ASIS, and mediated between them. The *oiik* punished humans who upset the balance of nature. Bail, the Supreme God of the Dilling and

Nuba of Sudan, entrusted the work of guiding the affairs of human beings to spirits called *arro*. The *arro* advised the chiefs of human communities, looked after humans, and rewarded or punished humans depending on how the humans had behaved.

For the Anang of Nigeria, spirits called *nnem* had special significance. The 54 *nnem* served religious, social, political, and economic functions. They carried sacrifices to the Supreme God, ABASSI, in order for him to make decisions about how to reward the supplicants.

The Nyoro of Uganda have a PANTHEON of spirits called CHWEZI. Each of the Chwezi spirits is identified with one of the long-dead (perhaps mythical) Chwezi, who ruled the kingdom of Bunyoro around A.D. 1300–1500. These spirits are not thought of as the spirits of actual people who lived long ago but as supernatural powers. They are variously associated with plenty, harvest, healing, weather, cattle, and smallpox.

STARS Myths abound about the stars and their origin. According to the Ewe of Benin, Ghana, and Togo, the stars were the MOON's children. The SUN and the Moon had large families and decided one day to kill their children. First, Sun killed her children and used their bodies to prepare a large meal that she shared with Moon. Moon was supposed to reciprocate by killing her children and preparing a meal to share with Sun. However, she changed her mind and hid her children. She let them out only at night when it was safe. Sun, who no longer had any children, was alone in the daytime sky.

In a Hausa tale about the origin of stars, some boys threw stones at an elderly woman (the Earth), who became annoyed. She caused the boys to rise into the sky, where they became stars. In a different version of the myth, the stars already existed but were close to Earth. An elderly woman moved them far away when some boys threw stones at them.

In some traditions, the stars were associated with the dead. For the Zulu of South Africa, stars were the eyes of the dead looking down at the human world. The San of Botswana, Namibia, and South Africa also thought that the stars were formerly people or animals. For the Jukun of Nigeria, each star represented a person's soul.

SUDIKA-MBAMBI *Ambundu (Angola)* A legendary hero child, the grandson of the CULTURE HERO KIMANAUEZE, who is featured in a cycle of stories. Sudika-mbambi's father was also named Kimanaueze; his mother was the daughter of the SUN and the MOON. The story of Sudika-mbambi is in the ENFANT-TERRIBLE genre—stories of children with miraculous births and extraordinary powers.

Before Sudika-mbambi was born, his mother heard a voice coming from her womb. The voice said that his sword was coming, his knife, his *kilembe*, his staff, and he himself. (A *kilembe* is a mythical plant, a "life tree" that every individual is born with. The growth and fate of the *kilembe* reflects the life of the individual.) As soon as Sudika-mbambi was born, he told his mother his name. His mother then heard a second voice coming from her womb. It repeated the same words Sudika-mbambi had spoken. In moments, a second son was born, who told his mother he was Kabundungulu. Then the two boys miraculously created a new home for their parents, whose home had been destroyed by the *makishi*—many-headed MONSTERS that had killed their grandfather.

Sudika-mbambi told his brother to stay with their parents while he went off to fight the *makishi*. He said that if his *kilembe* withered, they would know he was dead. On his quest for the *makishi*, Sudika-mbambi met four Kipalendes—supernatural beings with magical powers. At first they helped him fight the *makishi*, but after the monsters were destroyed and Sudika-mbambi won a wife from a destructive elderly woman, the Kipalendes turned against him out of envy. They threw him into a deep hole and took his wife for their own.

Sudika-mbambi followed a path that opened up before him until he reached the realm of KALUNGA-ngombe, the god of the UNDERWORLD. He asked for Kalunga-ngombe's daughter in marriage. The god told him that first he had to rescue her from the great serpent, Kinioka kia Tumba. After Sudika-mbambi succeeded in killing the serpent, the god told him he next had to kill Kimbiji kia Malenda, the CROCODILE that was master of the underworld abyss. The powerful crocodile pulled Sudika-mbambi into the water and swallowed him whole.

At the same moment, Kabundungulu saw that his brother's life tree had withered. He set out to rescue him, following Sudika-mbambi's route to the underworld. Kabundungulu killed the crocodile and brought his brother back to life. Kalunga-ngombe gave his daughter to Sudika-mbambi. On their way home, the brothers drove off the Kipalendes and recovered Sudika-mbambi's first wife. Kabundungulu asked his brother for one of his wives, since he had none. The brothers fought, but since neither could overcome the other, they decided to separate. They both went to the heavens, Sudika-mbambi traveling east and his brother traveling west. Sudika-mbambi became the thunder, and Kabundungulu became the thunder's echo.

SULWE See TORTOISE.

SUN The Sun is symbolic of the eternal light of the godhead, which explains why for almost all African cultures the Sun is the symbol of the Supreme God. Typically, the Sun symbolized the male element. The MOON, which often appears in tales as the Sun's wife, symbolized the female element.

The Sun's cycle—its rising, setting, and rising again—is symbolic of the cycle of life. When the Sun sets, it descends into the darkness of the UNDERWORLD, the realm of the dead. Its rising symbolizes renewal and rebirth.

In most mythologies throughout Africa, the Creator made the Sun along with all the other heavenly bodies and the Earth. Some tales, such as the following story told by the San, attribute different origins to the Sun. The Sun was a human but not one of the San. In the beginning, the sky was dark. The Sun's light came from one of the man's armpits as he held up his arm, and it lit only the area around his own dwelling. When he put his arm down, darkness fell. An elder told the children of her tribe to lift the man up while he was sleeping and throw him into the sky. She instructed the children to tell him that he must become entirely the Sun and warm the whole Earth. The children carried out her instructions. The Sun became round and shone down on Earth. It never became a man again.

Some people believed that the Sun needed help to shine. In a myth told by the Lamba of Zambia, armies of workers were responsible for the Sun. One group dragged the Sun in its journey from east to

This Pende *gitenga* mask from Democratic Republic of the Congo represents the Sun, a symbol of life. (© *Werner Forman/Art Resource, NY*)

west. At night, another group returned it to the east. During the nighttime part of the journey, the workers polished the Sun to keep it shining brightly. At dawn they relit the Sun's fires. According to the Pygmies of Central Africa, the nightly task of the Supreme God, KHONVOUM, was to renew the Sun so that it could rise again the next day. To do this, he gathered fragments of the STARS and tossed them at the Sun, giving it new energy.

SUNDIATA (SON-JARA KEITA, SUNDJATA KEOTO, SUNJATA KAYTA) (d. 1255) *Mande, or Mandinka (Mali)* The legendary first king of the ancient kingdom of Mali. According to legend, Sundiata was the youngest of 11 brothers and was born crippled and weak. Once he learned to walk at the age of nine, however, he became a strong leader among his peers. He was the son of a Mandinka warrior chief, Nare Fa Maghan (or Fata Magan) and his second wife, Sogolon Conde (or Sugulon Konde). Following the death of Sundiata's father, the boy and his mother were forced to flee. The king of Mema offered them refuge.

Sumanguru (also written as Samanguru or Sumamuru), the last king of Ghana, was trying to reestablish the former glory of Ghana. He had regained control over all of the Ghana lands except Manding (Mali). According to one legend, Sumanguru killed all of Sundiata's brothers but let Sundiata live, believing he would die soon anyway. Another story says that Sumanguru conquered Manding, and the Mandinka rulers were killed or fled. Messengers brought the news to Sundiata in Mema. He decided it was time to reclaim his father's lands. The king of Mema gave Sundiata an army with which to regain his kingdom.

After returning to Manding, Sundiata continued to grow in power. Each clan raised an army to add to Sundiata's forces. Meanwhile, Sumanguru—who already had many wives—stole the sole wife of his chief general and nephew, Fa-Koli. Enraged, Fa-Koli joined Sundiata's forces.

The decisive battle between Sundiata and Sumanguru was fought at Kirina in 1235. According to legend, both men were sorcerers. The one whose magic was more powerful would win the fight. Sundiata had an advantage over Sumanguru—Sundiata's sister had been forced to marry Sumanguru and had discovered the secret of his magical power. She passed on to Sundiata the knowledge that although Sumanguru could not be harmed by iron, he was vulnerable to a white cock's spur. In the battle, Sundiata struck Sumanguru with an arrow tipped with a white cock's spur, draining his magic. Sumanguru fled, and his army was defeated.

Sundiata followed up this victory by taking over all the territory of Ghana. He became the *mansa*—the king of kings—of the new kingdom of Mali. Through Sundiata and his successors, Mali became West Africa's wealthiest trading empire. See also SON-JARA, the EPIC of the Mandinka people, which records the events that led to the foundation of the Mali empire.

SUNJATA KAYTA See SON-JARA; SUNDIATA.

SUPREME BEING Almost all African peoples believed in a Supreme God or Supreme Goddess who was both all-knowing and ever-present and from whom everything came. African religious traditions associate the Supreme Being with certain basic attributes: He or she is the Creator of all things, absolutely controls and sustains the universe, provides for his or her creations, and possesses all these creations.

For the most part, the Supreme Being—who according to most traditions lived in the SKY—played only an indirect role in human affairs. Beneath this being were lesser deities who acted as intermediaries between the Supreme Being and humans and who presided over the physical workings of the universe.

In many African traditions, the Supreme Being once lived among humans but—for various reasons—left and returned to the sky world. The explanations for this separation of the deity from humanity fall into several categories. In some traditions, women were the cause. According to the Ashanti, the sky god, NYAME, went away because a woman kept bumping him whenever she pounded her mortar with a pestle. In the Dinka tradition, the Supreme God, NHIALIC, left because a woman hit him with her hoe. In other traditions, the Supreme Being left because of dissatisfaction with human beings. AKONGO, the Supreme God of the Ngombe, left when people became quarrelsome. When the first people disobeyed IKAGGEN, the San Creator, he destroyed them with FIRE and returned to the sky. Mugasa, the god of the Bambuti, also left Earth and returned to the sky when humans ignored his commandments. Other Creators who left because of human disobedience or aggression include KANU, KIUMBI, LOMA, MULUNGU, and NYAMBE. Whatever the reason, the Creator withdrew from the world, usually returning to the sky. The Supreme Being became distant and no longer had any interest in human affairs.

A second theme relates to the dual (or even multiple) nature of the Supreme Being. In some traditions, God was both female and male, as in the cases of MAWU-LISA and NANA-BULUKU (Fon), Loma (Bongo), and MWARI (Shona). In other traditions, the god's dual nature reflected the contrast between sky and Earth. ABASSI, the Supreme God of the Efik, was both Abassi Onyong, "the god above," and Abassi Isong, "the god below." Similarly, NGUN, the Supreme God of the Bari and Fajulu, was both Ngun Lo Ki, the sky god, and Ngun Lo Kak, "God Below the Earth." For the Ekoi, the dual nature of OBASSI was represented by Obassi Osaw, the sky god, and Obassi Nsi, the earth god. Yet another duality was that represented by good and evil, as in ADROA, the Supreme God of the Lugbara. As Adroa, the sky god, he was *onyiru*, "good." As Adro, the earth god, he was *onzi*, "bad," and was associated with death. (See also DEATH, ORIGIN OF.)

In some cultures, the Supreme Being was perceived as a trinity, each part of which represented a different aspect of the whole. The three aspects of CHUKU, the Supreme Being of the Igbo of Nigeria, were Chukwu, the Great God; Chineke, the creative spirit; and Osebuluwa, who governed and directed all things. In the Ashanti trinity, the Supreme God NYAME represented the natural universe; NYANKOPON represented the *kra*, or life-giving power; and ODOMANKOMA represented the creative force that made the visible world. The Fang Supreme God, NZAME, was also a trinity. His two other aspects, Mebere and Nkwa, represented the male and female aspects of creation. The Supreme Being of the Bambara, Bemba, was four gods in one: Bemba, master of air; Nyale, master of fire; Faro, master of water; and Ndomadyiri, master of earth. Together, the four aspects of Bemba ruled all of the elements on which life is based.

SUPREME GOD See SUPREME BEING.

TALL TALE A humorous type of folktale characterized by exaggeration, with events that might have actually happened carried to ridiculous extremes. The humor of a tall tale lies in the narrator's stretching of believable reality. The main characters in tall tales are usually human, and events do not involve magic or supernatural powers. A tale in which a person accomplishes great feats by means of magic or MEDICINE is not a tall tale. A story of a man carried across a river by miraculous crocodiles would be treated seriously; a story in which he got across in a single bound would be regarded as humorous. Tall tales are common in the traditions of most African peoples. An example from the Mende people of Sierra Leone follows.

A young man was carrying a basket of millet on his head when it began to rain. The soil turned to mud, causing him to slip. He skidded from one village all the way to the next. The basket of millet on his head tipped and began to fall. Before it could hit the ground, the man grabbed a knife from a house he was sliding by, cut some reed grass, wove a mat from the grass, and laid the mat on the ground. The millet from the basket spilled onto the mat instead of into the mud. As he shook the millet back into the basket, the young man congratulated himself for his presence of mind in making the mat.

TANO (TA KORA) *Ashanti (Ghana); Agni (Côte d'Ivoire)* The second son of the Supreme God, NYAME. Tano was the god of the Tano River. Although primarily a nature god, he was also invoked as a war god in times of strife. Some myths say that Tano held a singing contest with Death, but neither could defeat the other. They reached a compromise and decided that when Tano visited the world of humans, Death would go with him. In a different ver-

sion of the myth, the compromise was that whoever reached an ill or injured person first could claim the person. If Tano arrived first, the person would live; if Death arrived first, the person would die. (See also DEATH, ORIGIN OF.)

Tano's older brother, Bia (or Bea), was their father's favorite. When Nyame decided to divide up the land between these two sons, he planned to give Bia the most fertile land, which was the land of the Ashanti (now Ghana). He planned to give to Tano the more barren coastal lands (now Côte d'Ivoire). Nyame sent his servant, a goat, to tell Tano and Bia to come for their gifts the next day. The goat preferred Tano to Bia, so it told Tano to go to Nyame earlier than Bia and to disguise himself as his brother. Nyame was fooled and awarded all the land through which the Tano River flows to Tano. Unfortunately for Bia, Nyame could not reverse his promise, so Bia received the poor land that was left.

TELIKO See BAMBARA CREATION ACCOUNT.

THARU *Venda (South Africa)* A PYTHON associated with the origin of the Venda people. In a time of great drought, Tharu, the Python, divided himself into two parts: Thoho, the Head, and Tsamutshila, the Tail. Thoho went east in search of food, and Tsamutshila went west. Tsamutshila came to a fertile land with rivers, springs, and plentiful RAIN. He became a human being, herded cattle, and married many wives who gave him numerous children. Under the name Ramabulana, Tsamutshila ruled as chief over the prosperous Venda people.

Thoho went east to what is now Mozambique, transformed himself into a human, and founded the Rongo people. His lands, however, were infertile and suffered drought, so he left. Thoho, then known as

Nyamusoro, became a wandering musician and entertainer. One day he arrived at the town where Ramabulana ruled, and he danced and sang at the gates. Ramabulana did not want to go see the entertainment, because he recognized Nyamusoro as his other half and was afraid that they would be rejoined. His people convinced him to go, and what he feared happened. The two parts joined together and became Tharu, the Python, again. Then the great snake left the town and went into the forest.

Left without a chief, Ramabulana's sons quarreled among themselves and disagreed on every issue. Eventually, each son left with his family and followers, traveling in different directions and settling in different places. In this way the Venda people spread across the country.

THINGO   See RAINBOW.

THUNDER AND LIGHTNING   Thunder and lightning are powerful and frightening forces of nature, which traditionally were under the control of powerful gods. SHANGO, the god of thunder and lightning of the Yoruba of Nigeria, was portrayed with a double ax—the symbol of the thunderbolt—on his head. His symbolic animal was the ram, whose bellowing resembles the sound of thunder. AGIPIE, the Supreme God of the Turkana of Tanzania, fought with another god (perhaps another aspect of himself) by hurling lightning bolts. DJAKOMBA, the Supreme God of the Bachwa of Democratic Republic of the Congo, spoke through thunder and struck humans down with lightning. Other Supreme Gods associated with thunder and lightning include CHIUTA, IIGAMAB, KATONDA, KWOTH, NGAI, UMVELINQANGI, UNKULUNKULU, and XU. SOGBO was the god of thunder and lightning of the Fon of Benin. Not all of those who controlled thunder and lightning were deities. MWINDO, an EPIC hero of the Nyanga of Democratic Republic of the Congo, could ally himself with thunder and lightning.

Many different concepts of lightning are presented in myths. According to the Yoruba, Shango created thunder and lightning by throwing thunderstones down to Earth. Wherever lightning struck, priests of Shango searched the surrounding area for

Lightning over the plains in South Africa   (© Charles O'Rear/CORBIS)

the thunderstone. The Yoruba believed these stones had special powers and enshrined them in temples to the god. The Ashanti of Ghana viewed thunderbolts as axes that plunged to the ground during a thunderstorm. According to the Suk of Kenya, thunder and lightning were created when the Supreme God, TORORUT, beat his wings.

According to the Xhosa of South Africa, lightning was a BIRD—Impundulu or Intakezulu—the "bird of heaven." When Impundulu beat its wings, thunder roared. Impundulu was regarded as the Supreme God's servant of death and was greatly feared as a messenger of death. The Vugusu of Kenya also viewed lightning as a bird—a rooster that created lightning by beating its wings and whose crow caused the thunder. (See also TILO.) SNAKES are frequently associated with lightning because of their rapid, zigzagging movement. For the Lunda of Angola and Democratic Republic of the Congo, lightning was Nkuba, the husband of CHINAWEZI, the cosmic serpent.

TIANZA NGOMBE See CHINAWEZI.

TIKDOSHE See MONSTERS.

TILO (Blue Sky) *Shangaan, Thonga, Tonga (Mozambique, South Africa, Zimbabwe)* The Supreme God, whose name designates the heavens from which come both life-giving RAIN and THUNDER AND LIGHTNING. In some tales, a fowl, either the cock or hen of heaven, created thunder and lightning.

According to the CREATION ACCOUNTS of the Shangaan, Thonga, and Tonga, the first humans emerged from reeds. In one version, a reed exploded, releasing a man and a woman. In other versions, people of different tribes emerged from a marsh of reeds, each tribe with its own customs. (See also HUMANS, ORIGIN OF.)

After humans emerged, the chief of the marsh sent a CHAMELEON to them with the message that they would die but be reborn. Shortly afterward, the chief sent a LIZARD with the message that when humans died, they would not be reborn. In keeping with the theme of the "failed message," the lizard arrived first. When the chameleon arrived, the people told it that they had accepted the lizard's message. That is why death is permanent. (See also DEATH, ORIGIN OF.)

TIMI See SHANGO.

TOAD The lowly toad, with its bumpy, dry skin and squat appearance, is not held in high esteem. In African myths, the toad frequently attempts to punish humans for their attitude toward and treatment of it. In many traditions, a toad was associated with the ORIGIN OF DEATH. In a myth told by the Igbo of Nigeria, humans sent a DOG to the Supreme God, CHUKU, to ask him to restore the dead to life. The dog meandered along slowly and was overtaken by a toad that had overheard the message. The toad wanted to punish humans, so it gave Chuku the mes-

sage that humans did not wish to be restored to life. Chuku agreed to that request and could not reverse himself when the dog arrived with the correct message. Death became permanent. In a myth told by the Isoko and Urhobo of Nigeria, people once lived forever, and the world became overpopulated. Humans and animals argued over what should be done. A toad said that the solution was for people to die. A dog disagreed and argued that the Supreme God, OGHENE, should just make the world larger. The humans sent the dog and the toad to Oghene. The argument presented by the one that arrived first would be accepted. Convinced that his speed would make him the winner, the dog stopped for a meal and fell asleep. The toad arrived first, and Oghene accepted its opinion.

In a Mende myth, the Supreme God, NGEWO, sent a dog and a toad to humans to carry the news of life and death. The dog carried the message that people would not die, and the toad carried the message that death would come. Although both started out at the same time, the dog stopped in hope of getting some food from a woman, and the toad continued on. The toad arrived first, saying that death had come. The dog arrived too late; the people had accepted the message of death. In an Efe myth, a toad was given a pot containing death and was warned not to let anything happen to it. Tired of carrying the heavy pot, the toad accepted a FROG's offer to carry the pot for him. Unfortunately, the frog dropped the pot and it broke, letting death escape.

The Efe of Democratic Republic of the Congo say that the Supreme God, AREBATI, once brought dead people back to life. When Arebati was about to revive a dead woman, a toad demanded that he be permitted to move the body. Arebati allowed the toad to sit with the woman's body on the edge of a pit (symbolic of the grave). He warned the toad that if they fell into the pit, great misfortune would come. The clumsy toad knocked the woman's body into the pit and fell in after her. As Arebati had warned, misfortune came. The woman did not come back to life, and from then on all people were fated to die.

According to the Soko of Democratic Republic of the Congo, the MOON and a toad created the first humans. The Moon warned the toad that his creations would be inferior to the Moon's and would die after just one of the Moon's trips around the Earth. Later, the Moon relented and decided to give humans longer life and higher intelligence. First, though, he killed the toad.

TORE See AREBATI.

TORORUT *Suk (Kenya)* The Supreme God and Creator, who made Earth and was responsible for the birth of humans and animals. According to one legend, Tororut was human in form but had gigantic wings. When he beat his wings, their sound created thunder and their movement flashed like lightning. (See also THUNDER AND LIGHTNING.)

The heavenly bodies were all related to Tororut—the SUN was his younger brother, the PLEIADES were his wife, and the MOON was his first-born son. RAIN was another son, and the STARS were also his children. The Evening Star (the evening phase of the planet VENUS) was his firstborn daughter. These deities were all viewed as benevolent and positively inclined toward human beings. Only the Sun—who became angry during the dry season—was not entirely benevolent.

One myth explains how livestock—cattle, sheep, and goats—came to live with humans. Long ago, all the animals lived in the forest. Tororut built a large fire and called the animals to come to him. Most of the animals were afraid of the fire and ran away. Only the cattle, sheep, and goats came when Tororut called. Pleased by them, Tororut decreed that from then on they would live with humans.

TORTOISE Tortoise appears in stories of many African cultures. The TORTOISE's armored shell, ageless appearance, and deliberate gait give an impression of wisdom, determination, and dignity. For the Yoruba of Nigeria, IJAPA the Tortoise was a TRICKSTER-hero. Other tortoise tricksters are Ikaki, who appears in the tales of the Kalabari of southeastern Nigeria; Ekaga, the tortoise trickster of the Mpongwe of Equatorial Guinea and Gabon; and Sulwe, the subject of tales of the Ila of Zambia.

According to the Benga of Equatorial Guinea and Gabon, a tortoise named Kudu was a wise hero who brought knowledge of the Tree of Life to the animals. Long ago there was a famine, and the animals did not know where to find food. The PYTHON guarded a tree called *bojabi*, but the animals did not know whether its food was good to eat. Various animals went to the python to find out, but when they returned, none of them could remember what the python had told them. At last Kudu went to the python and was told that the tree's fruit was edible. He made up a song about the tree and its fruit, and in this way he was able to let the animals know that they could eat the fruit of the *bojabi* tree.

TOTEM Something that serves as the symbol of a family, clan, or tribe. A totem is often an animal or a plant. The ELAND, for example, is the totem animal of the San of southern Africa. Totems have strong spirit power.

Images of tortoises and a crocodile are woven into this cotton wrapper of the Djerema (or Djerina) people of Burkina Faso. (© *The Newark Museum/Art Resource, NY*)

A brass plaque that decorated the palace of the *obas* (rulers) of Benin depicts a palm tree—the source of oil and the sacred palm nuts used in divination. *(© Werner Forman/Art Resource, NY)*

TREES

Trees provide humans with wood for fire-making, shelters, furniture, tools, and innumerable other purposes. They provide food in the form of fruit and nuts. They are the home of many animals and birds. Consequently, trees play a significant role in the mythology of tribes throughout Africa.

In many traditions, a tree was the LINK BETWEEN HEAVEN AND EARTH—the means by which people kept in touch with the SUPREME BEING in the heavens. When this link was severed, the Supreme Being became distant from humanity, and suffering and death entered the world. According to the Uduk of Ethiopia, the *birapinya* tree linked heaven and Earth until an angry woman cut it down. A tree was also the link between heaven and Earth in myths of the Holoholo and Yombe of Democratic Republic of the

Congo and Tanzania, the Ovimbundu of Angola, and the Nuer of Sudan. In a story told by the Boloki of Central African Republic, LIBANZA—the hero of a cycle of tales—climbed a palm tree that grew until it reached the heavens.

For people of many cultures, certain trees are sacred. These trees are treated with respect, and offerings are made to them. The silk-cotton tree is sacred to the Ngombe of Democratic Republic of the Congo. They call the tree Libaka ("union"); it is a symbol of the unity of the seen—the living community—and the unseen—the ANCESTORS who have died. Whenever a new village was built, it was not considered a village until the chief planted a silk-cotton tree in front of his house. Covenants, or pacts, of peace and friendship were made at Libaka so that the ancestors could witness them. In the tradition of the Fon of Benin, the *ayan* tree is sacred to the god SHANGO. Sacrifices were made to him under this tree.

In the tradition of the Ambundu of Angola, every individual is born with a "life tree," or *kilembe*. The growth and fate of the *kilembe* reflects the person's life. When the person dies, the *kilembe* also dies.

In some traditions, the first humans emerged from trees. According to the Damara and Herero of Namibia, the first people and cattle originated from the mythic *omumborombonga* tree—the Tree of Life. In a myth of the San of southern Africa, the ancestors emerged from a hole in the ground among the roots of an enormous tree, followed by the animals.

TRICKSTER

A mythic figure distinguished by skill at trickery and deceit, frequently portrayed as a comical and amoral character. Tricksters are greedy, gluttonous, cunning, predatory, lazy, unpredictable, and unscrupulous and often combine opposing traits, such as wisdom and stupidity. The trickster mimics human needs, drives, and weaknesses. His tricks often fail and frequently backfire on him. It is sometimes hard to know whether the trickster is really ignorant or intends his elaborate schemes to fail in order to reap benefits from what appears to be catastrophe.

Sometimes the trickster introduces FIRE, agriculture, tools, or even death to the world. (See also DEATH, ORIGIN OF.) As such the trickster plays the part of another mythic archetype—the CULTURE HERO, who at the beginning of the world helps shape human culture. (See TURE for an example.) According to myth, the trickster existed in the beginning when the world was still taking shape. As one of the primordial supernatural beings, the trickster had extraordinary powers and was frequently able to thwart the SUPREME BEING's creative efforts.

Although occasionally human (see ABU NUWAS, HLAKANYANA, and HUVEANE), the trickster is more often an animal noted for its special characteristics. The crafty SPIDER, which inspires awe because of its mysterious ability to secrete the silken thread it uses to create its web, is one of the most popular tricksters in African folklore. ANANSI is the spider trickster of the Ashanti and other Akan-speaking tribes of Ghana, GIZO is the subject of tales told by the Hausa of Niger and Nigeria, and the Jo Luo of Sudan have WAC. The TORTOISE's armored shell, ageless appearance, and deliberate gait give an impression of wisdom and dignity. IJAPA reigns as a trickster among the Yoruba of Nigeria. Other tortoise tricksters are Ikaki, who appears in the tales of the Kalabari in southeastern Nigeria; Ekaga, the tortoise trickster of the Mpongwe of Equatorial Guinea and Gabon; and Sulwe, the subject of tales of the Ila of Zambia. The wily HARE, with its long ears and powerful hind legs, is found in stories in most parts of Africa. KADIMBA is the trickster hare of the southern Bantu-speaking peoples of Angola, Botswana, and Namibia. The sly and clever JACKAL is a trickster figure of the Khoikhoi and San people of the Kalahari Desert. The clever and elusive FOX is both a trickster and a culture hero for the Uduk of Ethiopia.

Deities themselves sometimes appear as tricksters. The divine trickster is at the same time both a spirit of order and a spirit of disorder. He is a symbol of transformation from the perfection of God to the imperfect, flawed human. In some traditions, the divine trickster is a lesser god, such as ESHU, the Yoruba god of chance, and LEGBA, the messenger god of the Fon. The Supreme God may also be a divine trickster, as in tales about IKAGGEN, the SUPREME BEING of the San.

Several reasons have been given for the popularity of trickster tales. One reason, of course, is that they are amusing and make people laugh. A perhaps deeper reason is the creativity that lies behind the trickster's mischief. A third reason is that trickster tales teach lessons about the consequences of vanity and greed. The characters that are the butt of the trickster's schemes—and frequently the trickster himself—come away from the experience wiser after having learned a hard lesson.

TSODILO HILLS *San (Botswana, Namibia, South Africa); Mbukushu (Angola, Botswana, Namibia)* Four sheer, quartzite hills that rise dramatically out of the flat plain of the western Kalahari Desert in Botswana. The San call the three largest hills Male Hill, Female Hill, and Child Hill. Male and Female Hill are considered to be husband and wife and Child Hill the result of their union. Legend has it that the unnamed fourth hill was Male Hill's argumentative first wife. He discarded her and sent her away when he married Female Hill.

According to San tradition, the Tsodilo Hills are the sacred location of the first creation. The most sacred place is near the top of Male Hill, where, legend says, the Creator knelt to pray after creating the world. At that time the rocks were still soft, and the impression of the Creator's knees can be seen in the rock. San tradition also says that the hills are a resting place for the SPIRITS of the dead. Various San gods are said to live in caverns inside Female Hill, from where they rule the world.

Located at more than 350 different sites in the hills are about 3,500 San rock paintings, some of which are more than 30,000 years old. Many depict wild and domestic animals, particularly the ELAND, the MASTER ANIMAL of the San. One of the most common images is of male dancers, most likely associated with the San trance DANCE, during which dancers acquire spiritual power used to heal the sick and control natural and supernatural forces. Some paintings depict SNAKES, which in San mythology are associated with RAIN. Many paintings are on high, nearly inaccessible cliffs with sweeping views over the surrounding landscape. This might indicate an authority and control over the SKY and Earth or protection for those living on Earth.

Because of the area's spiritual significance for the San, there are prohibitions against hunting and killing near the hills. When the South African writer Sir Laurens van der Post (1906–66) was researching his book *Lost World of the Kalahari*, his party

In the Tsodilo Hills of Botswana, Male Hill *(left)* and Female Hill *(right)*—sacred to the San and Mbukushu peoples— rise above the grasslands. *(© Peter Johnson/CORBIS)*

encountered inexplicable difficulties. Cameras jammed, tape recorders stopped working, and his party was attacked by swarms of bees three mornings in a row. The group's guide told Sir Laurens that two members of the party had disturbed the spirits by killing a warthog and a steenbok while approaching the hills. Sir Laurens buried a note of apology beneath some rock paintings. From then on, the problems ceased.

The Mbukushu (or Hambukushu) people migrated into the area in the early 1800s. According to Mbukushu tradition, Female Hill was where the Supreme God, NYAMBE, lowered their tribe and live-stock to Earth. Evidence of this is said to be seen in hoofprints etched into rock high on the hill.

TSOEDE (fl. 1500s) *Nupe (Nigeria)* A CULTURE HERO and the half-mythical, half-historical founder of the Nupe kingdom. Before the 16th century, the Nupe had no kingdom of their own; small chieftain-ships were subjects of the Igala, who were themselves subject to the Kingdom of Benin. Every year, the Nupe had to pay tribute to the Igala in the form of slaves. Each family had to contribute one male mem-ber of the household.

According to legend, a son of the *atta* (king) of the Igala went on a hunting trip into the Nupe lands. He fell in love with the daughter of a local chieftain, and she became pregnant. On hearing of his father's death, the young man returned to Idah, the capital of the Igala, to take the throne. Before he left, he gave the woman a charm and a ring to give their child when it was born. The child was a boy, who was named Tsoede (Edegi in the Hausa version of the legend). When he grew up, he was sent to Idah as a slave, part of that year's tribute to the Igala.

Tsoede's father recognized Tsoede as his son by the charm and ring he wore. He took Tsoede into his household and treated him the same as his other sons. This aroused the resentment of Tsoede's half-brothers, who became jealous of the favor shown him. When the *atta* grew old and felt that death was near, he gave the chieftancy of Nupe to Tsoede and presented him with all the regalia of that office. On hearing of this, Tsoede's half-brothers pursued him with the intention of killing him, but he managed to elude them and reached home in safety. Tsoede assumed the title of Etsu Nupe ("king of Nupe") and set about uniting the separate chieftainships. By about 1530 he had subdued the entire country. He withdrew the Nupe's allegiance to Igala and became the founder of an independent dynasty—the Kingdom of Nupe.

According to one account, Tsoede seized the throne by killing his uncle; then he extended the frontiers of the Nupe kingdom. In addition to creating this kingdom, he is credited with introducing technology to his people. He showed them how to build canoes and work metal.

TURE   *Zande (Democratic Republic of the Congo, Sudan)*   A divine TRICKSTER; the hero of a cycle of stories known as the *Sangbwa Ture*. One story in the cycle tells how Ture stole FIRE to give to humans. Ture's uncles, the Abare people, were divine blacksmiths who possessed the secret of fire. One day, Ture visited the Abare and worked the bellows of their forge for them, blowing air to keep the fire burning hot. Ture told his uncles that he would come again the next day and dance for them. He returned dressed in barkcloth and danced around the fire until the barkcloth caught on fire. The Abare tried to put out the fire, but they were unable to. Ture ran off. Wher-

ever he ran, the dried grasses caught fire and spread. That is how people came to have fire.

TWINS   Twins play important roles in some African cultures, especially that of the Yoruba of Nigeria. Births of twins are exceptionally common among the Yoruba, who surround them with a host of traditions, rituals, and beliefs. The term *IBEJI* is used to refer to twins and is also the name of the god of twins. SHANGO, the Yoruba god of THUNDER AND LIGHTNING, was considered to be the supernatural father of twins, who were called Thunderchildren. Twins were sacred to him and were under his protection. Because twins were thought to have special powers to bring good or bad fortune to their families, the parents of twins did everything possible to please them. If the twins' displeasure was aroused, the god Ibeji might punish the parents with illness, death, or disaster.

Among some cultures, twins were considered omens of bad fortune, perhaps because of the higher mortality rate of twins as opposed to single births. According to some legends, twins were children who had died and returned to torment their parents.

In many traditions, deities were created as sets of twins, who were frequently husband and wife. In the PANTHEON of deities of the Fon of Benin (known as the VODUN), DA ZODJI, the chief of the Earth Pantheon, had a female twin named Nyohwè Ananu, who was his wife. AGBÈ, the chief of the Sea Pantheon, had a female twin named Naètè, who was his wife. In the BAMBARA CREATION ACCOUNT, the Supreme God created two sets of twins, each of which were husband and wife. The first twins were PEMBA and MUSOKORONI; the second twins were FARO and her husband, Koni.

According to the Lugbara of Democratic Republic of the Congo, Sudan, and Uganda, before the first humans were created, a series of supernatural twins were born; see ADROA.

UKQILI See UNKULUNKULU.

UMVELINQANGI (MVELINQANGI) *Zulu (South Africa)* The SKY Father, an all-present god who manifested himself as thunder and earthquakes. He descended from the heavens to the vast swamp Uthlanga (or Uhlanga) and created the primeval reeds from which the Supreme God UNKULUNKULU emerged.

In one version of the ZULU CREATION ACCOUNT, Umvelinqangi brought out men, women, animals, grain, and all the fruits of the Earth from the reeds. People did not have to eat or drink, and they did not die. Although crops grew, people did not have any use for them. Then one day a new thing happened—a woman became ill. Unsure what to do, the people fed her some of the things they saw growing. When she grew well again, the other people decided to try eating the food. From that time on, people ate the crops that grew and the meat of animals.

In a myth about the ORIGIN OF DEATH, Umvelinqangi sent a CHAMELEON to give people the message that when they died, they would be reborn. The chameleon went along very slowly and stopped at a bush to eat, so Umvelinqangi sent a LIZARD with a second message: Death would be the end, and people would not be reborn. The lizard arrived first with the message of death. Not knowing what death was, the people accepted it. When the chameleon arrived, they would not listen to its message. (In another version of the myth, the messages were sent by Unkulunkulu.)

UMWA See JEN PANTHEON.

UNCAMA *Zulu (South Africa)* A mythic hero who made an accidental journey to the UNDER-WORLD. Uncama had planted a millet garden, but when the millet ripened, a porcupine came each night and ate it. One morning, when there was dew on the ground, Uncama was able to follow the porcupine's trail. The trail led to a hole in the ground, into which Uncama descended.

Uncama went on and on. He was no longer hunting the porcupine but seeking to reach the end of the hole. After a time, he came to a village. He heard dogs barking and children crying, saw smoke rising from cooking fires and people walking around. Unaware, Uncama had crossed over into the land of the dead. He became frightened and returned along the path he had taken, walking backward.

When Uncama returned to his village, he discovered that he had been gone so long that his family had believed he was dead. They had already burned his clothes and other belongings. Uncama then told his amazed family about his strange journey.

UNDERWORLD A subterranean world to which souls of the dead went. Commonly, the underworld was a reflection of the world of the living. In their subterranean village, dead souls carried out their customary daily activities—cultivating the fields, clearing brush, preparing food, and so on. (See KALUNGA; OGHENE; UNCAMA.) The ruler of the underworld was usually a deity, in some cases a male god (see WALUMBE), in others, a female goddess (see ALA; AMA). Sometimes, as in the case of the Ashanti underworld, ASAMANDO, a guardian received the souls of the dead (see AMOKYE).

The theme of a hunter or traveler who followed a strange trail or descended into an animal burrow and ended up in the land of the dead is widespread in African mythology. In some traditions, the story is told simply as an adventure tale to be enjoyed. In other traditions, the story is considered to be a true account of events that happened to a real person. Uncama, the hero of a Zulu tale, followed a porcupine underground, where he came upon the village of dead souls. In a Baganda myth, a hunter named Mpobe pursued some rats into a hole in the ground that led to the underworld ruled over by Walumbe, the god of death.

The Ambundu hero SUDIKA-MBAMBI was thrown into a hole by enemies. By following a path that led from the hole, he reached the realm of the god of the dead, KALUNGA-ngombe. The Ashanti hero KWASI BENEFO made a deliberate journey to the underworld to see his four dead wives.

UNKULUNKULU (NKULUNKULU, The Great Oldest One, Ancestor) *Zulu (South Africa)*   The Supreme God and Creator of all things. Unkulunkulu grew upon a reed in the mythical swamp Uthlanga (Uhlanga) and fell to Earth when he became too heavy. He broke off the people, cattle, and other animals from the reeds, and they followed him out of the reeds. Unkulunkulu created everything that exists on Earth—mountains, rivers, and all living things. He named the animals and taught humans how to hunt, make FIRE with sticks, and cultivate grain. (See also ZULU CREATION ACCOUNT.)

Unkulunkulu is sometimes called uKqili (The Wise One) and as such controls the lightning. (See also THUNDER AND LIGHTNING.) The Zulu consider that all cattle belong to him; they are his gift to humans. When lightning strikes and kills one of the cattle, the Zulu say that Unkulunkulu has slaughtered food for himself.

Unkulunkulu was responsible for the ORIGIN OF DEATH. He sent a CHAMELEON named Unwaba to give people the message that when they died, they would be reborn. Unwaba went along very slowly and stopped at a bush to eat. So Unkulunkulu sent a LIZARD with a second message—death would be the end, and people would not be reborn. The lizard arrived first with the message of death. Not knowing what death was, the people accepted it. When Unwaba arrived, they would not listen to its message. (In another version of the myth, the messages were sent by UMVELINQANGI, the SKY Father.)

According to Zulu tradition, when people die, their SPIRITS go to the sky to live. It is said that the STARS are the eyes of the dead looking at the human world.

UNWABA   See UNKULUNKULU.

UTHLANGA   See ZULU CREATION ACCOUNT.

VENUS The brilliant planet Venus, second from the Sun in our solar system, appears part of the time as an evening STAR and part of the time as a morning star. Tribes in Gabon regarded these two appearances of Venus as two different wives of the MOON. This myth is related to the Moon's phases. The Morning Star, Chekechani, met with the Moon in the morning. Because she never prepared meals for her husband, he lost weight and became thinner. When his hunger became too great, he left to visit his other wife, Puikani, the Evening Star. She fed her husband well, and he began to put on weight again. For the Makoni of Zimbabwe, the two phases of Venus were also wives of the Moon, who was the first man. (See MAKONI CREATION ACCOUNT.)

VODUN *Fon (Benin)* The name for the PANTHEON—the term for all the deities of a particular people taken together—of the Fon, or Dahomean, people, as well as for the members of the pantheon themselves. The Vodun includes both the great gods and the lesser gods who stem from the greater pantheon. The great gods are divided into four pantheons: the Sky Pantheon, the Earth Pantheon, the Sea Pantheon, and the Thunder Pantheon. The Thunder and Sea Pantheons are sometimes considered one pantheon. For the Fon, both the sea and THUNDER AND LIGHTNING were powerful and mysterious supernatural forces ruled by thunder gods.

The supreme deity of the Fon, NANA-BULUKU, ruled over all the *voduns* (the members of the Vodun pantheon) as the Originator, the creator of the beginnings of the universe. Nana-Buluku gave birth to MAWU-LISA, the Great God, a Creator with two aspects—female (MAWU) and male (LISA). Mawu-Lisa completed the creation of the universe and gave birth to other deities (see FON CREATION ACCOUNT).

Among the members of the Vodun are deities representing natural phenomena and elements of nature, as well as abstract concepts such as foretelling destiny. Some *voduns* appear to have come into being as the result of the deification of ANCESTORS. The stories of the *voduns*, their conflicts with one another, and their special characteristics and powers provide the rationale of Fon religious belief. Vodun is a living religion in Benin, Cuba, Haiti, and areas of the United States where Haitians settled.

The following list gives the attributes of some of the Fon pantheon deities. (See also AIDO-HWEDO.)

Agbè Third-born son of Mawu-Lisa; chief of the Sea Pantheon. AGBÈ had a twin sister named Naètè, who was also his wife.

Agè Fourth-born son of Mawu-Lisa; god of the hunt. (See also AGÈ.)

Da Zodji Firstborn son of Mawu-Lisa; the great serpent power and chief of the Earth Pantheon. DA ZODJI had a TWIN sister, Nyohwè Ananu, who was also his wife. The two produced several children who were the SAGBATA gods—the gods of the Earth Pantheon. Mawu-Lisa divided the realms of the universe among the children of Da Zodji and Nyohwè Ananu.

Djo Sixth-born son of Mawu-Lisa; god of the air. (See also DJO.)

Gbadu Daughter of Mawu-Lisa; goddess of fate.

Gu Fifth-born son of Mawu-Lisa; god of iron, war, weapons, and tools. (See also GU.)

Hevioso The general name given to the Thunder Pantheon and another name for Sogbo.

Legba Seventh-born and youngest son of Mawu-Lisa; the divine TRICKSTER. When Mawu-Lisa divided the universe among her offspring, there was no realm left for Legba.

118

The Fon of Benin created iron and brass staffs like the one above to honor and make offerings to the dead and the gods of the Vodun. (© *The Hamill Gallery of African Art, Boston, MA*)

Mawu-Lisa gave LEGBA the role of messenger between her and her other children.

Lisa   The male aspect of Mawu-Lisa; associated with the SKY, the east, the SUN, and the day.

Mawu   The female aspect of the androgynous Great God Mawu-Lisa; associated with the Earth, the west, the MOON, and the night.

Nana-Buluku   The SUPREME BEING, creator of the beginnings of the universe; parent of Mawu-Lisa.

Sagbata   The general name given to the Earth Pantheon and the name of one of the sons of Da Zodji and his sister-wife, Nyohwè Ananu.

SAGBATA went to live on Earth, taking his parents' riches with him.

Se   The *vodun* who represents the souls of humans.

Segbo (Da Segbo, Dada Segbo; Supreme Soul) King of the gods; early ruler of the world of humans.

Sogbo   Second-born son of Mawu-Lisa; god of thunder and chief of the Thunder Pantheon. SOGBO was androgynous—at the same time both male and female—and gave birth to the deities of the Thunder Pantheon.

WAC *Jo Luo (Sudan)* SPIDER, the divine TRICKSTER, the equivalent of the Ashanti trickster, ANANSI the Spider. Like Ananasi, Wac also had good qualities. In one tale, when the Supreme God, JUOK, wanted to create a second SUN so that the Sun would not be alone, Wac saved humans' lives by pointing out that with two suns, humans would be roasted. Juok was persuaded by the argument, but the angry Sun condemned spiders to hide during the day when the Sun was out.

Another tale explains why there are so many spiders in the world. Wac wanted to go to the heavens to find Juok. At this time, people were living in the SKY. Wac hung a small drum under his arm and asked the people to pull him up to the sky on a rope. He told them that he would beat his drum when he reached the sky, and they could then cut the rope. On the way up, however, Wac accidentally hit the drum with his elbow. Hearing the sound, the people cut the rope. Wac fell back to Earth and broke into many small pieces, each of which became a spider.

WAGA (WAQA) *Konso (Ethiopia)* The Supreme God and Creator, who brought the RAIN and established the social order under which humans live. Konso explanations of the ORIGIN OF HUMANS vary. Some tales say that SNAKES gave birth to humans; other tales say that humans emerged from a gourd. The tales agree that however humans came to be, it was Waga who gave them the breath of life. Before he did this, although humans were fully formed, they did not move, speak, or eat. When people died, their breath was returned to Waga.

As with the majority of African deities, Waga withdrew from the world at some point and became remote. However, he continued to judge people who called on him in disputes and to punish wrongdoers.

His presence was manifested in natural phenomena such as the RAINBOW.

WAGADU *Soninke (Mauritania)* The Soninke goddess, whose disappearance and rediscovery are the subject of the ancient *DAUSI* EPIC.

WAKA (WAQA, QAK) *Galla (Ethiopia)* The Supreme God, Creator and ruler of the Earth. When Waka created night, he ordered humans and animals to cover their eyes with their hands while he did so. However, the LION, LEOPARD, and HYENA peeped through their fingers. This myth explains why these three animals can see in the dark.

In many African cultures, the shedding of a SNAKE's skin symbolizes renewal and rebirth. A Galla myth about the ORIGIN OF DEATH also explains the supposed immortality of snakes. Waka sent a BIRD to tell humans that they would not die. When humans became old, they would shed their skins and be restored to youthfulness. On the way, the bird met a snake that was eating some meat. The bird offered to tell the snake Waka's message if it would give him some of the meat. Either by mistake or out of malice, the bird told the snake that when people grew old they would die, but that when the snake grew old, it would shed its skin and become young again. In this way, death became permanent for humans.

WALUMBE (Death) *Baganda (Uganda)* In the Baganda PANTHEON of deities (the LUBAALE), the god of death. Once, Walumbe lived in the SKY with his father, GULU, the sky god. The following story explains how Death came to Earth.

Walumbe's sister Nambi married KINTU, the first king of the Baganda, and the couple went to live on Earth. Gulu warned them never to return to the heavens. If they did, he said, Nambi's brother Walumbe—Death—would follow them back to Earth. The couple brought many things with them from the heavens, among them goats, sheep, and chickens. Nambi realized that they had forgotten grain to feed the chickens. Despite Kintu's efforts to stop her, she returned to the heavens for the grain. Walumbe saw her and followed her home. He asked for the couple's children, but Nambi and Kintu refused to give them up. When they begged Gulu for help, he sent Nambi's brother Kaikuzi to confront Walumbe. The brothers fought. In the end, Walumbe fled into the ground, where he became ruler of the UNDERWORLD. Since then, Death has lived on Earth.

WAMARA   See CHWEZI.

WANGA *Baganda (Uganda)* In the Baganda PAN-THEON of deities (known as the LUBAALE), one of the oldest of the deified heroes. Earthly deities such as Wanga were lower ranking than the SKY gods that ruled in the heavens. However, they were the deities to whom people turned on a daily basis. Wanga was consulted about illness and disease and foretold ways to prevent common community problems.

According to one legend, one day the SUN fell from the sky. The king called upon Wanga for help. Wanga was able to set the Sun back in its place. To thank Wanga, the king built a temple to him.

WANTU SU *Sara (Chad, Sudan)* The Supreme God, who lived in the SKY. Wantu Su gave his nephew, Wantu, a drum that contained a little of all he had in the sky. Wantu was to bring these things to Earth for humans. He announced his arrival by beating the drum. As Wantu slid down a rope from heaven, a CROW struck the drum. Startled, Wantu dropped the drum. It fell to Earth and broke, scattering animals, fish, and plants all over the world.

WITCH DOCTOR   See SHAMAN.

WOYENGI *Ijo (Nigeria)* The Creator goddess. One day, in a large field containing a huge *iroko* tree, a large table with soil on it, a chair, and a sacred creation stone came down from the heavens. In a burst of THUNDER AND LIGHTNING, Woyengi, the Mother, descended. She sat in the chair and her feet on the sacred stone. She took the earth from the table and molded human beings from it. They had no life until Woyengi held them one by one and breathed her breath into them. The humans came to life, but they were neither men nor women. One by one, Woyengi let them choose their sex. She also let them choose their way of life and how they would die.

One woman, Ogboinba, had asked for supernatural powers. When other women produced children, all Ogboinba could produce was magic. Dissatisfied with life, she traveled to Woyengi to ask that her fate be changed so that she could have children. Woyengi refused, because Ogboinba had already chosen her way of life. Ogboinba became angry and challenged Woyengi. To punish Ogboinba for her arrogance, Woyengi took away her magical powers.

WULBARI *Krachi (Togo)* The Supreme God and Creator. Wulbari once lived on Earth but retreated to the SKY. Various reasons are given for Wulbari's separation from humans. In one account, a woman kept bumping him with her pestle as she prepared food. This was painful, so he went higher to get out of her reach. Other reasons given were that Earth became too crowded, that people used Wulbari as a towel and wiped their soiled hands on him, and that the smoke of cooking fires irritated him. In another account, a woman cut off a piece of Wulbari each time she made soup to give the soup more flavor. Wulbari retreated to avoid the pain she caused him.

In a tale about the ORIGIN OF DEATH, a ground toucan had begun to kill and eat humans. The people begged Wulbari to help them. Because DOGS are closely associated with people, Wulbari gave a dog MEDICINE that would restore to life the people the toucan killed. On his way to deliver the medicine, the dog saw a bone in the road and set the medicine down. While the dog was busy gnawing on the bone, a goat took the medicine and scattered it all over the grass. This is why death is permanent for people, but grass dies and comes back to life each year.

WUTUTU   See BIRDS; SOGBO.

XHOSA CREATION ACCOUNT *Xhosa (South Africa)* In the beginning, humans and animals emerged from a hole in the ground. The marks left by their feet can be seen in the surrounding rocks. The cattle were the first to emerge, followed by humans and then by all the other animals and birds. The cavern from which they emerged, called *uhlanga*, is said to be in the east. The association with the east has a ritual significance for the Xhosa people. Traditionally, the entrance to the main house in a Xhosa homestead faced east, and chiefs were buried facing east.

XU *Heikum (Namibia)* The Supreme God and Creator, who made everything, including humans. (Xu is another name for the San Creator, IKAGGEN. The Heikum are one of the main groups of San.) Xu lived in the SKY on the first floor of a two-story house. The upper story was occupied by the souls of the dead. Xu was a benevolent weather god; he brought the RAIN and ruled over THUNDER AND LIGHTNING. He was also the lord of the SPIRITS, the IIgaunab. Xu sent people good luck in hunting and food gathering through the chief of the spirits.

YANSAN See ORISA.

YEHWE ZOGBANU See MONSTERS.

YEMAJA (YEMANJA, YEMAYAH, YEMOJA)
Yoruba (Nigeria) In the Yoruba PANTHEON of deities
(known as the ORISA), the *orisa*, or goddess, of the
Ogun River. She was thought of as the mother goddess—the patroness of birth—and was worshiped primarily by women. Yemaja was associated with the
Ogun River because its waters were believed to be a
remedy for infertility. In one account, Yemaja was
raped by her son, Orungan. When he tried to rape
her again, her body burst open and 15 gods sprang
forth, among them OGUN and SHANGO. In some
accounts, she was identified as a wife of Ogun.

YO *Bambara (Mali)* The primeval world-spirit that
created the structure of the heavens, the Earth, and
all living and nonliving things. According to legend,
in the beginning there was nothing but the emptiness
of the void. The universe began from a single point of
sound—the sound Yo. Everything—including human
consciousness—came from this root sound. Yo
brought into being the creator figures FARO, PEMBA,
and Teliko. See also BAMBARA CREATION ACCOUNT.

YORUBA CREATION ACCOUNT *Yoruba
(Nigeria)* In the beginning, there were only the SKY
above, where the ORISAS—the gods and goddesses of
the Yoruba PANTHEON—lived, and a world of water,
mist, and swamps below. The sky was ruled by the
Supreme God, OLORUN; the watery world was ruled
by the goddess of the sea, OLOKUN. One day, the *orisa*
OBATALA suggested to Olorun that the world below
would be greatly improved if there were solid land on
which *orisas* and other forms of life could live. Olorun

agreed, and Obatala said that he would undertake the
task of creating land.

Obatala went to ORUNMILA, the god of divination, who could foresee the best way to proceed with
any undertaking, and asked him how to begin. Orunmila instructed Obatala to have a golden chain made
on which he could descend to Earth. (See also LINK
BETWEEN HEAVEN AND EARTH.) He was to bring with
him a snail shell full of soil, a hen to scatter the soil
(in some versions a pigeon as well), a black cat as a
companion, and a palm nut. Obatala followed Orunmila's instructions. From the sky, Orunmila's voice
directed Obatala through the process of creating the
land. Obatala poured the soil onto the waters. He
then placed the hen on the soil. The bird scratched at
the soil, scattering it in all directions. Where the soil
fell, the waters turned into dry land. Obatala stepped
down onto the land, which he named Ife. He planted
the palm nut, which grew into a tree that dropped
many nuts and created many more palm trees. Olorun
sent his servant, AGEMO the CHAMELEON, to Earth to
ask how Obatala was doing. Obatala said that Earth
would be improved with more light, so Olorun created the SUN.

After a while, Obatala grew lonely with just the
cat as his companion. He decided that things would
be better if there were people on Earth. He shaped
human figures out of clay and called on Olorun to
breathe life into them. However, while Obatala was
forming the humans, he had become thirsty and had
drunk too much palm wine (the TRICKSTER, ESHU,
was said to have tempted him with the wine). His
drunkenness caused him to misshape some of the figures. When Obatala sobered up, he saw that some of
his creations had twisted limbs, hunched backs, and
other deformities. He was filled with remorse and
resolved to be the special protector of all humans

with disabilities. Obatala then gave people the tools they needed for life. Humanity flourished and grew in number. Obatala ruled Ife for many years. Eventually he became homesick, ascended the golden chain, and returned to the sky. In another account, while Obatala was sleeping off the effects of the palm wine, Olorun saw that he had left his work undone. Olorun sent ODUDUWA to complete the task of creation. Oduduwa created his own humans and became the first ruler of Ife. See also HUMANS, ORIGIN OF.

YORUBA PANTHEON   See *ORISA*.

Z

ZIMU *Ndebele (South Africa)* The Supreme God, who sent a CHAMELEON and a LIZARD to humans with messages of life and death. The chameleon carried the message that people would die but would rise again. However, it moved so slowly that the lizard quickly overtook it. The lizard told humans that when they died, they would not rise again. When the chameleon finally arrived with its message of eternal life, the people told it that they had accepted the lizard's message. From that time on, death was permanent. See also DEATH, ORIGIN OF.

ZRA *Dan (Côte d'Ivoire)* The Supreme God and Creator. Among Zra's creations was Death. (See also DEATH, ORIGIN OF.) In the beginning, Death lived in wild places and killed only game animals. He did not enter the villages, so humans did not die. Then one day a hunter came across Death cooking meat over a fire. Death told the hunter that they were fellow hunters and offered him some meat. The hunter accepted, stayed with Death for several days, and brought some of Death's meat back to the village. Shortly afterward, Death appeared in the village and demanded payment for the meat the hunter had eaten and taken. The hunter offered one of his children as payment. Death took the child. From that time on, Death went to the villages, and people died.

ZULU CREATION ACCOUNT *Zulu (South Africa)* According to Zulu tradition, life began in Uthlanga (or Uhlanga), a vast primordial swamp. UMVELINQANGI, the SKY Father, descended from the heavens to Uthlanga. He created the reeds on which the Supreme God and creator of humanity, UNKULUNKULU, and all the people and animals grew. Unkulunkulu grew upon a reed until he became too heavy. Then he broke off from the reed and fell to Earth. (In a different version of the myth, Unkulunkulu and a woman emerged from a reed together.) Unkulunkulu created all the things of the world—mountains, lakes, and rivers. He broke off all the other people and the animals from the reeds, and they followed him out of the swamp. He taught the Zulu how to hunt, make FIRE with sticks, and cultivate grain. See also HUMANS, ORIGIN OF.

ZULU PANTHEON *Zulu (South Africa)* As with many other African tribal groups, the Zulu have a PANTHEON of deities. The first god, who existed before all other deities, was UMVELINQANGI, the SKY Father and the god of thunder and earthquakes. (See also THUNDER AND LIGHTNING.) Umvelinqangi created the primeval reeds from which the Supreme God UNKULUNKULU emerged. The following list presents the attributes of some of the deities in the Zulu pantheon.

> **Amadlozi** The ANCESTORS of the Zulu people. Humans can invoke the help of the SPIRIT world by calling on the AMADLOZI.
>
> **Inkosazana** The goddess of agriculture, who made the grain grow.
>
> **Mamlambo** The goddess of rivers.
>
> **Mbaba Mwana Waresa** The goddess of the RAINBOW, RAIN, and harvest. MBABA MWANA WARESA was well loved because she gave the Zulu the gift of beer.
>
> **Unkulunkulu** (Ancestor) Both the first man and the Creator. He created humans, animals, and everything in the world. He is sometimes called uKqili, "The Wise One." In that aspect, he controlled the lightning.

SELECTED BIBLIOGRAPHY

Abrahams, Roger D. *African Folktales*. New York: Pantheon Books, 1983.

Afrika World. "African Peoples and Their Names for God," Afrika World. Available on-line. URL: http://www.afrikaworld.net/afrel/afnames.htm. Downloaded on March 4, 2003.

Agatucci, Cora. "African Storytelling: Oral Traditions," Humanities Department, Central Oregon Community College. Available on-line. URL: http://www.cocc.edu/cagatucci/ classes/hum211/afrstory.htm. Updated on October 31, 2002.

Alland, Alexander, Jr. *When the Spider Danced*. Garden City, N.Y.: Anchor Press/Doubleday, 1975.

Appiah, Kwame Anthony, and Henry Louis Gates, Jr., eds. *Africana: The Encyclopedia of the African and African American Experience*. New York: Basic Civitas Books, 1999.

Beier, Ulli, ed. *The Origin of Life and Death: African Creation Myths*. London: Heinemann, 1966.

Bently, Peter, ed. *The Dictionary of World Myth*. New York: Facts On File, 1995.

Biebuyck, Daniel P. "The African Heroic Epic." In *Heroic Epic and Saga: An Introduction to the World's Great Folk Epics*, edited by Felix J. Oinas, 336–67. Bloomington: Indiana University Press, 1978.

Biebuyck, Daniel P., and Kahombo C. Mateene. *The Mwindo Epic*. Berkeley: University of California Press, 1969.

Bleek, W. H. I. *Zulu Legends*. Edited by J. A. Engelbrecht. Pretoria, South Africa: J. L. Van Schaik, 1952.

Campbell, Joseph. *The Masks of God: Primitive Mythology*. New York: Viking Press, 1959.

Clark-Bekederemo, John P. *The Ozidi Saga*. Washington, D.C.: Howard University Press, 1991.

Cotterell, Arthur. *Oxford Dictionary of World Mythology*. Oxford: Oxford University Press, 1979.

Courlander, Harold. *The King's Drum and Other African Stories*. New York: Harcourt Brace Jovanovich, 1962.

———. *Tales of Yoruba Gods and Heroes*. New York: Crown Publishers, 1973.

———. *A Treasury of African Folklore*. 2d ed. New York: Marlowe & Company, 1996.

Davidson, Basil, and Editors of Time-Life Books. *Great Ages of Man: African Kingdoms*. New York: Time-Life Books, 1966.

Dowling, Mike. "The Electronic Passport to Ancient Africa," Mr. Dowling's Electronic Passport. Available on-line. URL: http://www.mrdowling.com/609ancafr.html. Updated on April 30, 2002.

Edgar, Frank. *Hausa Tales and Traditions: An English Translation of Tatsuniyoyi Na Hausa*. Translated by Neil Skinner. Madison: University of Wisconsin Press, 1977.

Editors of Time-Life Books. *Lost Civilizations: Africa's Glorious Legacy*. Alexandria, Va.: Time-Life Books, 1994.

Ford, Clyde W. *The Hero with an African Face: Mythic Wisdom of Traditional Africa*. New York: Bantam Books, 1999.

Frobenius, Leo, and Douglas C. Fox. *African Genesis*. New York: Benjamin Blom, 1966.

Garvey, Marcus. "A Treasury of African Folktale," Marcus Garvey. Available on-line. URL: http://www.marcusgarvey.com. Downloaded on April 29, 2003.

Gateway Africa. "The San Tribe," Gateway Africa. Available on-line. URL: http://www.gateway-africa.com/countries/namibia/bushmen.htm. Downloaded on May 26, 2003.

Green Sponsors. "The Rock Art of the San People," Green Sponsors. Available on-line. URL: http://www.greensponsors.com/html/San/san.html. Downloaded on May 26, 2003.

Huet, Michel. *The Dance, Art and Ritual of Africa*. New York: Pantheon Books, 1978.

Innes, Gordon. *Sunjata: Three Mandinka Versions*. London: School of Oriental and African Studies, University of London, 1974.

Isaak, Mark. "Flood Stories from Around the World," The Talk.Origins Archive. Available on-line. URL: http://www.talkorigins.org/faqs/flood-myths.html. Updated on September 2, 2002.

Johnson, John Williams. *The Epic of Son-Jara*. Bloomington: Indiana University Press, 1992.

K'Okiri, Oguda. *The Death of Lwanda Magere*. Nairobi, Kenya: Equatorial, 1970.

Krupp, E. C. *Beyond the Blue Horizon: Myths & Legends of the Sun, Moon, Stars, & Planets*. New York: HarperCollins, 1991.

Laney, David. "African Starlore," South African Astronomical Observatory. Available on-line. URL: http://www.saao.ac.za/starlore/legends.html. Updated on November 22, 2000.

Leach, Maria. *Creation Myths Around the World.* New York: Crowell, 1956.

Leeming, David, and Margaret Leeming. *A Dictionary of Creation Myths.* Oxford: Oxford University Press, 1994.

Lindemans, M. F., ed. "African Mythology," Encyclopedia Mythica. Available on-line. URL: http://www.pantheon.org/areas/mythology/africa/african.html. Downloaded on February 28, 2003.

Lugira, Aloysius M. *African Religion.* New York: Facts On File, 1999.

Makhuphula, Nambulelo. *Xhosa Fireside Tales.* Johannesburg, South Africa: Seriti sa Sechaba, 1988.

Mythome. "African Creation Myths," Mythome. Available on-line. URL: http://www.mythome.org/creatafr.html. Updated on July 24, 1999.

———. "African Flood Myths," Mythome. Available on-line. URL: http://www.mythome.org/fludmyt5.html. Updated on August 27, 1999.

Niane, D. T. *Sundiata: An Epic of Old Mali.* Translated by G. D. Pickett. Harlow, England: Longman Drumbeat, 1982.

Omtatah, Andrew Okoiti. *Lwanda Magere.* London: Heinemann, 1991.

Owomoyela, Oyekan. *Yoruba Trickster Tales.* Lincoln: University of Nebraska Press, 1997.

Radin, Paul, ed. *African Folktales.* New York: Stockmen Books, 1983.

Scheub, Harold. *A Dictionary of African Mythology: The Mythmaker as Storyteller.* Oxford, England: Oxford University Press, 2000.

Vernon-Jackson, Hugh. *West African Folk Tales.* London: University of London Press, 1958.

Werner, Alice. *Myths and Legends of the Bantu.* London: George G. Harrap, 1933; Frank Cass, 1968.

———. "Myths and Legends of the Bantu," The Internet Sacred Text Archive. Available on-line. URL: http://www.sacred-texts.com/afr/mlb. Downloaded on May 21, 2003.

Willis, Roy, ed. *World Mythology.* New York: Henry Holt, 1993.

INDEX

Boldface page numbers indicate main headings; *italic* page numbers indicate illustrations.